The Planning of Investment Programs in the Fertilizer Industry

A WORLD BANK RESEARCH PUBLICATION

Volume Two of
THE PLANNING OF INVESTMENT PROGRAMS
Alexander Meeraus and Ardy J. Stoutjesdijk, Editors

Armeane M. Choksi
Alexander Meeraus
Ardy J. Stoutjesdijk

The Planning of Investment Programs in the Fertilizer Industry

Published for the World Bank
THE JOHNS HOPKINS UNIVERSITY PRESS
Baltimore and London

The views and interpretations in this book are the authors' and should not be attributed to the World Bank, to its affiliated organizations, or to any individual acting in their behalf. The map on page 185 has been prepared exclusively for the convenience of readers of this book; the denominations used and the boundaries shown do not imply, on the part of the World Bank and its affiliates, any judgment on the legal status of any territory or any endorsement or acceptance of such boundaries.

Library of Congress Cataloging in Publication Data

Choksi, Armeane M 1944–
The planning of investment programs in the fertilizer industry.
(The Planning of investment programs; v. 2)
Includes index.
1. Fertilizer industry. 2. Fertilizer industry—Egypt.
I. Meeraus, Alexander, 1943– joint author.
II. Stoutjesdijk, Ardy J., 1938– joint author.
III. Title. IV. Series: Planning of investment programs; v. 2.
HD9483.A2C47 338.4′366862 78–8436
ISBN 0–8018–2138–X
ISBN 0–8018–2153–3 pbk.

Contents

Text Tables

Text Figures

Map

Editors' Note to the Series

THIS IS THE SECOND VOLUME in a series dealing with the use of mathematical programming methods in investment analysis. The volume focuses on the use of such methods to analyze production and investment problems in the chemical fertilizer industry. The exposition of the methodology follows closely that adopted in the first volume of the series, *The Planning of Industrial Investment Programs: A Methodology*, by David A. Kendrick and Ardy J. Stoutjesdijk.

The series relies essentially on one among a number of possible approaches to investment planning; specifically, it employs mixed-integer programming to analyze investment problems in the presence of economies of scale. Alternative approaches, such as dynamic programming, are successfully used by other investigators to address selected aspects of the investment planning problem. For sectorwide investment analysis, however, we believe that mathematical programming offers the best prospects for operational use.

ALEXANDER MEERAUS
ARDY J. STOUTJESDIJK

Preface

MOST PROJECTIONS OF FERTILIZER USE around the world, and particularly in the developing countries, imply continuing rapid growth in fertilizer demand. To meet such increased levels of demand, substantial investments are being made in new production capacity, in both developed and developing countries. Among the latter, many have some or all of the important raw materials for fertilizer production. That circumstance, combined with high growth rates of fertilizer demand and a fear of real or perceived shortages of supply worldwide, has led many developing countries to consider producing fertilizer domestically. In several parts of the world, investment plans for the fertilizer sector are being drawn up in the context of regional endeavors to gain self-sufficiency in this critical agricultural input.

Against this background, it appeared appropriate to devote the first sector-specific volume in this series to the chemical fertilizer industry in the hope that it will assist planners in the developing countries in drawing up efficient investment programs in this sector. For those not familiar with the fertilizer industry, a few chapters that give the most important technical information regarding the sector have been included; without this information, it might be difficult to understand the rationale and structure of the planning models proposed. In many respects, however, these chapters are no more than an overview; more detailed technical background will often be desirable.

The planning methods are set out in great detail in several chapters. The layout of these chapters is similar to the corresponding ones in volume 1, but all the models presented here are specific to the fertilizer industry. Moreover, attention has been paid to variants of the standard investment planning model to fit particular situations.

Finally, a case study of the Egyptian fertilizer industry is presented in the second part of this volume. Several of the models discussed in the first part are used to address a number of typical problems encountered by sector planners in Egypt. The study was carried out in close collaboration with Egyptian sector planners as well as with colleagues in the Industrial Projects Department of the World Bank.

We would like to acknowledge the helpful suggestions and criticism of a number of individuals who have read part or all of the manuscript in various stages of preparation. These include, first of all, Frederick Moore and William Sheldrick, both (at the time) of the World Bank's Industrial Projects Department. Moore, a fervent supporter of the research program in general from its inception, made it possible for us to carry out the Egyptian case study. Sheldrick, head of the World Bank's Fertilizer Unit, provided us with numerous suggestions for improving our description of the fertilizer sector. Although we do not assign any responsibility for the final product to him, we believe that, because of his help, the relevant chapters are a better and more up-to-date introduction to fertilizer technology than would otherwise have been the case.

A number of other colleagues at the World Bank provided us with comments and suggestions; in particular, Donald Brown, Neithard Petry, and Harald Stier, all of the Industrial Projects Department, should be mentioned. Outside the World Bank, a number of individuals played an important role at various stages in the research. John Couston, of the Food and Agriculture Organization of the United Nations in Rome, commented on earlier drafts of this volume, as did Bernard Raistrick; we are grateful to them for their help.

Numerous persons in Egypt, including staff of the (then) General Organization for Industrialization, the Organization for Chemical Industries, and the Ministry of Agriculture, were involved in various stages of the case study. Furthermore, we gratefully acknowledge the cooperation we received from the managers and staff of the fertilizer production facilities we visited in Egypt during the data collection phase of the study.

J. S. Rogers, of the University of Toronto, made many valuable suggestions for improving the manuscript. The final manuscript was edited by Robert L. Faherty. The charts were prepared by Pensri Kimpitak, proofs were read and corrected by Marie Hergt through the Word Guild, and the index was prepared by Nancy E. MacClintock. The map was compiled by Hans Stolle and was drawn by Larry A. Bowring under the supervision of the World Bank's Cartography Division.

ARMEANE M. CHOKSI
ALEXANDER MEERAUS
ARDY J. STOUTJESDIJK

PART ONE

General Methodology

1

Introduction

THE PROVISION OF ADEQUATE FOOD SUPPLIES for a rapidly growing world population has become inconceivable without substantial increases in the supply of chemical fertilizers. Also, the increased use of fertilizers in the production of cash crops is often a contributing factor to increased income for the grower. Fertilizers must be made available to the farmer at the lowest possible delivered cost for two basic reasons. First, since fertilizer is a crucial input in the agricultural production process, its cost is a component of the production cost and thus of the supply price of agricultural produce. Second, the price of fertilizers is an important element in the individual farmer's decision about how much fertilizer to use. Not only does the purchase of a fertilizer constitute an important short-term investment, but its price is also a critical determinant of the expected return on its use.

The delivered cost of fertilizers at the farm gate is the ultimate result of an intricate process of decisions at many different levels. Should a given country produce its own fertilizers or import them from abroad? Which fertilizers should be produced or imported? In the case of domestic production, which feedstocks should be used? At what scale and at which time and location should productive capacity be installed? If technological choice exists, how should the appropriate production process be selected? What is the most efficient transport and distribution pattern for products in the fertilizer industry?

These questions arise during the initial phase in the project planning process for the chemical fertilizer industry. This phase—that is, selecting the broad outlines of an investment, production, and trade pattern—should be distinguished from the phase in which a given project or set of projects are engineered and appraised in detail. At that time, many of the important decisions relating to the structure of the industry have already been made, either implicitly or explicitly, and although sensitivity analysis may frequently lead to modification of the project, such changes are small compared with those that should normally be allowed for during the project or program selection phase.

One of the most difficult problems to handle during the project selection phase is that many of the questions which come up at that time are highly interdependent: decisions in one area affect decisions in other areas. To give one particularly obvious example, whether a given product should be produced domestically or imported from abroad depends, among other things, on the size of the market for the product in question since economies of scale, which are characteristic of the fertilizer industry, tend to lead to lower production costs per unit as the output level increases. In turn, since fertilizer demand can normally be expected to increase over time, the timing of new capacity construction will be of crucial importance in deciding on the appropriate scale. It is not difficult to see how other issues such as technology, location, and transportation would enter this decisionmaking process and influence the "make–buy" choice.

Primarily because such interdependencies exist, the number of options at the project selection phase is frequently large, and literally thousands of project combinations can be technically feasible. The know-how and judgment of the sector specialist form an important guide to decisionmaking during this time. More often than not, rules of thumb assist the project planner in choosing from among the many alternatives normally available. Nevertheless, the validity of such rules of thumb can be doubted in any given situation, and sector specialists are increasingly dissatisfied with the absence of more systematic planning tools to assist in selecting the appropriate investment project or program. The primary objective of this volume is to describe a planning approach for the analysis of the most important aspects of the investment planning problem in the chemical fertilizer industry.

The Basic Approach

This volume describes the planning tools that are designed to analyze the implications of alternative investment, production, trade, and distribution patterns for the fertilizer industry over time and in a given geographical context. Moreover, it provides criteria on the basis of which the project planner can rank alternative programs and, ultimately, decide about the attractiveness of one program as compared with others. This planning approach forms the basis for subsequent analysis during the project engineering, appraisal, and implementation phases of the project cycle.

The approach to be adopted is the following. The fertilizer industry is represented by a set of mathematical expressions that capture the essential technical and economic relations that characterize the industry. They concern primarily the relations among products at various levels of processing (in the form of input-output coefficients) and the investment and operating costs at various scales of production. The fact that fertilizer production costs are highly dependent on the scale of operations is explicitly modeled in the investment cost function. A further set of expressions describes the cost of transporting the various products in the model between producing sites, import and export points, and marketing centers. Given a set of projections of the demand for fertilizer nutrients, over time, and by marketing center, the model is used to find the least-cost pattern of investment, production, and transportation to meet those demands. The possibility of importing from abroad versus producing domestically is normally taken into account. Furthermore, a range of area-specific restrictions can be represented in the form of constraints. Some of these may reflect industry-specific constraints, such as the availability of raw materials, whereas others may reflect government policies, such as a limitation on the investment resources available for expansion of the fertilizer industry. Also, choice among fertilizers may be constrained by more or less stringent fertilizer recommendations.

Planning problems in the fertilizer industry do not, however, always cover the entire range of issues outlined above. The planner may be interested only in alternative transport and distribution patterns for an existing industry, or in an efficient plan to expand the capacity of a given firm. In such cases, a much less complex problem is posed and a simplified model would be applicable. In what follows, this circumstance will be used and a series of planning models of slowly increasing complexity will be presented; the particular planning problem to which each variant of the model is applicable will be indicated. Moreover, guidelines will be provided about how each model can be modified further to handle specific problems.

The sector planner may not always be interested in finding the least-cost production pattern for the industry as a whole, but simply in costing out the implications of a given project proposal or of competing proposals. As is demonstrated later, the model provides a highly efficient framework for analyzing such questions.

One qualification must be noted. The models presented in this volume are simplified representations of reality, designed to guide decisionmaking, not to replace it. They are highly efficient tools to evaluate and quantify the implications of a certain understanding of the economic and technical relationships that typify the fertilizer industry and the environment in which the industry is supposed to function. Nevertheless, the decision process normally involves more elements than can or should be incorporated in a planning model. More or less important modifications of the initial investment program may therefore appear desirable in subsequent stages of the planning process. This is neither a weakness of the methodology nor something unique to this particular approach to project planning. All project planning methods proceed in phases, and it is inevitable that, as an investment project or program takes shape, greater attention is paid to detailed aspects. In the process, certain inconsistencies with earlier assumptions and judgments will frequently appear; in fact, one of the main advantages of the proposed approach is that, in such cases, a rapid and efficient reassessment of broad strategy options is possible.

The approach to the investment planning problem advocated in this series has limitations. These are discussed extensively in volume 1, but it may be useful to recapitulate the main limitations briefly here. First and foremost, the approach requires a set of projections of demand for the final products that are relevant to the investment planning problem. As the supply price for final products is not known at the outset, the demand projections need to be based on price assumptions that may turn out to be incorrect. Depending on the price elasticity of demand, it may be necessary to revise the demand projections in an iterative manner. In theory, demand schedules that are responsive to price may be incorporated into the model, in combination with a more sophisticated formulation of the objective function, but in practice this would lead to insuperable computational problems.

Normally, another limitation should be made explicit: namely, that by definition the demand projection for final products excludes the possibility of substitution among products on the basis of supply price considerations. Interestingly, the fertilizer sector is one of the few cases in which this limitation does not necessarily apply; the simple reason is that final demand for fertilizers can be expressed in terms of nutrient content—as will be explained shortly—so that the model can be used to select the least-cost fertilizer types. Substitution among inputs and among transport alternatives is permitted, on the basis of explicitly stated supply prices; the limitation is that, normally, most inputs are assumed to be available at a given price either in unlimited quantities or up to a given maximum.

Finally, the state of the art does not permit uncertainty to be incorporated. To a limited extent, sensitivity analysis can be carried out to determine the impact of projection errors on the least-cost investment program. The possible emergence of new products or new production technologies cannot be taken into account, but this is a limitation of investment planning in general rather than of any specific planning technique.

Previous Work

Until now, the major emphasis in investment analysis has undoubtedly been on project appraisal, and a substantial body of literature is available on this subject.[1] Most of this literature is of a general methodological nature, and it does not explicitly address appraisal problems and methods in the fertilizer sector.

In contrast, little systematic attention has been paid in the literature to formulating an investment program, and the fertilizer industry is no exception. It is true that the early experiments with the methodology

1. Several of the more important contributions in this area are: A. C. Harberger, *Project Evaluation* (Chicago: Markham Publishing Co., 1973), particularly chapter 2, pp. 23–67; I. M. D. Little and J. A. Mirrlees, *Project Appraisal and Planning for Developing Countries* (New York: Basic Books, 1974); Lyn Squire and Herman van der Tak, *Economic Analysis of Projects* (Baltimore: Johns Hopkins University Press, 1975); P. Dasgupta, A. Sen, and S. Marglin, *Guidelines for Project Evaluation* (New York: United Nations, 1972).

outlined in this volume included case studies relating to fertilizer manufacture, but these were specific, fairly restrictive, experimental formulations of the investment planning problem, and they are not sufficient to provide general guidelines to investment planning in the industry.[2] Generalizing these earlier studies into a standard approach to the planning of investment projects and programs in the fertilizer industry appears to be a logical extension of this experimental work.

The planning methodology outlined in this volume was developed by H. M. Markowitz and A. S. Manne;[3] it was applied by Thomas Vietorisz and Manne to analyze the optimal location of capacity in the South American fertilizer industry.[4] Manne and others took the methodology one step further, using it to study the optimal time-phasing, location, and scaling of nitrogenous fertilizer plants in India.[5] Ardy Stoutjesdijk, Charles Frank, Jr., and Alexander Meeraus extended the methodology to analyze the optimal investment, production, and trade pattern for the fertilizer industry within the East African Community, substantially increasing the number of products and regions covered in the analysis.[6]

On the basis of this early work, fairly substantial advances have been made in the art of modeling the essential characteristics of the fertilizer industry. At the same time, rapid progress has been made in computer hardware and software, permitting extensive experimentation with such models at continuously decreasing cost. Therefore, it appears to be the appropriate time to acquaint a wider audience of sector specialists with these modeling techniques so that their characteristics can be better understood and their applicability can be evaluated.

2. See Alan S. Manne, ed., *Investments for Capacity Expansion: Size, Location and Time-Phasing* (Cambridge, Mass.: The M.I.T. Press, 1967); and Thomas Vietorisz and Alan S. Manne, "Chemical Processes, Plant Location, and Economies of Scale," in *Studies in Process Analysis, Economy-wide Production Capabilities*, eds. Manne and H. M. Markowitz (New York: John Wiley, 1963).

3. H. M. Markowitz and Alan S. Manne, "On the Solution of Discrete Programming Problems," *Econometrica*, vol. 25 (January 1957), pp. 84–110.

4. Vietorisz and Manne, "Chemical Processes, Plant Location, and Economies of Scale."

5. Manne, ed., *Investments for Capacity Expansion*.

6. Ardy Stoutjesdijk, Charles Frank, Jr., and Alexander Meeraus, "Planning in the Chemical Sector," in *Industrial Investment Analysis under Increasing Returns*, eds., Stoutjesdijk and Larry E. Westphal (forthcoming).

A Reader's Guide to the Volume

This volume is written in two parts: the first part presents the general methodology, and the second part reports on an application of that methodology. Chapter 2 provides a brief general introduction to the fertilizer industry, and offers definitions of commonly used terms in the industry. The next four chapters describe the products and processes associated with particular categories of fertilizers—the nitrogenous, phosphatic, potassic, and multinutrient fertilizers. Chapter 7 treats the major decisionmaking problems concerning fertilizers faced by a planner or project analyst. Chapter 8 presents a series of planning models designed to assist the analyst in solving the problems outlined in chapter 7. The models are presented in order of slowly increasing complexity; the presentation is self-contained, however, in the sense that no prior familiarity with methods and techniques is assumed. Those who are familiar with these methods can turn immediately to chapter 9, which presents a complete statement of the fertilizer model. Chapter 9 also includes a brief discussion of alternative specifications of the model, to suit situations other than the standard one assumed.

In the second part of the volume, an extensive description is given of an application of the methodology to the Egyptian fertilizer sector.

2

The Fertilizer Industry: Some Terminology

GENERAL BACKGROUND INFORMATION on the fertilizer industry is presented in this chapter. The information provides only a summary overview of the industry, but it is sufficient to understand the major sector-specific features of the planning models presented later in the volume.[1]

Fertilizer Nutrients and Grades

Broadly speaking, the function of a fertilizer is to furnish one or more of the chemical elements that plants need to grow. The chemical

1. The following four chapters provide a more detailed description of products and processes in the industry. For more technical and comprehensive information, see: Vincent Sauchelli, ed., *Chemistry and Technology of Fertilizers* (New York and London: Holt, Reinhart, and Winston, 1960), a standard collection of reference papers on various aspects of fertilizer production; United Nations, *Fertilizer Manual* (New York: United Nations, 1967), a still largely up-to-date, comprehensive source of information; and numerous publications of the Tennessee Valley Authority, Muscle Shoals, Alabama.

Figure 1. The Chemical Elements Essential for Plant Growth

Macronutrients	Natural nutrients	Carbon Hydrogen Oxygen
	Primary nutrients	Nitrogen Phosphorus Potassium
	Secondary nutrients	Calcium Magnesium Sulfur
Micronutrients		Boron Chlorine Copper Iron Manganese Molybdenum Zinc

fertilizer industry produces a multitude of fertilizer materials that contain these elements, also called plant nutrients, in a wide range of combinations and compositions. Fertilizer materials are usually classified on the basis of their plant nutrient content. The number of these nutrients has increased over the years and now totals sixteen. They may be separated into two categories: macronutrients and micronutrients, or trace elements, as shown in figure 1. The first three macronutrients (carbon, hydrogen, and oxygen) are supplied in sufficient quantities by air and water. The other macronutrients are subdivided into primary nutrients (nitrogen, phosphorus, and potassium) and secondary nutrients (calcium, magnesium, and sulfur). The seven micronutrients are required in much smaller amounts. A commercial fertilizer contains at least one primary nutrient (with or without secondary nutrients and micronutrients).

In order for plants to grow, they need primary nutrients in substantial quantities, although the specific quantities vary widely among crops, and primary nutrients are the main nutrients provided by chemical fertilizers.[2] Fertilizer materials are therefore usually classified according to the primary nutrient or nutrients they contain; the presence of secondary nutrients and trace elements is often considered a bonus of somewhat varying importance. In this volume, fertilizer materials are classified by primary nutrient according to the following distinction: nitrogenous fertilizers, phosphatic fertilizers, potassic fertilizers, and multinutrient fertilizers.

Two further terminological conventions should be noted in this context. First, fertilizer material containing only one primary nutrient is usually referred to as straight fertilizer. Second, a fertilizer product may be qualified as a low-analysis fertilizer if the ratio of nutrients to other components is relatively low, or as a high-analysis fertilizer if the ratio is relatively high.

Commercial fertilizers are graded according to their content of available primary nutrients (and sometimes secondary nutrients), expressed as a percentage by weight, in the order presented in figure 1. Nitrogen is reported as the element N, whereas phosphorus and potassium are usually reported as the oxides P_2O_5 and K_2O, respectively. Thus, a 10–20–15 fertilizer contains 10 percent nitrogen, 20 percent phosphorus (expressed as P_2O_5), and 15 percent potassium (expressed as K_2O). When a fertilizer contains only two primary nutrients, the missing element is represented by a zero: for example, 10–20–0.

The nutrient ratio is the proportion of the nutrients to each other. Thus, a 10–10–10 grade of fertilizer has a ratio of 1–1–1 and a 10–20–10 has a ratio 1–2–1.

The Main Materials in Fertilizer Production

The fertilizer industry covers a great number of raw materials, intermediate products, and fertilizer products. These products, as well as the main production processes currently employed, are described in some detail in the subsequent four chapters. In this section, a brief description is given of nitrogenous fertilizers, phosphatic fertilizers, potassic fertilizers, and multinutrient fertilizers.

2. The primary nutrients are also provided by animal manures.

Nitrogenous fertilizers

Ammonia is the basis for almost all nitrogenous fertilizer production; in some technologically advanced situations, it is used directly as a fertilizer as well. The preferred feedstock to produce ammonia is natural gas; other raw materials include coal, naphtha, and fuel oil. Another important intermediate product in the nitrogenous fertilizer industry is nitric acid; at present, it is manufactured almost exclusively from ammonia.

The most important nitrogenous fertilizer products are:

- ammonia (82.5 percent N), which is produced primarily from natural gas, but also from naphtha, fuel oil, coal, refinery gas, liquefied petroleum gas, and the water-electrolysis process;
- urea (45 to 46 percent N), which is produced from ammonia and carbon dioxide;[3]
- ammonium nitrate (33.5 percent N), which is produced from ammonia and nitric acid, often when carbon dioxide is unavailable for urea production;[4]
- ammonium sulfate (20 to 21 percent N), which is produced either from ammonia and sulfuric acid, or as a by-product of the production of iron and steel in coking plants or of certain petrochemical processes such as the manufacture of caprolactam;
- calcium ammonium nitrate (usually between 21 and 33.5 percent), which is produced by adding limestone to ammonium nitrate, thereby reducing its explosive as well as its hygroscopic character.

Phosphatic fertilizers

Phosphate rock is the basic raw material for the production of phosphatic fertilizers; in fact, finely ground phosphate rock itself is used directly as a fertilizer. In addition to rock-based phosphates, basic slag, which is a by-product of iron and steel manufacture, is also used as a raw material.

3. Urea is almost always produced in conjunction with synthetic ammonia because carbon dioxide can be obtained as a by-product of synthesis gas purification.

4. Ammonium nitrate is also used as an explosive.

In most cases, phosphatic fertilizers are produced by reacting ground phosphate rock with either sulfuric or phosphoric acid. In turn, sulfuric acid is produced either from elemental sulfur, pyrites, or gypsum, or as a by-product of petroleum or metallurgical refining, while phosphoric acid is produced by combining phosphate rock and sulfuric acid. Depending on the type of acid used, and on the proportions of rock and acid, a variety of phosphatic fertilizers can be produced. The main ones, however, are single and triple superphosphate. In short, the main phosphatic fertilizers are the following:

- ground phosphate rock (variable P_2O_5 content, normally about 30 to 33 percent, but rarely of commercial interest unless more than 15 percent);
- basic slag (usually between 10 and 20 percent P_2O_5) which is a by-product of iron and steel manufacture;
- single superphosphate (16 to 21 percent P_2O_5), which is produced by combining ground phosphate rock and sulfuric acid;
- triple superphosphate (43 to 48 percent P_2O_5), which is produced by combining ground phosphate rock and phosphoric acid.

Potassic fertilizers

Virtually all potassic fertilizers are produced from potash-bearing brines or from underground deposits of potash. The main potassic fertilizers are:

- potassium chloride (60 to 62 percent K_2O);
- potassium sulfate (50 to 54 percent K_2O).

Multinutrient fertilizers

Multinutrient fertilizers contain more than one primary nutrient. Their manufacture may or may not involve a major chemical reaction. Essentially, two routes are available to produce multinutrient fertilizers. The first is dry-mixing or bulk-blending, in which mutually compatible fertilizers, preferably in granular or prilled form, are mechanically mixed. In technologically advanced countries, bulk-blending is frequently integrated into the marketing and distribution system for fertilizers. The second possible route is granulation of several fertilizer intermediates; this process is more flexible in terms of input products, and it does not pose subsequent segregation problems. A variety of processes are in use, and they permit the production of a wide range of fertilizer grades, including several of the highest concentration fertilizer products, such as diammonium phosphate (16 percent N, 46 to 48 percent P_2O_5) and monoammonium phosphate (11 percent N, 50 to 54 percent P_2O_5). These products enjoy a rapidly growing market around the world, both in direct use as a fertilizer and as material for further bulk-blending or granulation.

Conclusion

The chemical fertilizer industry comprises a large number of products and processes, and this number is continually increasing because of ongoing research efforts. Nevertheless, a rather small number of these possible products and processes predominate. Only the main products have been included in this chapter; products and processes that are used less frequently are included in the subsequent four chapters.

3

The Production of Nitrogenous Fertilizers

THE ATMOSPHERE IS AN INEXHAUSTIBLE SOURCE OF NITROGEN. But, because atmospheric nitrogen is extremely inert chemically, it must be converted into an available form before it is suitable for plant use. Although some nitrogen is continually being fixed in the air and in the soil as a result of natural processes, this natural fixation is inadequate to supply the world's need for nitrogenous nutrients. Hence, increasing quantities of chemically fixed nitrogen are needed.

Fixed nitrogen has three important natural sources: namely, by-product ammonium salts from the manufacture of coke, the Chilean deposits of sodium nitrate, and natural organic manures. Of the three well-known chemical processes for fixing nitrogen—the electric arc process, the cyanamide process, and synthetic ammonia production—only the last is important for the fertilizer industry. The electric arc process was formerly an important method for manufacturing nitric acid, which is now produced chiefly by ammonia oxidation. The cyanamide process is currently important only in the manufacture of organic nitrogen compounds (nonfertilizer petrochemical products), and hence it is not discussed here. Synthetic ammonia accounts for virtually all the nitrogen that is fixed chemically, and thus attention is focused on technological alternatives for producing it.

Ammonia

Ammonia has a crucial place in the manufacture of nitrogenous fertilizers. It is the principal form in which fixed nitrogen is available, and it is the basis for almost all nitrogenous fertilizers, including nitric acid, ammonium sulfate, ammonium nitrate, calcium nitrate, urea, ammoniating solutions, as well as fertilizer compounds and, indirectly, blends of fertilizer material containing nitrogen nutrients. Moreover, under certain conditions, ammonia—principally in the form of anhydrous ammonia—can be applied directly as a fertilizer.[1] Anhydrous ammonia contains 82.5 percent nitrogen by weight. Ammonia liquor (also known as aqua ammonia, ammoniacal liquor, or ammonia water) contains only 15 to 30 percent nitrogen, by weight in water; it is normally supplied to the fertilizer trade in a concentration of 29.4 percent ammonia in water.[2] Like the anhydrous form, the liquor has an alkaline reaction.

The raw material used most often nowadays in the manufacture of synthetic ammonia is natural gas, which is present in many regions of the world. Natural gas can be classified as "associated" if it occurs with crude oil from which it is liberated, or as "nonassociated" if it comes directly from the well. Its composition varies, depending on the geographical location and the type of deposit, but essentially the gas is methane (60 to 96 percent) mixed with ethane (4 to 40 percent) and other higher hydrocarbons, gaseous impurities, and inert gases. It is preferable that the natural gas used as a raw material for synthetic ammonia contain a high concentration of methane because methane

1. The use of anhydrous ammonia by direct injection depends much more on the suitability of the soil and on the way the crop is grown than on most other factors; for example, the soil should be free of stones. This form of nitrogen application is most useful for wide-row crops. It is not good for grass or for the top dressing of cereals, no matter how technologically advanced the country is.

2. In Europe, the description "ammonia liquor" is usually reserved for the crude liquor obtained from coal carbonization. The aqueous solution made from anhydrous ammonia is usually described as "aqueous ammonia" or "aqua ammonia."

has a lower ratio of carbon to hydrogen than higher hydrocarbons.[3] In the synthesis process, all the carbon in natural gas is converted to carbon dioxide, which is removed in purification steps. Hence, smaller and less expensive purification units are required for plants that use natural gas with a high methane content.

Until the early 1950s, fuel oils were commonly used in the production of ammonia, even in countries where natural gas was available, and even though fuel oil is more difficult to use than natural gas and the capital costs of plants using fuel oil are higher than those of plants using natural gas. Because of recent changes in relative prices, as well as in technology, however, there is currently renewed interest in using fuel oil.

Naphtha is also an important alternative hydrocarbon raw material for ammonia synthesis. For economic and technical reasons, the sulfur content of the naphtha should be as low as possible. The use of cracked naphtha is not recommended because of the difficulty that might be encountered in removing the sulfur. Naphtha is produced during the refining of crude oil, and it can be processed further to yield gasoline. It can be transported by pipeline or bulk carriers such as trucks and ships.

Until twenty to thirty years ago, coal was a major raw material for ammonia synthesis. Over the years, however, coal and lignite have given way to naphtha, natural gas, and fuel oil as the important feedstock. Consequently, old plants have been converted or shut down, and new ones have been designed for the use of these materials. Coal has not been economically competitive with liquid or gaseous petroleum materials; the quality of the competitive coal is low because of its high ash content and low calorific value. Further, the coal gasification processes are elaborate, and in general the plant investment, maintenance, and operating costs tend to be higher for them than for petroleum-based plants. The popularity of coal as a raw material for ammonia production may increase, however, because of the increasing costs of the petroleum materials.[4]

3. These considerations may not apply if the ammonia unit is part of a more comprehensive petrochemical complex.

4. Coal is only used as a raw material for ammonia synthesis today in those countries lacking oil or natural gas—South Africa is the main case. In the long term, however, producers are likely to be forced to use coal, and this is the reason for the keen interest in coal now being manifested in the United States as well as in other countries with substantial coal deposits, such as India, where two coal-based ammonia plants were scheduled to start production in 1978.

The manufacture of ammonia

The synthesis of ammonia is of considerable historical importance in the chemical industry because it represents a significant application of thermodynamic principles to the solution of a difficult commercial process. The basis of ammonia production is the reacting of hydrogen with atmospheric nitrogen. The first ammonia plant came on stream in 1913 and used what became known as the Haber-Bosch process, after its inventors. Although variations on the basic process have been developed since then, the main differences lie in the method of preparing the synthesis gas, which is a 3-to-1 mixture of hydrogen and nitrogen; the purification of synthesis gas; the design of the ammonia converter; and the method for recovering ammonia from the converter effluent gas.

The four major steps in the manufacture of ammonia are synthesis gas preparation, carbon monoxide conversion, gas purification, and ammonia synthesis. Each of these steps can be accomplished by several processes, which will be discussed below.

Figure 2 is a diagrammatic representation of the alternative processes available for the synthesis of ammonia. These processes are denoted by the rectangular boxes.

Synthesis gas preparation

The synthesis ammonia process depends on the availability of large quantities of extremely pure synthesis gas.[5] The major processes for preparing synthesis gas are steam reforming and partial oxidation; in addition, there are coal gasification, autothermal, and electrolytic processes.[6] Several variations of each process are also available. Each process produces a gas that is rich in hydrogen and carbon monoxide; the carbon monoxide is later converted to carbon dioxide, generating hydrogen by reaction with steam in the shift converter.

5. Sulfur, phosphorus, carbon monoxide, and arsenic are irreversible catalyst poisons and can only be present in the order of parts per million (ppm). Water, oxygen, and carbon dioxide are reversible poisons that can be removed by heating the catalyst; even here, however, the catalyst suffers some permanent damage, so these gases must also be present in very low concentrations.

6. The electrolytic process is not very common; it produces hydrogen for synthesis gas by electrolysis of water. This process is used where electric power is (or was) inexpensive—for example, at Aswan in Egypt, and near Cuzco in southern Peru.

Figure 2. Alternative Processes for Ammonia Synthesis

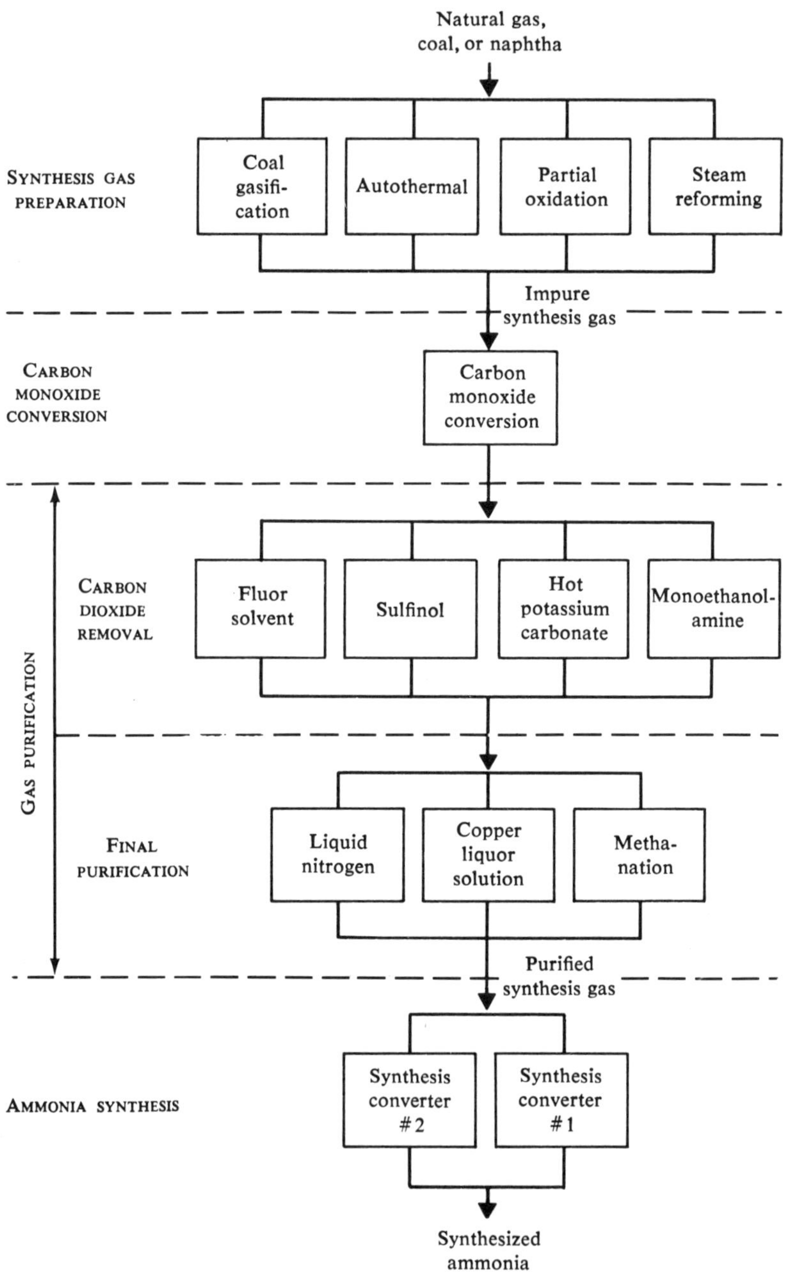

STEAM REFORMING. Steam reforming of natural gas (methane) is usually carried out in two stages, using primary and secondary reformers with a nickel catalyst. Since the reforming catalyst would be poisoned by sulfur, the first step in the process is desulfurization of the natural gas. The purified gases are then mixed with steam and sent to the primary reformer. The exit gases from the primary reformer are mixed with air and are sent directly to the secondary reformer. Heat liberated by the partial oxidation of hydrogen and methane raises the temperature, which essentially completes the reforming of the natural gas.

Until the early 1950s, the danger of tube failure restricted the process to a low-pressure operation. With the advent of new alloys and improved methods of fabrication, however, high-pressure operation is now common practice. This development has improved the efficiency of ammonia production by conserving the pressure of the incoming natural gas and eliminating the need to compress the process gas for the purification step, thus reducing the size of plant equipment and the volume of catalyst.

Naphtha is an alternative feedstock for steam reforming, but there are essential differences between natural gas reforming and naphtha reforming: because of its high sulfur content, naphtha must undergo a preliminary acid treatment to remove most of the sulfur; naphtha contains more unsaturates and aromatics (that is, various other hydrocarbons), thereby increasing the possibility of carbon deposits; a vaporizer must be added in naphtha reforming; additional capacity to remove carbon dioxide is required in naphtha reforming because of the higher ratio of carbon to hydrogen in the feedstock; and naphtha reforming requires a catalyst that contains a promoter to inhibit carbon formation and that is more resistant to poisoning by sulfur.

PARTIAL OXIDATION. Partial oxidation of hydrocarbons is another method of preparing synthesis gas, and several different forms of the method have been developed. One form of partial oxidation, which is very flexible, can be used for feedstocks ranging from natural gas to heavy fuel oils. The method does, however, require a source of oxygen, which is normally obtained from a liquid air plant.

This method offers four advantages over the steam reforming process: no catalysts are required; the heat requirements are lower; impurities in the feedstock are tolerated; and the process can be adapted to a wide range of hydrocarbon feedstocks. The process also has disadvantages: it requires a liquid air or air separation plant to produce oxygen, and the costs associated with such a plant are high; and substantial quantities of undesirable carbon are formed, and they must be removed from the combustion gases.

AUTOTHERMAL. The autothermal process is a combination of the steam reforming and partial oxidation processes. The feedstocks for the process range from natural gas and naphtha to refinery gas and liquefied petroleum gas (LPG). Steam, air, oxygen, and the hydrocarbon feedstock constitute the feed material of the reactor. The process operates at high pressures without difficulty. The major advantage of the process is that it does not require catalyst tubes, which can present problems for high-pressure operations. Its disadvantage is that it requires an air separation plant to provide oxygen and nitrogen.

COAL GASIFICATION. Many processes have been developed for coal gasification, but the two most important are the Lurgi process and the Koppers-Totzek process. Both use steam, oxygen, and coal or lignite as feed materials.

In the Lurgi process, a mixture of steam and oxygen is passed into a bed of coal that is maintained at a high temperature. Small lumps of coal are fed in batches as the gas flows from the generator. This process for the formation of synthesis gas is used in ammonia plants in South Korea and Turkey.

The Koppers-Totzek process uses pulverized coal as the feedstock. Oxygen and coal dust are passed into a gas generator into which steam is introduced. The gas flow is continuous. Gaseous or liquid hydrocarbons can be used instead of coal as feed material; this is a significant advantage. Among the countries using this process are France, Japan, and Spain.

Carbon monoxide conversion

The second step in the process of producing ammonia is the catalytic reaction between carbon monoxide, obtained in the first step, and steam to form hydrogen. Exit gases from the preparation unit (the secondary reformer in the case of the steam reforming process) contain appreciable quantities of carbon monoxide, which are converted to hydrogen by passing the gases through a converter containing a catalyst made of a mixture of iron and chromium oxide.

For economic reasons, the conversion to hydrogen should be as high as possible. Variables affecting this conversion are: concentrations of carbon dioxide, carbon monoxide, and steam in the gas entering the converter; temperature of the catalyst; pressure; catalytic activity; and gas velocity.

Initial gas purification

The third stage in the production of ammonia is to purify the process gas by removing carbon dioxide and carbon monoxide.

In older ammonia plants, carbon dioxide was removed by scrubbing the process with water. This method, however, proved to be relatively inefficient and possessed several disadvantages; hence, all new processes employ solvents that absorb carbon dioxide more efficiently. Solvents commonly used are monoethanolamine, hot potassium carbonate, sulfinol, and fluorsolvent.

Final gas purification

Since carbon monoxide is an irreversible poison to the synthesis catalyst, its concentration must be reduced to a few parts per million in the synthesis gas. Carbon dioxide is still present in small amounts, and this must also be reduced before the gas is suitable for ammonia synthesis. Three processes are available to remove the traces of these oxides: methanation, copper liquor solution, and liquid nitrogen.

METHANATION. Most new plants use catalytic methanation to remove carbon monoxide, carbon dioxide, and oxygen. In this process, the gas stream is heated and passed through a nickel-base catalyst. The carbon monoxide and carbon dioxide react with hydrogen to form methane and water. The equipment cost for this process is low, and the only operating cost is the initial charge of the catalyst. The major disadvantage is the hydrogen loss caused by the reaction with carbon monoxide and carbon dioxide and by the purging required to control the concentration of methane in the recirculating gas of the synthesis loop.

COPPER LIQUOR SOLUTION. Scrubbing with copper liquor is one of the oldest processes for removing carbon monoxide, but it has been used very little in new construction. The operation of this process is more complex than the methanation process, and the corrosiveness of the solution results in higher maintenance costs.

LIQUID NITROGEN. Scrubbing with nitrogen is economical only in conjunction with partial oxidation plants, since the nitrogen is available from the liquid air plant. In this process, the gases are first dried and then washed directly with liquid nitrogen, which removes not only carbon monoxide and dioxide but also methane and argon. The resulting synthesis gas is so free of impurities that little purging is required. This is a low-temperature operation, however, and considerable heat exchange is needed to make the process economical.

Ammonia synthesis

Ammonia synthesis is a reaction between hydrogen and nitrogen at elevated pressure and temperature in the presence of a catalyst that is composed of iron oxides and contains promoters of aluminium, potassium, magnesium, and calcium oxides.

Synthesis gas from the methanator is cooled, condensed water is removed, and the gas is then compressed to the final synthesis pressure. In the past, reciprocating compressors were used for the high-pressure compression; now, however, there is a trend toward centrifugal compressors and larger plants. The high-pressure synthesis gas is mixed with recycled gas from the ammonia converter; this mixture is passed through an oil trap to remove any entrained oil from the reciprocating compressors, and it is then sent to an ammonia refrigeration exchanger that condenses out ammonia from the recycled gas and removes nearly all traces of water from the synthesis gas. The purified synthesis gas passes to a separator and heat exchanger before entering the ammonia converter. The design of this converter is quite critical because fairly large quantities of heat are given off in the synthesis reaction.

Two general types of synthesis converters are in use, and the major difference is in the method of temperature control. One type employs multiple beds of catalyst with provisions for cooling the gas between the beds by means of cooling coils or quenching with cold gas. The other type uses gas flow and heat exchangers to control the temperature.

Nitric Acid

Nitric acid is a strong acid and a powerful oxidizing agent that is normally manufactured as a product containing 55 to 60 percent acid. Approximately 75 percent of the manufactured nitric acid is used for fertilizer production, 15 percent for the manufacture of explosives (nitrates and nitro compounds), and 10 percent for numerous other purposes by the chemical industry.

Three different processes can be used to manufacture nitric acid—ammonia oxidation, the electric arc process, and a process based on the reaction between sodium nitrate and sulfuric acid—but only the first is significant today.

Basically, ammonia oxidation involves the oxidation of nitric oxide, which is itself produced by burning ammonia in air over a platinum catalyst, and the absorption of the oxides of nitrogen in water to form nitric acid. This process has three general forms: oxidation and absorption at atmospheric pressure; oxidation and absorption at elevated pressure; oxidation at atmospheric pressure but absorption at elevated pressure. There are numerous proprietory processes for nitric acid manufacture, which differ mainly in design details or selected operating conditions. Their major features are:

- vaporization, superheating, and filtration of anhydrous ammonia;
- preheating filtration and compression of process air;
- catalytic oxidation of ammonia;
- oxidation of nitric oxide to higher oxides;
- absorption of the nitrogen oxides in water to form nitric acid;
- acid bleaching;
- tail-gas treatment;
- energy recovery;
- recovery of the catalyst.

Urea

Urea is the diamide of carbonic acid and in its pure state contains 46.66 percent nitrogen. It is sold in the form of crystals, granules (1.5 to 4 millimeters), or prills (1 to 2.5 millimeters), with or without a mineral coating. Crystal urea and uncoated prills contain 46 percent nitrogen, and coated prills average 45 percent nitrogen. Synthetic urea is chemically identical with organically produced urea, and its high nitrogen content makes it the most concentrated solid nitrogen fertilizer material in the world fertilizer market.[7] Accordingly, it is

7. For use as a straight nitrogen fertilizer, prills hold most of the world market. A typical specification for prilled urea is 95 percent concentration and 1 to 2.5 millimeters with no oversize.

increasingly favored among manufacturers of high-analysis grades of NP and NPK fertilizers.

Generally, urea must be used with caution in mixtures because it is hygroscopic and incompatible with triple superphosphate. Because of its hygroscopicity, urea should never be mixed with ammonium nitrate in solid fertilizers. One of the most popular uses of urea in the manufacture of mixed liquid fertilizers is its application in solution with ammonia as ammonia-urea liquor or as ammonia-ammonium nitrate-urea solution.

Urea is sold under various trade names. Uramon is a processed form that contains 42 percent nitrogen. Ureor and Caliureor are trade names used in Europe to designate processed types of crystalline urea that are coated with a finely ground limestone to reduce the tendency to absorb moisture.

The manufacture of urea

Urea was the first organic compound to be synthesized from inorganic materials, and thus it is of considerable historical interest. At one time, substantial quantities of urea were made by the hydrolysis of cyanamide produced from calcium carbide. At present, however, virtually all urea is based on the dehydration of ammonium carbamate. Most urea is manufactured in conjunction with synthetic ammonia since the necessary carbon dioxide is available from the synthesis gas purification system at essentially zero cost.

Urea can be manufactured by various processes, which are classified according to the degree of recycling of the unconverted ammonia and carbon dioxide. The processes are referred to as the once-through process, the partial-recycle process, and the total-recycle process. These alternative processes are diagrammed in figure 3. The only difference among the processes is in the handling of the gases evolved during the decomposition of the ammonium carbamate. The choice of the process depends upon the location of the plant and whether or not the urea process can be integrated with other plant operations. Thus, the once-through and partial-recycle processes might be most economical if the urea off-gases could be used to produce ammonium sulfate or ammonium nitrate, and if carbon dioxide is available in ample supply at low cost. On the other hand, the total-recycle process would be used if there were no place to dispose of the off-gas ammonia. The most serious problems associated with any method of urea synthesis are the corrosion of equipment, the formation of biuret

Figure 3. Alternative Processes for the Manufacture of Urea

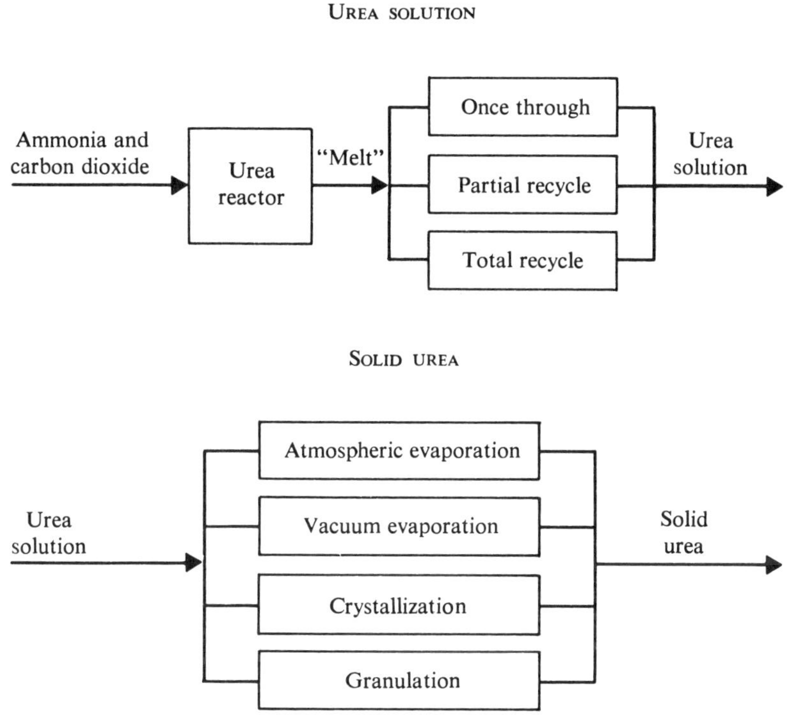

(which is toxic to some plants), and the presence of unconverted ammonia and carbon dioxide.

THE ONCE-THROUGH PROCESS. In the once-through process, the solution or melt from the urea reactor is flashed to a lower pressure and is heated to drive off ammonia and decompose the unreacted carbamate. The resulting solution is 80 percent urea, which can be either utilized directly or concentrated to crystalline urea. Although this is the simplest process, it is the least flexible and cannot be operated unless some provision is made to utilize the large amount of off-gas ammonia. This off-gas can be absorbed in acid to produce ammonium nitrate, ammonium sulfate, or ammonium phosphates. Only about 32 percent of the ammonia is converted, and thus several tons of ammonium sulfate or nitrate are produced for each ton of urea. Even though the carbon dioxide in the off-gas is lost and hence must be available in sufficient supply, this is the least expensive process in both capital investment and operating costs.

THE PARTIAL-RECYCLE PROCESS. In the partial-recycle process, part of the off-gas ammonia and carbon dioxide from the carbamate strippers is recycled to the urea reactor and part is used to produce a coproduct nitrogen material, as in the once-through process. Although the rate of coproduction is greatly reduced in this process, the operation of the urea plant must still coincide with that of the coproduct plant.

THE TOTAL-RECYCLE PROCESS. In the total-recycle process, all the unconverted ammonia and carbon dioxide mixture is recycled to the urea reactor, where about 99 percent of the mixture is then converted. No by-products are produced, and hence no nitrogen coproducts are necessary. Of the three urea synthesis processes, this is the most flexible because it depends only upon its supporting ammonia plant for operation. It is also the most expensive process in investment and operating costs; hence, if the production of other materials requiring ammonia is planned, either of the other two processes would have lower investment and operating costs. Synchronizing the operation of the urea and the nitrogen coproducts plant presents difficulties, however, and this has often biased the decision in favor of the total-recycle process, despite the lack of by-products.

Total-recycle systems are of two general types: the gas-separation system and the carbamate-solution-recycle system. Comparing these two types of processes is difficult, but there are indications that the requirements of the gas-separation unit for utilities such as water and electricity are significantly higher than those of some solution-recycle processes.

Special processes

Three special processes that have been developed deserve mention: the carbamate-recycle process, the thermo-urea process, and the "integrated-loop" process.

THE CARBAMATE-RECYCLE PROCESS. In the carbamate-recycle process, most of the unreacted feed-gases (from the reactor effluent at synthesis pressure) are stripped by a fresh carbon dioxide feed in a special, indirectly heated stripper. The remaining unreacted gases are stripped and recycled by the aqueous carbonate solution method. Ninety percent of the ammonia can be converted in this way. It is claimed that the requirements for steam, electricity, and cooling water are reduced significantly in this process. A similar process has been developed with gaseous ammonia as the stripping agent.

THE THERMO-UREA PROCESS. In the thermo-urea process, also known as the hot-gas recycle, sufficient heat is produced to eliminate the need for steam but the electrical power requirements offset some of this saving. Because of the high temperatures, centrifugal compressors rather than reciprocating compressors must be used, to avoid maintenance problems. But centrifugal compressors are not practical in small sizes, and thus 1,500 tons of urea a day would need to be produced for their best use.

THE "INTEGRATED-LOOP" PROCESS. The integrated-loop process combines urea and ammonia production into a single unit. There are three combined steps: carbon dioxide is scrubbed from the converted gas in the ammonia train by carbamate-recycle solution (from the urea plant absorbers) and by fresh ammonia; the resulting scrubbing liquor is fed by its own pressure to the urea reactor; the hot gas from the carbon monoxide shift converter is cooled by heating the urea effluent in the decomposers to strip off the unreacted ammonia and the carbon dioxide. In general, more carbon dioxide is produced than is needed to convert all ammonia to urea; hence, an auxiliary system to remove carbon dioxide must be provided.

The principal advantages of this process are the substantial savings in plant investment and operating costs that arise because: the need for a carbon dioxide compressor is eliminated; the size of the urea reactor is reduced; the requirements for carbon dioxide regeneration equipment and steam are eliminated; the heat of converted gas is utilized in the urea plant; the ammonia purge-gas recovery system is eliminated; and the ammonia pumping requirements are reduced. Some disadvantages are also associated with this process namely, the ammonia plant is completely dependent upon the urea plant operation, and the production rate of the urea plant must be matched with that of the ammonia plant, unless a large standby carbon dioxide removal system is provided.

Prilled urea

The synthesis processes described above produce an aqueous solution containing between 70 and 80 percent urea, with the proportion depending on the extent of recycling. This solution must be concentrated if solid urea is to be produced, and it is in the concentration step that biuret is formed, unless provisions are made to prevent a harmful combination of high temperature and long retention time. In practice, some compromise is made between the biuret content of the urea and the size and costs (both operation and investment) of the evaporation equipment. The method of evaporation and solidification should be chosen to give the maximum acceptable biuret content at the minimum cost. For most commercial crop applications, a biuret content of 1 percent is acceptable.

Prilled urea is produced by four methods: atmospheric evaporation, vacuum evaporation, crystallization, and granulation. The differences among the first three lie in the method of producing the concentrated melt required for the prilling operation.

ATMOSPHERIC EVAPORATION. The moisture from a continuously replenished film of stripped urea reactor effluent is evaporated. These evaporation units have either rotating discs to spray the feed against the jacketed walls or rotating blades that wipe the walls continuously. Both present maintenance problems associated with bearing lubrication. In some units, a current of inert, dry gas is passed through to carry out the water vapor. The resulting "melt" is sprayed into the top of a prilling tower, and the droplets from the spray solidify upon cooling during their descent. Despite the short retention time (few seconds) in the evaporator, the biuret content is about 0.8 to 1.5 percent.

VACUUM EVAPORATION. Water is evaporated at the melting point of urea in a conventional heat exchanger operating under a vacuum. Though the retention time is short because of the flash evaporation, the biuret content is generally 0.7 to 1.0 percent. Two or more stages of evaporation may be used. This process is widely used because it does not have the maintenance problems of the atmospheric evaporation unit.

CRYSTALLIZATION. A circulating vacuum crystallizer is used to produce a saturated solution of urea, from which urea crystallizes. A side stream of the suspension is withdrawn and fed into a centrifuge, where the crystals are separated. They are then dried in a rotary drier. The mother liquor is recycled through the off-gas absorbers to the urea reactor. Since the biuret does not crystallize with the urea, any that is formed is recycled with the molten liquor. Under the reactor conditions, the biuret is reconverted to urea.

GRANULATION. The granulation process, which has been developed recently, uses a tilted-pan granulator.[8] The stripped urea effluent solution is concentrated to about 95 percent in a vacuum evaporator. The solution is then sprayed onto a tumbling bed of urea granules. The sprayed solution agglomerates or coats the particles, the tumbling action rounds off the agglomerates, and the classifying action of the tilted pan produces urea granules that are substantially on-size—that is, 1.5 to 3.5 millimeters. These granules are then dried, cooled, and screened. Investments and operating costs of this process are lower than those of the prilling operation, and the particles are of larger size. The biuret content is about the same, however. A granulation process has also been developed using rotary drums instead of the tilted-pan granulator.

Ammonium Sulfate

Pure ammonium sulfate contains 21.2 percent nitrogen. The commercial grade ordinarily used by fertilizer producers contains small amounts of moisture-free sulfuric acid and other impurities, and it is guaranteed to contain 20 to 21 percent nitrogen. It contains about 24 percent sulfur, and this is often seen as a valuable plant nutrient. In the formulation of granular mixed fertilizers and bulk blends, ammonium sulfate is highly esteemed as a nitrogen source because of its low hygroscopicity. It can be mixed in all proportions with practically all the solid raw materials of the trade. It is not,

8. The tilted-form granulator has been used in the fertilizer industry for at least twenty-five years, but it has only been applied to urea in recent years. Its main advantage is that it gives a product which is the same size as granular diammonium phosphate. Bulk blends can therefore be made without significant segregation problems.

however, compatible with alkaline materials such as lime, cyanamide, calcium nitrate, and basic slag. It can be mixed with urea, provided the mixture is used shortly after mixing.

Ammonium sulfate is produced by six principal methods, which are described below.

COMBINED REACTION-EVAPORATION METHODS. In the combined reaction-evaporation methods, anhydrous ammonia and sulfuric acid are reacted in a continuous saturator-evaporator under vacuum or at atmospheric pressure. The resulting crystals are recovered by means of a centrifuge or a filter.

GAS-WORKS BY-PRODUCT METHODS. Before synthetic ammonia was available, most ammonia was obtained from solid-fuel carbonization. The bituminous coals used to produce gas and coke contain about 2 percent nitrogen, of which 15 to 20 percent can be recovered (at high temperature) as ammonia; that is, 5 to 6 pounds of ammonia per ton of coal. Hence, most by-product ammonia is associated with high-temperature carbonization units—for example, at coking plants for iron and steel production, about 35 to 40 pounds of ammonium sulfate can be produced for each ton of steel. There are three principal methods for ammonia recovery and the subsequent production of ammonium sulfate or other ammonium salts: the direct, indirect, and semidirect processes. The two main processes currently in use are the indirect and semidirect ones.

THE AMMONIUM CARBONATE-GYPSUM PROCESS. Ammonium carbonate and calcium sulfate (anhydrite or gypsum) can be made to react in a series of wooden vessels or mild steel tanks fitted with steam coils and agitators.[9] The gypsum can be derived from natural sources or by-product sources (for example, phosphoric acid production), and the ammonium carbonate is obtained by absorbing ammonia gas in water and carbonating the solution in carbonating towers.

RECOVERY OF BY-PRODUCT LIQUOR. The waste liquor stream from the processes for the production of caprolactam, acrylonitrile, and some other products contain at least 35 percent ammonium sulfate in solution. This can be recovered as a nearly pure salt by crystallization

9. Almost all plants using this process have now been shut down.

of the waste liquor and subsequent centrifuging. Spent sulfuric acid from petroleum refineries, petrochemical plants, and soap factories can also be used, if the impurities present in the acid do not cause frothing or corrosion problems. An alternative is to ammoniate the contaminated acid and granulate the slurry on a moving bed or in a drum and to recycle the products in a drier-screening system to produce granules of the required size range.

SPRAY TOWER AMMONIATION. Sulfuric acid can be sprayed into ammonia vapor inside a spray tower. The heat of reaction produces a dry, amorphous product, which is removed continuously from the base of the tower. This form of ammonium sulfate is particularly suitable for dry-mixed and granulated-mixed fertilizers.

MISCELLANEOUS PROCESSES. One method utilizes an organic solvent that absorbs sulfurous gases. After the absorption, the liquor is blown with air to form a basic sulfate, and ammonia is added to produce ammonium sulfate. This salt separates from the organic base and is centrifuged, dried, and sent to storage. The organic absorbent (for example, xylidine or monomethylaniline) is recycled for further use. This process can be useful where sulfur is costly or where air pollution is a serious problem, since it does not require a source of sulfuric acid and it can operate on rich or lean sulfurous gases from roasters, boiler flues, and other sources. Other proposals for recovering sulfur from flue gases are based on scrubbing with ammonia to yield mixtures of ammonium bisulfite and ammonium sulfate.

Ammonium Nitrate

Next to urea, ammonium nitrate is the most concentrated solid nitrogen compound used in the fertilizer industry. It is available as granules, flakes or crystals, and prills, which, when mixed with kieselguhr or kaolin to improve the compound's caking behavior, contain about 33.5 percent nitrogen as a commercial product. One-half of this nitrogen content is in the nitrate form. Ammonium nitrate is hygroscopic and prone to fire or explosion unless some suitable precautions are taken. It is very soluble in water and aqueous ammonia and is the principal solid nitrogen material used in the preparation of ammoniating solutions. In its liquid form, it is available as an 80–90 percent concentrated solution. It is used in solution form

Figure 4. Alternative Processes for the Manufacture of Ammonium Nitrate

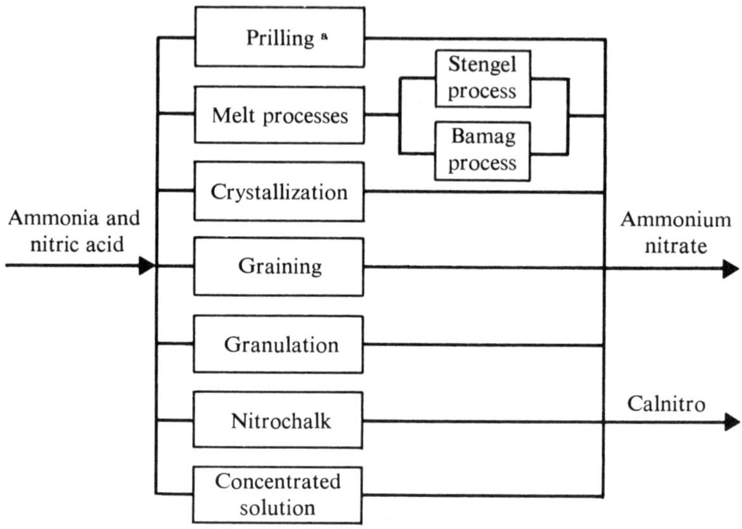

a. Prilling is also a melt process.

for direct application to the soil and in solid form for bulk-blending. Increasing quantities are used in conjunction with fuel oil for blasting purposes, and relatively small amounts are consumed by the brewing and chemical industries.

Ammonium nitrate is produced from ammonia and nitric acid by several processes that vary only in their combinations of different neutralization, evaporation, drying, and finishing methods. The alternative manufacturing processes are diagrammed in figure 4.

PRILLING. Prilled ammonium nitrate is made by reacting nitric acid with ammonia in a circulating stream of ammonium nitrate solution. This produces an 83 percent solution of ammonium nitrate, which salts out at 71 degrees centigrade. The solution is then pumped to an evaporator. Concentrated ammonium nitrate solution containing less than 5 percent water is pumped from the evaporator to the top of the prilling tower and sprayed down inside the tower. The droplets of nitrate cool and harden during the fall to spherical pellets (or prills).[10] These are carried off from the base of the tower by a conveyor and, if necessary, are further dried to below 0.5 percent moisture. The pellets are coated with a dry powder to keep them free-flowing.

MELT PROCESSES. Ammonium nitrate can also be produced in molten form. In one process, ammonia vapor and 58 percent nitric acid are preheated separately in specially designed heat exchangers and are fed continuously and simultaneously to a reactor. Ammonium nitrate and a trace of ammonia flow from the reactor into the separator, and the molten ammonium nitrate from the separator then enters a wire box that distributes it on an endless, stainless steel, watercooled belt. The chilled nitrate flake is fractured, coarse ground, screened, coated, and bagged as a 33.5 percent nitrogen, semigranular product.

In another process, gaseous ammonia and concentrated nitric acid are pumped into molten ammonium nitrate. The anhydrous molten salt is obtained after removal of the water vapor formed. The salt is then used to produce granules, prills, or other forms according to need.

CRYSTALLIZATION. In crystallization, ammonia is reacted with 60 percent nitric acid in a circulating loop, and thc ammonium nitrate formed is dissolved in the recirculating molten liquor from the crystallizer.[11] To avoid the possibility of hazard, a vacuum crystallizer is used at low temperatures. Evaporation is divided between the concentrator (evaporator) and the crystallizer. Concentrated liquor from the evaporator is fed into the crystallizer, where the solution is cooled under vacuum to effect crystallization. The crystals are centrifuged, passed through a rotary drier, coated, and bagged. The finished product contains about 33 percent nitrogen.

GRAINING. In graining, the nitrate solution is evaporated in batches to about 98 percent (almost a molten salt) and is then discharged into kettles equipped with heavy plows that knead the material as it cools

10. One of the major problems of prilling ammonium nitrate is that many of the spherical pellets are not solid. They contain internal cavities and the prill is correspondingly weak.

11. This process is not significant for fertilizers, but it is mentioned for the sake of completeness.

and solidifies.[12] Steam or cooling water is used to control the cooling rate. Additional moisture is evaporated during this treatment, and the mass first "fudges" and then breaks apart into small, rounded pellets or grains which are subsequently cooled, screened, mixed with clay, and bagged.

GRANULATION. Ammonium nitrate is also produced in granular form using rotary drums, pug mills, or combinations of these. The granules are then dried by the latent heat of crystallization. Air-swept rotary drums are used for final drying, cooling, and hardening. This is followed by coating and bagging in moisture-proof bags.

NITROCHALK. Adding powdered limestone or calcium carbonate to ammonium nitrate improves its storage properties and minimizes the risks of fire or explosion. The addition is made to the concentrated solution before prilling or granulating. The product, which is called calcium ammonium nitrate (CAN), "calnitro," or lime ammonium nitrate, contains between 15 and 30 percent nitrogen; the most common grade is 26 percent nitrogen.

AMMONIUM NITRATE SOLUTIONS. There are several ammonium nitrate solution processes. In one process, part of the ammonia from the once-through urea process is used to make nitric acid, and part is reacted with tail gas from the nitric acid unit to yield ammonium nitrate. This product is used alone or in combination with urea in the form of a fertilizer solution containing 32 percent nitrogen (UAL 32).

Ammonium Sulfate-Nitrate

Ammonium sulfate-nitrate, which is sold under the trade names Leunasalpeter and Montansalpeter, is a double salt with a nitrogen content of 26 percent. It is not hygroscopic, and its storage properties are superior to those of ammonium nitrate or mixtures of solid ammonium sulfate and ammonium nitrate, since no free ammonium nitrate is present. The importance of ammonium sulfate-nitrate has,

12. This process is also not significant for fertilizers.

however, diminished in most countries because of the large-scale manufacture of urea as well as of binary and tertiary high-analysis fertilizers.

Ammonium sulfate-nitrate can be produced by ammoniating mixtures of sulfuric and nitric acids or by combining ammonium nitrate and ammonium sulfate in special ways. In one process, it is made by ammoniating the requisite mixture of sulfuric and nitric acids, followed by evaporating and adding ferrous sulfate (to reduce caking), and then cooling, chilling, and flaking the products. After further conditioning by spraying with diluted ammonia solution, the salt is granulated, dried, cooled, and bagged. The product is a double salt containing 62 percent ammonium sulfate and 38 percent ammonium nitrate; its total nitrogen content is 26 percent.

In a simpler process, ammonium nitrate solution is evaporated under vacuum to a 95 percent concentration, cooled, and reacted with solid ammonium sulfate in a pug-mill granulator. The product is then dried, cooled, and bagged.

Ammonium Chloride

Ammonium chloride is the ammonium salt of hydrochloric acid and contains an average of 23.4 percent nitrogen—the range is from 18.6 to 26.1 percent. It is not used as a fertilizer in the United States, but in Japan and other Far Eastern countries it is applied to paddy on an appreciable scale and is usually produced when there is an abundant supply of hydrochloric acid. Its major disadvantages as a fertilizer material are: the resulting high acidities and chloride content in most soils, unless they are well irrigated and limed; the poor storage properties, unless the material is granulated and packed in moisture-proof bags; and a tendency to corrode handling and application equipment, unless certain components are suitably modified and protected with acid-resistant materials. If these precautions are observed, ammonium chloride fertilizer could become a useful outlet for surplus supplies of chlorine. Further, it can be safely applied to rice in the presence of certain fungi that would reduce ammonium sulfate to toxic sulfides. Ammonium chloride is also used in the manufacture of dry-cell batteries and as a flux for soldering and brazing.

Other Nitrogenous Fertilizers

Besides the nitrogenous fertilizers that have been treated above, others that are less important in the fertilizer industry deserve some mention because of their special nature.

Calcium nitrate

Calcium nitrate is the calcium salt of nitric acid and contains 17 percent nitrogen and 34.2 percent calcium, calculated as oxide. Because of its extreme hygroscopicity, even in moderately humid climates it is not used as a fertilizer, nor is it used in conjunction with other fertilizer intermediates. Also, precautions are usually taken to avoid impregnating organic material with calcium nitrate because of its tendency to explode in the presence of heat. It is used in explosives, fireworks, and inorganic chemical operations.

Calcium nitrate is made in two ways. In one method, calcium carbonate is reacted directly with nitric acid; in the other, calcium nitrate is produced as an important by-product in some nitrophosphate processes.

Sodium nitrate

Sodium nitrate has a nitrogen content of 15.4 to 16.5 percent. Although it has long been applied to the soil as a surface dressing for some vegetable crops, cotton, and tobacco, its use as a "straight" nitrogen fertilizer has declined. Like other nitrates, it tends to leach the soil.

Sodium nitrate can be produced from natural deposits or as a synthetic product.

Nitrogen solutions

A nitrogen solution is an aqueous solution of ammonia, ammonium nitrate, or urea—separately or in combination—used either for the manufacture of mixed fertilizers or for direct application. These nitrogen solutions include aqua ammonia but not anhydrous ammonia or liquid mixed fertilizers containing potash or phosphate. They have certain advantages over solid fertilizers: they can be applied accurately to the soil without problems of caking or dusting; they can be incorporated in irrigation water more readily than solids; and they are easy to handle since there is no need to lift or move fertilizer bags. They can be manufactured in an independent process or in an accessory operation integrated with the manufacture of synthetic ammonia, ammonium nitrate, or urea. Their disadvantages are: they are expensive to store, they need expensive application equipment, and they often contain less nitrogen than solids. At the moment, it is unlikely that these solutions will be used significantly in developing countries.

The most important nitrogen solution is aqua ammonia. Other relatively less important nitrogen solutions are: solutions containing ammonia and ammonium nitrate; solutions containing ammonia and urea; solutions containing ammonia, ammonium nitrate, and urea; and solutions containing ammonium nitrate and urea but not ammonia.

Aqua ammonia is used primarily as a direct-application fertilizer. It is a good source of nitrogen under many conditions and is sometimes superior to other sources. Its nitrogen content is between 15 and 30 percent by weight. It is generally applied subsurface to avoid loss by evaporation.

A simple operation that can be carried out independently of an ammonia synthesis plant is to add anhydrous ammonia to water. The operation requires facilities for proportioning the flows of water and ammonia, cooling the freshly formed aqua ammonia, and measuring its concentration. The rough proportioning of the flows of water and anhydrous ammonia can be regulated by the heat of solution using a temperature recorder-controller that adjusts the water flow based on temperature. Other methods of proportioning the flows of water and ammonia are based on the concentration of a recirculating stream of aqua ammonia, as indicated by a hydrometer. The aqua ammonia can be cooled using heat exchangers or refrigeration. Local conditions such as the availability and temperature of the cooling water may affect the choice of method.

Ureaform

Ureaform is a generic name for a type of nitrogen fertilizer that has the valuable property of controlled nitrogen release to plants. These urea-formaldehyde fertilizer materials are reaction products of urea and formaldehyde and contain at least 35 percent nitrogen, largely in insoluble but slowly available form. Most ureaform products contain a small amount of unreacted urea which, along with the simpler methylene ureas, make up a soluble and relatively quickly available nitrogen portion. The more complex methylene urea molecules constitute the less soluble and predominant fraction of ureaform, and they provide the slow-release supply of nitrogen for plants. Ureaform of high quality is, therefore, a mixture of methylene ureas, ranging from methylene diurea to forms containing about six urea molecules. In general, this type of fertilizer tends to be expensive and is most often used for horticultural purposes.[13]

13. Ureaform is much too expensive to be used in agriculture. A more promising approach to controlled-release nitrogen fertilizers may be use of sulfur-coated urea or use of very large urea granules.

4

The Production of Phosphatic Fertilizers

PHOSPHORUS IS ESSENTIAL TO THE GROWTH OF PLANTS, and fertilizers containing this element are applied to improve yields and hasten plant maturity. Phosphate is fixed quite quickly by most soils, and the resulting phosphorus complexes are only slightly soluble in the soil solution. Phosphorus is absorbed from the soil solution by plants as the orthophosphate ion rather than as the element. Deposits of phosphate rock exist in nature because of the low solubility of the phosphorus compounds. A primary objective of the fertilizer industry is to convert the rock phosphates into more available compounds—that is, into forms of the element that can be more readily absorbed by plants. The processes involved in this conversion are the subject of this section.

Phosphate Rock

Phosphate rock is a term applied to naturally occurring phosphate minerals containing 10 percent P_2O_5 or more. Chemically, the phosphate minerals present are variants of apatite, with fluoropatite and hydroxyapatite predominating. Certain iron ore deposits also have a significant phosphorus content, and a fertilizer (basic slag) is obtained as a by-product of the steel industry. Phosphate rocks can be converted into a form that is available to plants by various methods, but in general these methods can be classified as thermal or acidulation. The latter is far more important because it produces a fertilizer that is cheaper and agronomically more effective.

Most phosphate rock undergoes three general stages of treatment —mining, washing, and beneficiation—in order to upgrade the P_2O_5 content of the phosphate rock. Although the methods and technologies vary according to the type of deposit, general descriptions of the three stages can be given.

MINING. The mining operations can be surface mining or underground mining.[1] In surface mining, the tasks of removing overburden (deposits of unconsolidated quartz sand), digging the ore, and delivering it to a sump are normally carried out by dragline operations, bulldozers, or other digging methods. In underground mining, several methods can be used, depending on the type of ground and the wall conditions. Where both walls are firm, room-and-pillar or stull stopes are employed. If the bed is thin, however, underground mining may be uneconomical, and the mines may either close down or resort to strip mining. Strip operations have become the major method of mining in the western United States.

WASHING AND BENEFICIATION. After the matrix has been broken up in the pit and sluiced to the suction of the sand pump, it is pumped to the head of the washer plant.[2] In the United States, it used to be customary to move a washer plant to the site of the mine. The changes in plant construction, however, and the upgrading of equipment may now require that the feed be transported to the plant. Under such circumstances, careful selection of the construction material of both pumps and pipelines is an important economic decision. Clearly,

1. Most mining operations are surface mining because underground mining is usually much more costly. The proportion of underground mining is falling, and this trend is likely to continue.

2. Washing and beneficiation can be done together or separately, depending on the P_2O_5 content of the rock.

this need not be the case in all countries. After the slurry has reached the feedbox on top of the washer plant, it is generally split into three fractions: the oversized particles go to the log washers and hammer mills, the fines go to the flotation plant, and the middlings are scrubbed and screened.

When the middling fraction is screened, clay, sand, and fines are separated from the pebbles, which are retained on the screens. The discharge through the screens contains all the clay slimes in the matrix, in addition to the silica and the phosphate particles. These slimes tend to absorb reagents and make flotation costs prohibitive. The removal of the slimes before further concentration is thus very important.

Before the flotation process was discovered, the pebble fraction was the only phosphate value recovered. Since there was no known method to separate the small phosphate particles from sand and clay, they were discarded with the slimes. In the method of fatty acid flotation, however, the fine phosphate particles are separated from silica sand by a froth-flotation process. After the pebble rock is recovered, the remaining plant feed is separated into two fractions: agglomeration flotation of the material larger than 29 mesh, and cell flotation of the material smaller than 29 mesh.[3] The first fraction is conditioned with flotation reagents and is treated by mechanical separation to separate the phosphate from the silica sand. The tailings from this separation join the tailings from the cell-flotation fraction and go to the general mill-tailing pond. The concentrate is washed and then dried for shipment.

Sulfuric Acid

To be converted to an available form, phosphate rock must be acidulated; hence, sulfuric or phosphoric acid is needed. The fertilizer industry consumes more than 45 percent of the world production of elemental sulfur and sulfur equivalents from pyrites and other sources, primarily as sulfuric acid for the manufacture of phosphatic fertilizers. The cost of producing sulfuric acid is lower

3. The mesh number refers to the openings per linear inch.

than that of any other mineral acid. Sulfuric acid is normally manufactured from elemental sulfur, pyrites, anhydrite, and the sulfur-containing gases produced by roasting sulfide ores such as zinc and copper.

Crude sulfur is produced mainly by the Frasch process, which involves drilling a well and running three concentric pipes down to the sulfur deposits. Water at high temperature and pressure is pumped down the center pipe to melt the sulfur, which collects in a pool at the base of the well. Air at high pressure is forced down the central pipe and the mixture of air and molten sulfur is brought to the surface in the annular space of the two outside pipes. The molten sulfur is distributed to vats, where it solidifies and can later be broken up.[4] Crude sulfur mined in this way is 97 percent pure. Although this sulfur can be shipped in open railroad cars and barges, for economic reasons it is often shipped in liquid form in insulated tank cars, barges, and ocean vessels.

The sulfide minerals—such as iron, zinc, and copper sulfide—are normally obtained as concentrates by flotation from the crude ore. The chief problem with using sulfide ore as the basis for sulfuric acid is that the mineral industry is often located at a considerable distance from potential markets for the acid. Sulfuric acid is so inexpensive that it is usually impractical to ship the chemical over large distances because the shipping costs would be more than the value of the acid. Thus, large quantities of sulfur are wasted in the refining of the ore.[5]

The main processes for manufacturing sulfuric acid are from sulfur by means of either the contact process or the chamber process; they are diagrammed in figure 5. The differences between them lie in the manner in which sulfur dioxide is converted to sulfur trioxide and then reacted with water to produce sulfuric acid. Sulfuric acid can also be made as a coproduct in the manufacture of cement. Anhydrite is used in place of limestone in a cement kiln, coke is

4. The increasing tendency is to convert the molten sulfur into forms that do not need to be broken up and that can be handled easily. Two important forms are flakes and pellets.

5. Of the three sulfide minerals mentioned, zinc and copper are smelted to recover the metals, and the sulfuric acid is a by-product. In the case of iron sulfide (pyrites), the mineral is normally shipped to the location where the sulfuric acid is required.

Figure 5. Alternative Processes for the Manufacture of Sulfuric Acid

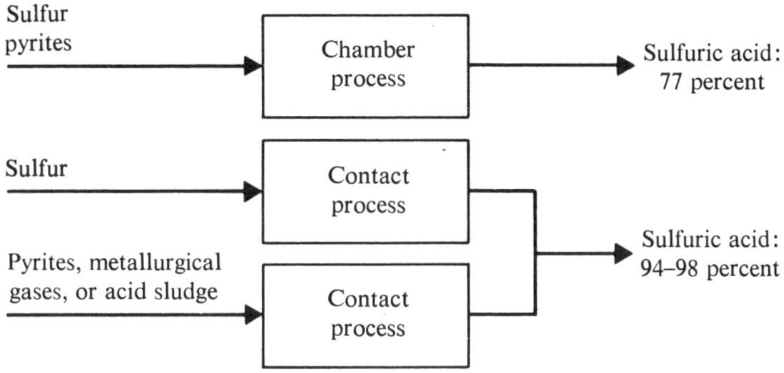

added to reduce the sulfate, and the sulfur dioxide in the kiln gases is converted to the trioxide by the contact process.[6]

THE CONTACT PROCESS. The success of the contact process depends on the catalytic oxidation of sulfur dioxide to sulfur trioxide. The common catalysts are iron oxide and vanadium pentoxide, although new plants use the latter almost exclusively. The sulfur trioxide is then passed to a tower, where it is absorbed in recycling concentrated sulfuric acid to which an equivalent amount of water is added.

6. When sulfuric acid is made via the cement route, anhydrite is normally used as the source of calcium sulfate; using gypsum results in a more costly production operation because of its water content. But phosphogypsum can be regarded as a by-product, and using it is often less expensive than mining anhydrite. The production of acid by the cement/sulfuric route is tending to diminish at present because the capital costs of the plant are much higher than those for making sulfuric acid from sulfur and the quality of the cement produced tends to be lower than that of conventional cement. Moreover, the quantity of cement made annually by a reasonably sized plant is large; therefore, some of the product has to be shipped long distances and the cost of transport becomes progressively higher.

The basic design of the plants has become more or less standardized, and descriptions of modern plants are easily available. All plants perform the following operations: produce sulfur dioxide from a suitable raw material; cool, purify, and dry the sulfur dioxide gas; preheat the gases to the kindling temperature for conversion to sulfur trioxide; catalytically oxidize the gases to sulfur trioxide; cool the converted gases; and absorb the sulfur trioxide in strong sulfuric acid.

Contact sulfuric acid plants are of two types, depending on the raw material used. The first type, referred to as the "hot-gas-purification" plants, includes those plants operating on Frasch or recovered sulfur. These are the least expensive and easiest to operate if there is an abundance of sulfur deposits. In countries where pyrites are the major source of sulfur, however, the "metallurgical" type of plant is built. These plants can also use metallurgical gases and acid sludge as the source of sulfur. In metallurgical plants, sulfur dioxide is contaminated with water vapor, dust, sulfuric acid mist, and other impurities which must be removed by cooling the gases, condensing out moisture, filtering, and drying before sending the purified gas to converters. Although the initial cost and the operating cost are higher for such plants, the cost of the sulfuric acid product may be lower if sulfur dioxide is available as a by-product or waste product from some other operation or if the pyrites are available at low cost.

THE CHAMBER PROCESS. The chamber process, which is the oldest method for manufacturing sulfuric acid, utilizes brimstone or pyrites as the raw material. This process gets its name from the fact that the reactions which produce sulfur trioxide, and then sulfuric acid, take place in lead chambers, in which oxides of nitrogen are the catalysts. The gases from the final chamber pass to a Gay-Lussac tower, countercurrent to cold sulfuric acid, which recovers the oxides of nitrogen before discharging the gases to the stack.

The chamber process is becoming obsolete in the United States, partly because of the increase in demand for strong acid and oleum which cannot be supplied by this method, and partly because contact plants with high throughput capacity can be constructed at a lower cost, require less floor space, and produce a pure, concentrated acid. Thus, contact acid has become less expensive than chamber acid, even for use in the manufacture of fertilizer, which does not usually require the stronger acid.

Phosphoric Acid

Phosphoric acid may be categorized either as wet-process acid or as furnace or thermal acid. The former is less expensive but quite impure; it is used for the manufacture of fertilizer and, after upgrading, for phosphate chemicals. Furnace acid is more expensive, but it is very pure and can be produced from certain low-grade phosphate rocks. The use of thermal acid has become much more limited as new processes for cleaning wet-process acid have been developed.[7] A third category is superphosphoric acid, which is a concentrated form of the acid that can be made by the two alternative processes. These processes are diagrammed in figure 6.

WET-PROCESS PHOSPHORIC ACID. Phosphoric acid can be made by completely acidulating phosphate rock, using a strong acid such as hydrochloric or sulfuric acid.[8] For economic and technical reasons, sulfuric acid is the one most commonly used. Since the purity of the sulfuric acid is unimportant, contact acid, chamber acid, and even spent acid from petroleum refining can be used, as long as no appreciable amount of organic sludge, chloride, or metallic impurities is present.[9] A fairly good grade rock is required, however, or else water-insoluble phosphates may be produced for fertilizers.[10]

The acidulation process has used nitric and hydrochloric acid, but these acids are more expensive and there is the problem of sepa-

7. The article of commerce normally sold as wet-process acid contains 54 percent P_2O_5—that is, 75 percent H_3PO_4. A common grade of furnace acid is 1.75 density—that is, 90 percent H_3PO_4. Within reason, any concentration can be produced by either process, because there are no constraints limiting the strength, as occurs, for example, with nitric or hydrochloric acid. But no dilute acids find their way into the market—mainly because it would be too costly to transport them.

8. Phosphoric acid is never made by acidulating phosphate rock with nitric acid—the separation problems are too great.

9. The purity of the acid is becoming important in some locations, mainly because of the gypsum disposal problem—for example, acid from pyrites sometimes contains cadmium and mercury.

10. The question of whether difficult impurities are present in rock is often much more important than the question of grade. For example, a low-grade rock can be tolerated if the diluent is silica, but not if it is a component of iron or aluminum.

Figure 6. Alternative Processes for the Manufacture of Phosphoric Acids

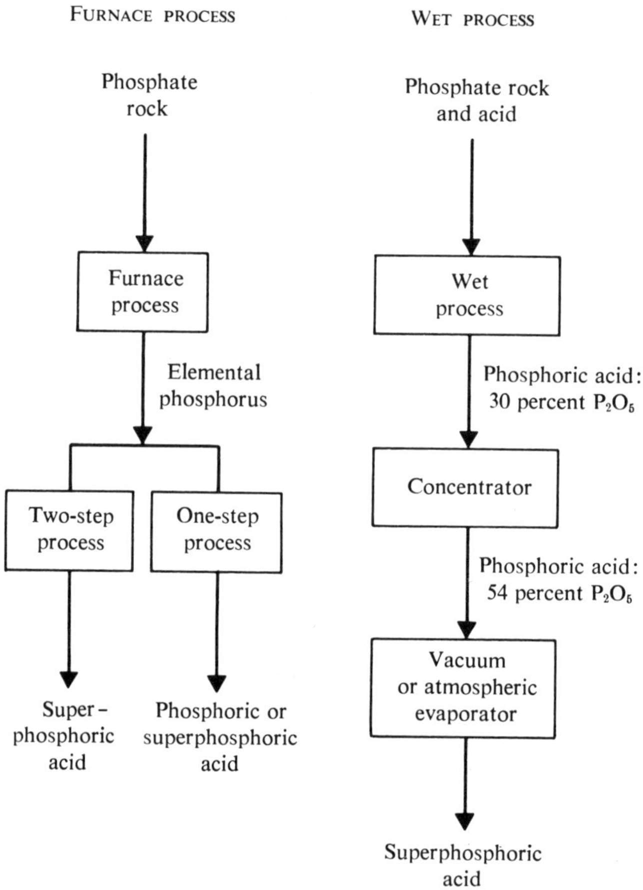

rating calcium salts from the acid product. In the case of hydrochloric acid, however, the calcium chloride has been separated from the acid by means of a solvent that is subsequently separated from the acid and recycled to the process. Although this use of solvent provides phosphoric acid of higher purity than that produced by the standard wet process, this process is not significant for fertilizer manufacture.

CONCENTRATION OF WET-PROCESS PHOSPHORIC ACID. Most wet-process acid is used to manufacture triple superphosphate, for which a strength of 54 percent P_2O_5 is normally required, and to manufacture monoammonium phosphate (MAP), diammonium phosphate (DAP), and multinutrient fertilizers (NPK). The usual wet-process acid has a strength of only 30 to 32 percent P_2O_5 when it leaves the gypsum filter. Hence, the acid must be concentrated to the strength of up to 54 percent P_2O_5, depending on the use of the material. This evaporation used to be difficult and expensive because of the corrosive nature of the acid and the presence of other impurities, but it is no longer so.

FURNACE PHOSPHORIC ACID. The furnace process grew rapidly in the past, particularly during the period from about 1945 to 1955. The growth has moderated over recent years, however, and virtually all new fertilizer phosphoric acid has come from the wet process. A world shortage of sulfur or the development of low-cost nuclear or hydroelectric power could result in greater use of the furnace method for fertilizer production. But large wet-process phosphoric acid plants today are so economic that the power would have to be very inexpensive indeed to justify using the furnace method for fertilizer production.

SUPERPHOSPHORIC ACID. Superphosphoric acid can be prepared either from elemental phosphorus (the furnace method) or by concentrating the wet-process acid (the wet method). In the former process, the acid is prepared merely by limiting the amount of water added to the phosphorus pentoxide. The resulting acid contains 76 percent P_2O_5, and the production cost per unit of P_2O_5 is essentially the same as that of the furnace acid already described.

The wet method produces a similar acid of about 71 percent P_2O_5, equivalent to 98 percent phosphoric acid. The wet-process phosphoric acid (54 percent P_2O_5 content) is concentrated in vacuum and atmospheric evaporators, and an acid of improved quality is thus obtained.[11]

Superphosphoric acid has six advantages over phosphoric acid manufactured by either the furnace method or the wet method: the acid contains 40 percent more P_2O_5 than ordinary acid; large savings in freight and other transport costs are possible; it is less corrosive; the trend to higher analysis fertilizers has created a demand for stronger acids;[12] the presence of the polyphosphoric acids is an advantage for the production of these high-analysis fertilizers;[13] and the acid can be used directly for liquid fertilizer applications.

Ground Phosphate Rock

Phosphate rock used for direct application must be ground to the proper particle size (200 to 300 mesh). The grinding can be done at the mining site or near the location of use.[14] The rock is stored until it is transferred to the millfeeder which controls the flow of the rock to the mill—either a roller mill or a ball mill. After the rock is ground to the desired size, it is carried out of the mill by an air stream to a centrifugal separator and then it is discharged to a storage silo. Some types of phosphate rock, however, are not suitable for direct application. Rocks of igneous origin, for example, are virtually useless. The usable ones are those with a high specific surface containing 3 to 5 percent carbonate substituted in the rock structure.

11. When making superphosphoric acid from either the wet process or elemental phosphorus, the acid produced can have any strength in a range. It is easiest to make the highest concentrations from elemental phosphorus because, in the case of wet acid, impurities increase viscosity and prevent the highest concentrations being achieved.

12. High-strength acids are necessary to minimize the cost of transportation, evaporation, and the like. They do not lead to fertilizers of significantly higher analysis.

13. Polyphosphoric acids are advantageous mainly because of this sequestering property, which makes it easier to obtain liquid fertilizers and suspension fertilizers of higher strength than can be achieved with orthophosphoric acid.

14. If the grinding is done at the mining site, the problem of dust in transit is aggravated.

Single or Normal Superphosphate

The term "superphosphate" applies to the mixture of finely ground phosphate rock and sulfuric acid, phosphoric acid, or the mixture of the two. The product obtained using sulfuric acid is called ordinary or single superphosphate (SSP) and contains between 16 and 21 percent P_2O_5. The phosphoric acid product is referred to as double, treble, multiple, concentrated, or triple superphosphate and contains between 43 and 48 percent P_2O_5. Both single and triple superphosphates are used as straight fertilizers; large proportions, however, are further processed into multinutrient fertilizers.

Single superphosphate is a product obtained by mixing finely ground phosphate rock with sulfuric acid. It has a composition of 30 percent monocalcium phosphate, 10 percent dicalcium phosphate, and 45 percent calcium sulfate, with the remainder being iron and aluminum phosphates plus some moisture.[15]

The manufacture of superphosphate involves four mechanical or physical operations:

- Preparation or grinding of the phosphate rock for acid treatment. When the rock is finely divided, quick and complete reaction with sulfuric acid can occur.
- Mixing of the finely ground phosphate with sulfuric acid. A thorough mixing of the rock and the acid is necessary to obtain a good reaction and the maximum yield of available P_2O_5. Unless this operation is efficiently performed, a larger quantity of sulfuric acid may be used than is actually required. As a result, the product will have a high content of free acid, will be in poor mechanical condition, and will be difficult to handle.
- Curing and drying of the acidulated material. This is performed by the closed-chamber, or den, method which promotes a good reaction between the rock dust and the acid, resulting in the production of a dry, porous type of superphosphate.[16]
- Excavation, milling, and bagging of the final product.

15. Superphosphate manufacturers that produce to a water-soluble specification could not tolerate 10 percent dicalcium phosphate in the product.

16. Some types of dens can be used for both single superphosphate (SSP) and triple superphosphate (TSP) and even, with some modification, for monoammonium phosphate (MAP).

These various mechanical processes can be conducted as a number of separate steps, or they can be carried out continuously in complete, self-contained units. Also, several different makes and designs of mixers are available. Regardless of the mixing process employed, the manufacture of this product is a relatively simple operation.

Triple Superphosphate

Triple superphosphate (TSP) is obtained by acidulating finely ground phosphate rock with phosphoric acid. It consists almost entirely of monocalcium phosphate and thus differs from single superphosphate, which contains a large proportion of calcium sulfate. Although TSP may be made with any phosphoric acid, it is most commonly made from wet-process acid. The P_2O_5 content of the product may range from 43 to 48 percent, depending on the purity of the acid and the rock and on the efficiency of the manufacturing process.[17]

Triple superphosphate is manufactured by three principal processes, which are diagrammed in figure 7.

"RUN-OF-PILE" TRIPLE SUPERPHOSPHATE. The "run-of-pile" (ROP) process mixes the phosphoric acid (50 to 54 percent P_2O_5) and phosphate rock in a cone mixer.[18] The slurry produced is discharged either into a den or onto a conveyer belt, where it is hardened.[19] It is then disintegrated mechanically and stored on the curing pile. Although this product is normally used for ammoniated fertilizers, it can be granulated after the curing period is over. Normally, the capital investment and labor and maintenance costs for ROP triple superphosphate are lower than those for the granular variety phosphate, but an extensive gas scrubbing system is frequently required for ROP, and then the cost differential might be narrowed.

17. The efficiency of the process is not a significant factor in determining the P_2O_5 content of TSP. The efficiency is important, however, to ensure good conversion to water-soluble or citrate-soluble P_2O_5.

18. Run-of-pile triple superphosphate is a mixture of all sizes of phosphate rock, from small lumps to dust.

19. Most TSP can be made in the same den that is used for SSP.

Figure 7. Alternative Processes for the Manufacture of Triple Superphosphate

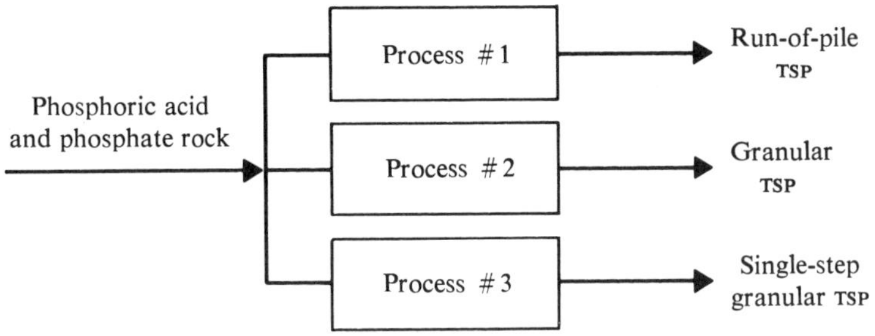

GRANULAR TRIPLE SUPERPHOSPHATE. The granular process produces a granulated product in a multistep process. It is well-suited for direct application as a phosphate fertilizer or for inclusion in mixed bulk blends made by dry-blending solid raw materials. The process employs 45 to 48 percent phosphoric acid and phosphate rock, which are reacted in a series of reaction tanks. Quick drying is facilitated by blending the slurry into a bed or by recycling crushed, oversized particles and product. The partially dried granules are then fed to a rotary drier. A multilayered, dense product with excellent handling qualities is thus built up.

SINGLE-STEP GRANULAR TRIPLE SUPERPHOSPHATE. The single-step granular method combines the features of quick drying and granulation in a single step. Acidulation and granulation are accomplished simultaneously in a rotary-drum mixer. Wet-process phosphoric acid and steam are fed through distributors under a rolling bed of material in the drum. The product has a short curing time, can be readily ammoniated, and has good storage properties. The process has the advantage of low equipment and processing costs, and it can be adapted to use existing continuous ammoniators.

ENRICHED SUPERPHOSPHATE. The manufacture of enriched superphosphate is similar to that of TSP, but a mixture of sulfuric and phosphoric acid is used for acidulation. The acid mixture is chosen so that the product will have an adequate amount of sulfur which is not as diluted as in the case of single superphosphate.

Dicalcium Phosphate

Dicalcium phosphate has valuable properties as a fertilizer,[20] as an ingredient in animal feedstocks, and as a source of calcium and phosphorus in human foods and restoratives. It is normally marketed as the dihydrate, containing 41.26 percent P_2O_5 when pure. In this form, it is citrate-soluble, but if dehydrated, it can be citrate-insoluble. When dicalcium phosphate with a high standard of purity is required, it is usually made from thermal acid and limestone or lime. Less pure grades can be made from bones or from phosphate rock. Normally, bones are not used to make this fertilizer, but they are frequently used to produce feedstock supplements.

PREPARATION FROM BONES. When dicalcium phosphate is prepared from bones, the grease in the bones is usually extracted by a solvent, and they are then leached with a weak solution of hydrochloric acid to separate the tricalcium phosphate component from the organic material. The tricalcium phosphate passes into solution as monocalcium phosphate and calcium chloride.

In another process for manufacturing dicalcium phosphate from bones, a sulfur dioxide solution is used to extract the calcium and phosphorus as monocalcium phosphate and calcium sulfate. Subsequent treatment with steam, followed by hydrochloric acid, leaves a precipitate of dicalcium phosphate in a solution of calcium chloride. The dicalcium salt is filtered, washed, dried, and packed.

PREPARATION FROM MINERAL PHOSPHATES. Dicalcium phosphate is also prepared on a large scale from mineral phosphates by the action of hydrochloric acid on phosphate rock. One process utilizes hydrochloric acid available from the production of potassium sulfate. The phosphate rock is mixed with the acid in agitators. With many African rocks, grinding is unnecessary, because relatively coarse rock dissolves quite easily and the reaction can be controlled to get com-

20. To date, however, it has not found much use as an agricultural fertilizer.

plete dissolution of the P_2O_5 in the rock. The clear liquor overflows from the agitators to a first stage of dicalcium phosphate precipitation, where lime slurry is added. The solution overflowing is treated with more lime slurry, which precipitates the remaining P_2O_5, primarily as tricalcium phosphate. The precipitate is dewatered and returned to the dicalcium phosphate precipitation step, where the tricalcium is converted to dicalcium phosphate. If total recovery of the P_2O_5 is attempted in a single liming stage, the final product will contain tricalcium phosphate that is low in both grade and citrate solubility. The dicalcium phosphate dihydrate is filtered and carefully dried to avoid losing water of hydration, which in turn would cause loss of citrate solubility. Small amounts of some type of binder can be added during the drying stage to reduce the tendency of the material to dust. Since this material is insoluble in water, coarse granules are undesirable for use as a fertilizer.

Thermal Phosphate Fertilizers: Basic Slag

One of the oldest thermal phosphate fertilizers is basic slag, a by-product of iron and steel manufacture. Basic slags differ considerably in quality, depending on the process and raw materials used. A converter slag might contain 16 to 20 percent P_2O_5, whereas an open-hearth slag might contain 10 to 12 percent P_2O_5. The liberal use of fluorspar may reduce the P_2O_5 content to 2 to 3 percent, unless tapping is undertaken before the spar is added. The increased use of scrap metal can also reduce the yield and value of slag. Although the reactions between impurities in molten iron and basic furnace linings are quite complex, iron phosphide is removed from the metal, with the assistance of oxygen, lime, and the basic lining of the converter or furnace.

Since many steelmakers believe that the production of a superior slag is of secondary importance, developments in steel technology have not resulted in improvement of the quality of basic slag. In particular, the use of fluorspar as a flux is of great benefit to the steel industry, but it gives an inferior basic slag, since fluorapatites are formed, and these compounds are insoluble when applied to the soil. Attempts to raise the P_2O_5 content of slags, by adding ground phosphate rock either to the furnace charge or to the slag, have not been widely made except in Europe. Such attempts have not been made in the United States because of the fear of handicapping steel production. The Duplex process, however, is one method of compromising between high steel production and good quality slag yields. In this operation, iron that is high in phosphorus is first treated in an acid-line converter and blower. The charge is then treated in a basic open-hearth furnace to yield a slag high in basic phosphates, which is cooled or chilled, cracked, and ground to a fineness of 95 percent or better. Other thermal phosphate fertilizers include Rhenania phosphate, Rochling phosphate, calcium magnesium phosphate, and calcium metaphosphate. Since these are not important products of the fertilizer industry, they are not discussed in detail.

5

Production of Potassic Fertilizers

POTASH, OR POTASSIUM, which is one of the major nutrients, is widely dispersed in nature, occurring in highly soluble salts such as potassium chloride, in insoluble minerals such as potassium-bearing silicates, and in marine and land plants. The principal minerals currently used as fertilizers are potassium chloride (muriate of potash), potassium sulfate, potassium nitrate, and a mixture of potassium and magnesium sulfate. The potassium content of the minerals is stated in terms of potassium oxide (K_2O).

Production and Processing of Potash Ores

Virtually all commercial potash is produced from potash-bearing brines or from underground deposits of soluble minerals. The brines are available from surface deposits, and their compositions are widely known. The underground deposits, which are often difficult to exploit, are vastly more important because of their high content of potash and generally more favorable locations. Subterranean deposits of potash occurring as sylvinite (a mixture of potassium chloride and sodium chloride) or carnallite (a mixture of potassium chloride and magnesium chloride) are usually exploited as underground mines. There are also a few operations that mine solutions. Mineral langbeinite, a double salt of potassium magnesium sulfate, occurs in underground beds mixed with halite and sylvite. Langbeinite and the chloride salts are both soluble in water, but the chlorides dissolve at a much faster rate, and this is the basis of the separation. After the minerals are crushed, they are washed at a rate sufficient to remove most of the chloride salts, while the langbeinite remains largely unchanged. The langbeinite is then separated from the wash waters by centrifuging, and it is kiln-dried and conveyed to finished product storage.

Potassium Chloride

Pure potassium chloride has an equivalent K_2O content of 63.1 percent; sylvinite usually contains 15 to 30 percent K_2O. The muriate of potash used for fertilizer manufacture is not pure potassium chloride, and its K_2O content is between 60 and 62 percent (95 to 98 percent KCl). Fertilizer and agricultural grades of muriate of potash are sold in various particle sizes and concentrations, usually containing 60 to 62 percent K_2O. Crude salts containing 20 to 25 percent K_2O are also available, and they find a market for direct application to agricultural land.

Two principal processes are used to produce potassium chloride: solar evaporation and mining methods.

SOLAR EVAPORATION OF BRINES. Solar evaporation is used mainly in Israel and the United States. Basically, in this process brine is evaporated in solar pans. Sodium sulfate and chloride are the first salts to crystallize. At this stage, the solution contains magnesium and potassium with some sodium chloride. The concentrated brine is then moved into harvesting pans where carnallite—a double salt of magnesium and potassium chloride—crystallizes. After the carnallite has crystallized, it is sent to a plant to be separated by flotation.

MINING METHODS. Two types of mining methods are employed:

shaft mining and solution mining.[1] There are several forms of shaft mining. The room-and-pillar mining method is generally used to recover sylvinite and carnallite; it is also used for langbeinite. Coal mining methods are used for underground recovery; continuous mining machines are used to extract the ore, and belt conveyers are employed for underground haulage.

Solution mining is utilized at depths considered less practical to mine by conventional shaft mining. Essentially, water is pumped through drilled holes to the potash deposits. The water dissolves the potash and sodium chloride, and the solution is forced to the surface. The difficulty with this method is to obtain a relatively pure solution of potash. A solution to this problem that has been used in Canada is to inject a blanket of natural gas over the potash deposit to prevent the dissolution of the sodium chloride.

Refining methods for potassium chloride

Two methods are used to refine the potassium chloride: one is solution and recrystallization; the other is flotation. These methods are diagrammed in figure 8.

SOLUTION AND RECRYSTALLIZATION. Solution and recrystallization is an old, refined process that, with some modifications, can produce relatively pure potassium chloride from a wide variety of ores. Among its disadvantages are that it demands high-temperature processing of corrosive brines, expensive equipment, and large fuel and cooling requirements. It was favored in Europe, but it is being superseded by flotation separation methods.

The process is based on the different solubilities of sodium and potassium chloride in hot and cold saturated brines. Sodium chloride is an unusual salt because its solubility increases only slightly with temperature; with most salts, the solubility increases much more as the temperature increases, and this is the case with potassium chloride. The procedure is to take a brine that is saturated with sodium and potassium chloride at a high temperature and to cool it so that potassium chloride crystallizes and can be separated as a solid. The brine mother liquor is reheated and used to dissolve more

1. Shaft mining usually has high capital costs and low operating costs; the reverse is true for solution mining.

Figure 8. Alternative Methods for Refining Potassium Chloride

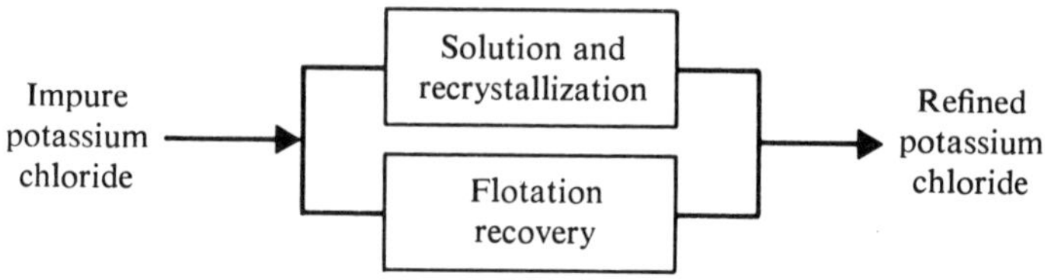

crushed sylvinite. The last brine is removed along with small quantities of insoluble clays and similar impurities. The solid is usually discarded or sold for ice control on roads and similar applications. The hot solution is cooled once more, and the cycle of operations continues.

Crude carnallite ore containing sylvite is leached in a vat with a hot saturated brine solution. Potassium chloride and the carnallite dissolve, leaving common salt and insoluble matter in the residue. The hot liquor is cooled in vacuum crystallizers that yield a low-analysis potassium chloride product. The mother liquor is evaporated and cooled to form carnallite. Potassium values are recovered from the crystallized carnallite by a hot leach followed by vacuum crystallization. The potash deposited in this step is of high purity.

FLOTATION RECOVERY. A widely practiced method is to separate potash from its ore by froth flotation.[2] In this separation process, a selectively reagentized solid is suspended in an aerated aqueous liquid. The potassium chloride adheres to the bubbles of the air and is removed from the suspension as a froth. The froth is mechanically removed, and the unreagentized sodium chloride is removed as a pulp. The floated froth is concentrated in a thickener, centrifuged or filtered, washed with water to displace the brine, and then dried. The product generally averages 97 percent purity, and the recovery efficiency of this process is greater than 96 percent.

2. In the United States, the term "mineral flotation" is widely used rather than "froth flotation."

Potassium Sulfate

Potassium sulfate, also known as arcanite, is a white crystalline compound. The dissolved solids in water form a neutral solution. The potash content is 54.06 percent K_2O, and the compound contains 55.13 percent sulfate. Potassium sulfate is the least hygroscopic of the common fertilizer materials. It is often associated with other salts in potash deposits. When it is present with calcium and magnesium sulfate, the stable salt is called polyhalite, which has a 15.5 percent K_2O content. When calcium is not present, the double salt of potassium and magnesium sulfate is called langbeinite, which has a K_2O content of 22.6 percent. With the exception of specialized crops, potash fertilizers are equally effective. Tobacco is a common exception; it is sensitive to chlorides and is often fertilized by potassium sulfate.[3] The latter is also considered to be a superior fertilizer for potatoes and citrus fruits in certain soils.

Three methods can be used to produce potassium sulfate, and they are diagrammed in figure 9.

3. In fact, any chloride-free fertilizer can be used for chloride-sensitive crops, and the nitrate is widely used in the United States and Denmark.

Figure 9. Alternative Processes for the Production of Potassium Sulfate

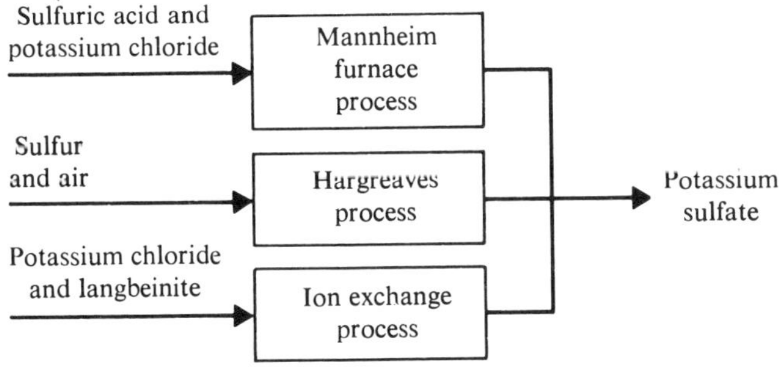

THE MANNHEIM FURNACE PROCESS. Sulfuric acid is made to react with potassium chloride in the Mannheim furnace process. First, potassium bisulfate is formed and then potassium sulfate. Hydrochloric acid is evolved as the by-product.

THE HARGREAVES PROCESS. The Hargreaves process depends upon the burning of sulfur in air to produce sulfur dioxide. Water vapor is added and the composite gas is then passed countercurrent through a series of chambers. Each chamber contains approximately 80 tons of potassium chloride, which are converted by the sulfur dioxide to approximately 90 tons of potassium sulfate.

PRODUCTION BY ION EXCHANGE. A third process produces potassium sulfate from naturally occurring salts by an exchange of ions. It requires the slurrying of potassium chloride and ground langbeinite and water. The potassium sulfate liquor is saturated with potassium chloride and leonite; after allowing time for the solution to approach equilibrium, potassium sulfate is separated from the slurry, dried, and stored.

6

The Production of Multinutrient Fertilizers

MULTINUTRIENT FERTILIZERS—that is, those containing more than one of the primary nutrients—comprise a wide range of chemical compositions and nutrient ratios, and they can be produced by many different processes. In their final form, however, they can usually be categorized either as compound fertilizers or as dry-mixed or bulk-blended fertilizers.

Compound fertilizers are prepared by granulating together solid or liquid fertilizer ingredients or intermediates.[1] In some cases, the intermediates are prepared at their sources immediately before granulation. The composition of each granule is the same, and a wide range of ingredients can be used and fertilizers produced.

Dry-mixed or bulk-blended fertilizers are obtained by mechanical mixing of fertilizer materials already in the granulated or prilled

This chapter has benefited from substantial redrafting by William T. Sheldrick, Head, Fertilizer Unit, World Bank. His help is gratefully acknowledged.

1. Compound fertilizers are also known as complex or mixed fertilizers.

form. Individual granules do not necessarily have the same composition, and the technique requires careful matching of sizes to avoid segregation and ensure an acceptably uniform product.

Granulation Processes

In order to produce fertilizers that have good storage and distribution properties, it is now customary to produce compound fertilizers or blend components in a granular form. In this context, the term "granulation" is used to describe processes that produce large fertilizer particles within the range of 1 to 4 millimeters: for example, prilling, agglomerating, solidification from the melt, compacting, and flaking.

SLURRY GRANULATION. In the slurry granulation process, most of the feed enters as a slurry or liquid, and granulation is achieved by operating a large recycle and building up successive layers of solid on each recycled granule. This process is most commonly used for compounds based on ammonium phosphate and for nitrophosphates. Granulation is achieved in a pug mill or paddle mixer operating with high recycle ratios.

AGGLOMERATION GRANULATION. In the agglomeration granulation process, the feeds are normally in powder form, although liquid feeds may be used. Granulation is achieved by adding steam or water to cause the particles to adhere. The granulation recycle ratios are small—normally of the order 1:1—and granulation is carried out in a rotary drum or pan granulator.

MELT GRANULATION. Molten mixtures of salts are granulated by controlled solidification in a rotating drum or pan granulator. This process is usually applied to ammonium-phosphate-nitrate mixtures.

PRILLING. Melts of ammonium nitrate phosphate or other pure salt melts can be solidified by spraying the melt down a void or dust-filled tower. Prilling can also be achieved by spraying the melt into oil followed by centrifugal separation.

COMPACTING. Compacting is used on a small scale to prepare multinutrient fertilizers, although its major use is to upgrade potash to a size in which it can be bulk-blended. Powder material is forced between rolls under pressure to produce a sheet of compacted material. This material is disintegrated and screened to the desired size range.

Multinutrient Fertilizer Materials

Although a large number of compound fertilizers can be produced, their formulation generally tends to be based on two or more chemically compatible materials. For example, potassium chloride and, to a lesser extent, potassium sulfate are used as a source of potash; superphosphate or ammonium phosphates, as a source of phosphate. Urea, ammonium nitrate, and ammonium sulfate are the principal sources of nitrogen.

Ammonium phosphate

Ammonium phosphate—which can exist as monoammonium phosphate (MAP), diammonium phosphate (DAP), or a combination of the two—is one of the most concentrated fertilizers. Because of this, it has become an important fertilizer intermediate in recent years, and it is used both as a bulk-blending component and as an ingredient for compound fertilizers. Monoammonium phosphate contains 11 percent nitrogen and 48 to 54 percent P_2O_5, depending on the purity of the ingredients. It is made by granulating wet-process phosphoric acid. The degree of ammoniation can be controlled in the process to yield MAP or a mixture of MAP and DAP. Diammonium phosphate usually contains 16 to 18 percent nitrogen and 46 to 48 percent P_2O_5.

RAW MATERIALS. Ammonium phosphates are now normally produced from wet-process phosphoric acid. There is a growing trend for both phosphoric acid and ammonium phosphates to be produced in large plants near the phosphate rock sources. Ammonia is usually provided to the site as anhydrous liquid ammonia, although either liquid or gaseous ammonia can be used for neutralization. In a few cases, phosphoric acid is used to neutralize ammonia present in the gases from coke ovens.

PROCESSES FOR THE MANUFACTURE OF AMMONIUM PHOSPHATES. Most

ammonium phosphate is made from wet-process phosphoric acid using slurry granulation to produce a granular product or by one of the newer processes developed in the last few years to produce ammonium phosphate powders. Some ammonium phosphates, mainly from furnace-grade acid, have been produced using crystallization techniques, but this process is now rarely used.

The slurry granulation process was developed by Dorr Oliver more than forty years ago and, although improvements and changes have been made, the basic process remains the same. The slurry granulation plant can also be used to make granular triple superphosphate or ammonium phosphate nitrates. In the ammonium phosphate process, wet-process phosphoric acid of between 38 and 50 percent P_2O_5 is fed to a reaction system and neutralized with ammonia. Ammonia leaving the reactors is scrubbed with incoming phosphoric acid. In some variations of the process, the second-stage ammoniation from MAP to DAP can be carried out in the granulator. Normally, a high recycle ratio is employed in this process, and after granulation the product is dried and screened.

In recent years, several processes have been developed to produce ammonium phosphate powder as a fertilizer intermediate. These processes usually have low investment cost and are inexpensive to operate; their main object is to provide a simple phosphate intermediate for transport as an alternative to phosphoric acid. The MAP powder is used as an ingredient in compound fertilizers.

The first process of this type was the Scottish Agricultural Industries' (SAI) "Phos AI" process; another is Fison's "Miniphos" process. Other not-so-well-known processes have been developed by Swift, Norsk Hydro, and Gardinier. About forty plants of this type have been built in the last ten years. One major variant of this process is to ammoniate phosphoric acid under pressure in either a pipe or a tank reactor, followed by a simple spray-drying process. The product is normally of a coarse powder or minigranular form with good properties for agglomeration granulation.

SOME ECONOMIC CONSIDERATIONS FOR AMMONIUM PHOSPHATE. The main advantage of ammonium phosphate is that it can be produced simply as a high-concentration fertilizer which has good storage properties and can be shipped in bulk either as a fertilizer intermediate or as a finished product. Increasingly, the trend is to build ammonium phosphate plants near the phosphate rock mines so that low-grade rocks can be utilized. Most such developments are occurring in North Africa and the United States.

Ammonium phosphate is a valuable ingredient for mixed fertilizers because of its compatibility—superphosphates, for example, do not have this property to the same extent because they contain calcium. Three useful products of ammonium phosphate mixed with other salts are given below.

Ammonium phosphate sulfate is formed by ammoniating mixtures of phosphoric acid and sulfuric acid to form products such as 13–39–0 and 16–20–0. Potash can be added as required, and this process is popular where sulfuric acid is inexpensively available as a by-product from smelting operations.

Ammonium phosphate nitrate is produced by neutralizing mixtures of phosphoric acid and nitric acid—or, alternatively, mixtures of ammonium nitrate and phosphoric acid—with ammonia. Under certain pH conditions, ammonium phosphate nitrate forms a eutectic mixture that can be melt granulated, and a number of processes have been developed to achieve this. Typical grades that can be achieved are: 30–10–0, 27–14–0, and 25–25–0. Adding potash yields nitrogen-phosphorus-potassium fertilizers such as 17–17–17.

Ammonium phosphate nitrate fertilizers are popular in Europe and the United States, where nitrate-based compounds are preferred to urea-based compounds for agronomic reasons.

Finally, concentrated fertilizers can be produced using urea and ammonium phosphate, and several plants have been built recently to make these compounds. In view of the rapid growth of urea and ammonium phosphates as fertilizer intermediates, the manufacture of ammonium phosphate urea (APU) fertilizers is expected to increase. These materials are particularly suitable for paddy and, since they are the most concentrated compounds possible from conventional materials, they offer savings in transport and storage. Unlike ammonia-nitrate-based compounds, they offer no hazard from fire or decomposition.

Ammoniated superphosphate

Ammoniated single and triple superphosphate have been produced for many years in the United States and elsewhere. Ammoniation improves the storage properties of fertilizers containing superphosphates, but it also reduces their water solubility. Normally, about 3 or 4 units of nitrogen are added to 20 units of P_2O_5 in this process.

Nitrophosphates

Nitrophosphates are produced by acidulating phosphate rock with nitric acid. The main advantage of this process is that it eliminates the use of sulfur. Nitrophosphates were developed mostly in Europe during periods of sulfur shortages, but the availability of inexpensive sulfur and sulfuric acid within Europe and certain inherent disadvantages have tended to reduce the general impact that these processes once had.

The major disadvantage of nitrophosphate processes is that calcium nitrate, which is a product of the acidulation stage, is extremely hygroscopic and must be treated in some way to produce a fertilizer than can be stored. Although many processes have been developed to do this, they fall into four main types:

- Separation method. In variations of the Odda process, excess calcium nitrate is crystallized from the acidulation mass by cooling and is separated by centrifuging. Various degrees of concentration and water solubility of product can be achieved, depending on the quantity of calcium nitrate removed. The calcium nitrate so removed can be sold separately as a fertilizer, or it can be reacted with carbon dioxide to produce ammonium nitrate, a more concentrated fertilizer.
- Sulfonitric and phosphonitric processes. These are mixed-acid processes in which the ratio of calcium to phosphate is adjusted by attacking the phosphate rock with a mixture of either nitric and sulfuric acids or nitric and phosphoric acids.
- Nitrocarbonic process. Free calcium nitrate is reacted with carbon dioxide after ammonia is added to convert the mixture into calcium carbonate. Products of this process are of low analysis and are water insoluble.
- Sulfate recycle process. In the sulfate precipitation process, either an outside source of ammonium sulfate is used to precipitate the calcium as calcium sulfate (by-product ammonium sulfate from caprolactam production is sometimes used for this purpose) or, alternatively, the ammonium sulfate can be regenerated from the calcium sulfate, in which case it is referred to as the sulfate recycle process. The excess calcium is eliminated as calcium carbonate.

These processes can be used in various combinations. After the acidulation and separation stages, the ammonia and potash are added to produce fertilizers of the required analysis.

Nitrophosphate processes have two further disadvantages. First, they are not flexible. It is not easy to obtain a wide range of products in these processes and $N:P_2O_5$ ratios of less than about 1.5:1 can only be achieved by using supplementary phosphoric acid or by removing the calcium nitrate as a concomitant product.

Second, most nitrophosphate processes produce fertilizers with phosphates that are water insoluble or only partly water soluble; these are regarded as less desirable than completely water soluble phosphates. Several new nitrophosphate processes can produce high degrees of water solubility either by additional separation of calcium nitrate or by use of the sulfate recycle process, but these processes are complex and have to be operated on a large scale to be economic.

SOME ECONOMIC CONSIDERATIONS FOR NITROPHOSPHATES. The controversy over the relative merits of nitrophosphates and ammonium phosphates has gone on for many years. The claims for nitrophosphate processes were probably justified when sulfur and phosphoric acid were expensive raw materials and when fertilizer concentrations were low. General international trends in the fertilizer industry, however, have made the arguments academic.

First, the need for high concentrations has, to a large extent, eliminated the low-grade nitrophosphate process as well as the arguments about the water insolubility of its products. Concentrated fertilizers now have most of their phosphate in the form of ammonium phosphate.

Second, the availability of relatively inexpensive phosphoric acid and ammonium phosphates and the differential pricing of phosphate rock and the intermediates makes it less favorable now than it was formerly for producers to import rock and process it with either sulfuric or nitric acid.

Third, in many areas urea has become the principal nitrogenous fertilizer for both technical and agronomic reasons, and it seems likely that this trend will continue. The worldwide availability of urea and ammonium phosphates—both of which are produced in large plants at the most economic locations and conditions—provides fertilizer intermediates that can be compounded to give a wide range of fertilizer analyses. Recent evaluations by the Tennessee Valley Authority (TVA) indicate that in most countries urea and diammonium phosphate would be a less expensive form of fertilizer than nitrophosphates.[2]

Moreover, under certain conditions, nitrophosphates undergo decomposition reaction and this necessitates more careful storage and handling than would be required for compounds based on ammonium phosphate urea.

As a result of these considerations, it seems unlikely that the use of nitrophosphate processes will grow significantly. An exception might be in Eastern Europe and the Soviet Union, where state control and operation of fertilizer plants is more favorable to large, single-product plants than elsewhere.

Potassium nitrate

Potassium nitrate (KNO_3) can be used as a component of solid or solution fertilizers when nitrate nitrogen and potassium without the presence of chloride ions are required. The application of potassium nitrate has been limited, however, because of its relatively high cost in terms of plant-food units and its high-temperature solubility coefficient in water. The main nonfertilizer uses include explosives, fireworks, and chemical manufacture. It is available in various grades; the technical quality is 99 percent pure, and the fertilizer quality is 95 percent pure. The latter contains 13 percent N and 44 percent K_2O. Alternative names for the salt are niter and saltpeter.

The chemical means used to produce potassium nitrate are similar to those used to manufacture sodium nitrate, described in chapter 3. One recently developed process is based on the reaction of potash with nitric acid to yield potassium nitrate and chlorine. In another process, solid potash is added to a hot aqueous solution of sodium nitrate; the sodium chloride formed crystallizes in the hot mother liquor and is separated by filtration or centrifuging. The potassium nitrate liquor is concentrated and cooled to yield the crystalline product.[3]

A method that reacts solid potassium chloride and 60 to 65 percent nitric acid, without the use of heat, has been developed in Israel. It is based on the use of an organic solvent that separates the solid

2. T. P. Hignett, *Technical and Economic Comparison of Nitric and Sulphuric Acid Routes to Phosphate Fertilizers* (International Fertilizer Development Center).

3. The process is not generally used for agricultural fertilizers.

and liquid phases of the reaction, yielding solid potassium nitrate. The hydrochloric acid formed can be used for other purposes such as phosphoric acid manufacture or dicalcium phosphate production.

Granular Compound Fertilizers

The process of producing multinutrient fertilizers was developed as a convenient method to prepare solid materials from a solution or slurry and also because granulation allows fertilizer materials to be handled and stored more easily than mixed powders. Granulation of different nutrients into granules of the same composition also ensures that the growing plant receives the recommended nutrient ratio and that the effects of fertilizer segregation are minimized. The various processes that can be used to produce compound fertilizers are outlined above.

Dry-Mixed Fertilizers or Bulk Blends

Bulk-blending provides the best results if two or more granular materials having similar particle size are blended. The resulting blend, then, has little tendency toward segregation. The fertilizers used most often for bulk-blending are ammonium nitrate, ammonium sulfate, urea, triple superphosphate, diammonium phosphate, and potassium chloride. If mutually compatible fertilizers (in terms of particle size and moisture content) are used, bulk-blending is a simple and inexpensive operation; it can produce a wide range of mixtures. In the United States, bulk-blending is largely integrated into the fertilizer distribution sector, and it is used to supply fertilizer mixes that correspond exactly to the user's nutrient needs.

Since the mixing plant itself is usually inexpensive, does not exhibit significant economies of scale, and does not transform the intermediate (fertilizer) products into a new product, bulk-blending is not usually specified as a separate activity in the planning models described in this volume. The location of blending plants can appropriately be dealt with once the primary producing plants have been analyzed.

7

Problems in Fertilizer Sector Planning

THE GREAT VARIETY of raw materials, intermediate and final products, and productive processes that characterize the chemical fertilizer industry may pose a difficult planning problem for those selecting the appropriate products and processes for a sectoral investment program. This problem is aggravated by the wide range of possibilities for product substitution on the demand side; that is, specific nutrients can usually be provided by many different fertilizer products.

Other factors also complicate investment planning in the sector. Since most fertilizer products can be traded internationally, the choice between producing domestically and importing from abroad needs to be investigated.[1] Further, since most products associated with fertilizer manufacture are produced under economies of scale (that is, production cost per unit tends to fall as output level in-

1. Some products cannot be traded internationally today. The two main products are single superphosphate, which is too dilute, and fertilizers that are at a grade below international standards but are perfectly good for home use: for example, low-grade triple superphosphate made from a low-grade rock without much beneficiation.

creases), the question of the optimal scale and timing of new capacity must always be addressed during the planning phase.

Because the demand for fertilizer material is by nature geographically dispersed, the question of the optimal location of producing facilities, blending plants, granulation facilities, warehouses, and distribution points can have important implications for the supply price of the final product at the farm gate. Similarly, since alternative means of transportation (rail, highway, water) are often possible, the selection of the least-cost means and pattern of transportation should be based on careful analysis.

Thus, decisions may have to be made on major strategy options during the early project planning phase. Which products should be produced? Which are the appropriate feedstocks? Should specific raw materials and products be imported from abroad or produced domestically? Which is the most efficient investment, production, and trade pattern over time for the products to be produced domestically?

The analysis of these broad issues requires assumptions and judgments on many aspects of the planning problem. During later phases in the project planning cycle, several of these assumptions and judgments may be found not to stand the test of more detailed scrutiny. This is an inevitable characteristic of planning in phases, and it occurs frequently in investment project planning. One of the main advantages of the methodology described in this volume for planning investments in the fertilizer sector is that the initial broad strategy can be reformulated conveniently so that an intensive and meaningful interaction between different phases in the planning process is possible.

This chapter provides a systematic discussion of the major decisionmaking problems faced in fertilizer sector planning. Broadly speaking, these can be placed in two categories. The first category is decisions related to specifying the planning problem. Which feedstocks and end products should be included in the investigation? How many and which potential production sites should be specified? How many and which marketing centers should be selected to represent adequately the geographical dispersion of demand for fertilizer material? Which transport alternatives should be considered?

The second category of decisions relates to formulating an efficient investment program once the scope of the planning problem has been specified. The planning models described in this volume are specifically designed to address the second set of decisionmaking problems. But, because this second set of problems is an efficient screening device, they permit the basic planning problem to be specified more comprehensively than would be feasible with more conventional methods of project selection. Hence, many more products, production processes, transport alternatives, and the like, can be specified and assessed on their relative merits.

Specifying the Planning Problem

This section treats various factors involved in specifying the planning problem: feedstocks, fertilizer products, production processes, production sites, by-products, and means of transport. In addition, the questions of regional breakdown and number of time periods in the model are discussed.

Feedstocks

Many products in the fertilizer industry can be produced from several feedstocks. The choice may be among basically different raw materials or products (for example, coal, natural gas, or naphtha for ammonia manufacture) or among different grades of a given product (for example, grades of phosphate rock with different phosphorus and impurity contents).[2] In most cases, common sense suggests which feedstocks from among the likely candidates should be specified. Clearly, if abundant natural gas is available domestically, whereas coal is not, the latter need not be specified as a possible feedstock. Similarly, if high-grade phosphate rock is available locally, one does not need to consider imported low-grade rock. The situation is not always so clear-cut, however. For instance, even though pyrites are locally available for the production of sulfuric acid, it may be desirable to specify imported elemental sulfur as an alternative feedstock.

Fertilizer products

Since the fertilizer industry is characterized by a wide variety of end products, one of the most important problems at the project planning stage is selecting the appropriate product mix to be con-

2. Wet phosphoric acid is preeminent in the phosphate fertilizer industry. The grade of rock—that is, its P_2O_5 content—is usually much less important than the nature of the impurities it contains.

sidered. A related consideration is selecting a plant that is flexible enough to produce the proper mix.

The simplest case is the one in which stringent fertilizer recommendations have been drawn up for agricultural crops grown in the planning area. In that case, the fertilizer material that will be in demand is known in advance, and the product mix to be produced domestically depends fully on whether or not domestic production meets a given efficiency criterion.

Although the choice of end products to be produced by the fertilizer industry is frequently made on this basis, the validity of the approach can be questioned. Fertilizer recommendations are normally based on agronomic and economic considerations, and the price at which fertilizer is delivered to the farmer plays a considerable role in determining the most profitable type of fertilizer to be used in any one region for specific crops. Clearly, however, the attainable delivered price of fertilizer products is not known at the outset of the planning exercise. If fertilizer requirements are expressed in terms of major nutrients, then a priori a wide choice of products should be considered. In principle, therefore, as wide a range of end products as possible should be considered in the project selection phase.

The number of end products is very large, however, and normally it will be neither possible nor desirable to include all products in the planning problem. No simple rules can be proposed to make a final choice, and a combination of elements must enter the decision. These include: the range of fertilizers currently used, the range of fertilizers for which area-specific fertilizer recommendations have been drawn up, agronomic advice, and expert opinion of the sector specialist. The selection of the final products to be considered in the planning model—not to be confused with the selection of the products recommended for importation and production—is a typical example of an area in which judgment plays an important role. The use of a planning model is often mistakenly considered to be a procedure that does not allow for expert judgment. Nothing could be further from the truth, because both the specification of the planning problem and the interpretation of the results are primarily based on such judgments.

Production processes

Fertilizer manufacture has a much greater range of technological alternatives than is commonly assumed. In principle, if alternative manufacturing processes for the products selected for investigation exist, these should be explicitly taken into account. This can greatly expand the scope of the planning problem: if ten products can each be manufactured with five alternative processes, the total choice set amounts to fifty processes. In practice, it will hardly ever be necessary to complicate the planning problem to such an extent. First, many alternative processes for producing a given product may be competitive in the sense that they have similar implications for investment and operating cost and are simply different proprietary processes that represent minor modifications of a basic manufacturing process. In other cases, alternative processes are clearly associated with plant scales, so that for a given capacity range one process is dominant, whereas for another capacity range an alternative process is dominant. A typical example is the production of ammonia: motor-driven reciprocating compressors are used for capacities when the capacity is less than 600 short tons, whereas turbine-driven centrifugal compressors are used when the capacity is greater.

Sometimes, the choice of production process may be limited because of the nature, availability, and quality of the feedstock, or the quality requirements of the end product. For example, in the production of sulfuric acid for phosphatic fertilizers, processes using pyrites normally need not be specified if elemental sulfur is locally available. In the case of end products, the example of multinutrient fertilizers that can be produced by bulk-blending plants as well as by compounding plants can be cited. If transport distances are great, the compounding process may often be preferable, since today's bulk blends exhibit segregation problems.

The availability of processes may also restrict the number of processes that need to be considered in specifying the planning model. Some processes previously used in developed countries may no longer be operated. Even though such processes, under certain circumstances, may still be of interest to countries with different resources, difficulties in procuring equipment, replacement parts, and managerial expertise may make it undesirable to include them among the possible technological alternatives for a particular country.

Finally, certain processes may be more technically complicated than others, and hence require more highly trained manpower. Shortages of such manpower may often justify the a priori elimination of these processes. In fact, a host of other local conditions may render certain production processes more attractive than others, although it is difficult to generalize about this. As in the case of product choice, the judgment of the sector specialist is of great importance in deciding which production processes should be considered explicitly in the sector planning problem.

Production sites

Since all products in the fertilizer industry can be transported, there is, in principle at least, a wide choice of potential plant sites. Economies of scale in the production of most products will tend to restrict the number of sites where production actually takes place. On the other hand, because the demand for fertilizer products is dispersed geographically, there will be a countervailing tendency to disperse the location of plants in order to lower transport costs.

The major problem in site selection is to decide whether to locate a productive activity close to the raw material supply, close to the demand center, or close to transport facilities. Although the planning models discussed later are designed partly to answer this question, the answer depends to a large extent on which potential sites have been specified. In view of the dispersion of demand for fertilizer material, it will usually be desirable to specify the model as a regionally disaggregated planning model, with a number of demand regions and corresponding marketing centers. In principle, each marketing center can be specified as a potential site. Moreover, the major ports should often be regarded as potential sites. If the planning area is large, this approach can result in a large number of potential sites. Since this greatly complicates the planning problem, it is desirable to attempt to restrict the number of potential sites as much as possible. Once more, judgment plays an important role. Remote regions, with relatively modest fertilizer requirements and no relevant raw materials, will normally not have to be considered as sites for productive facilities. Two ports located in close proximity can be considered as one potential site. Other, similar decisions that limit the number of potential sites to a manageable few can also be made.

By-products

Certain by-products of the fertilizer industry find uses in other industries. Similarly, certain products required in the manufacture of fertilizers are required in the production of other commodities as well; for example, sulfuric acid is extensively used outside the fertilizer industry. In such cases, the market for such products outside the fertilizer industry should be specified. First, the sale of by-products directly benefits the operation of the fertilizer industry. Second, explicitly incorporating the sales volume outside the fertilizer industry allows larger production capacities and thus lower production cost per unit. Both activities can be specified as "by-product sales." Their inclusion provides an approximation for the possible links of the fertilizer sector with other industrial activities and is a potentially important aspect of the specification of the planning problem.

Means of transport

The correct specification of the transport alternatives facing the fertilizer industry is of considerable importance for several reasons:

- To a varying degree, all raw materials and products in the industry are mobile.
- Transport cost is usually a substantial portion of delivered cost.
- Transport cost is the main inhibiting factor for large-scale, geographically concentrated production units.[3]
- Even in some undeveloped regions, a number of transport alternatives are usually available.[4]

When the transport alternatives are being specified, it may often be useful to carry out a number of back-of-the-envelope calculations, and to decide on the basis of these whether any one form of transport is clearly more efficient than any other. With this approach, the least-cost means of transport between any two points in the planning area can usually be specified. If, however, the cost impact of economies of scale in transportation can be specified correctly, ignorance of the volume of trade between supply points and marketing centers (or plants) would require that alternatives be explicitly specified.

Marketing centers

Since demand for fertilizer material is by nature geographically dispersed, and since transport cost is an important component of

3. In many locations, however, the cost of providing infrastructure for the construction of several plants is even more inhibiting.

4. In the most underdeveloped regions, a dirt road is often the only possibility.

delivered cost, a number of demand regions within the planning area and a number of marketing centers within each region should be specified as the terms of reference for determining transport cost. It is difficult to generalize about the appropriate number of demand regions.[5] Often, the specification of demand regions will be based upon the availability of data, because a projection of fertilizer demand is required for each demand region. Administrative regions or districts can frequently form a reasonable basis for regional disaggregation.

Time periods

The dynamic properties of alternative investment programs in the fertilizer industry can be investigated, using the planning models discussed in this volume. In certain cases, it may not be necessary to analyze these properties, and a static model will suffice; for example, in investigating the efficiency of the domestic transport pattern for an existing fertilizer industry. In most cases, however, the planner is interested in drawing up an investment and production program for a particular period of time, and questions arise about which planning horizon should be chosen and for what time intervals results should be reported. The first aspect to be taken into account is that a certain amount of time will elapse between the moment an investment decision is made and the moment the new capacity is installed and in operation. Although local circumstances may be responsible for variations in the length of this so-called gestation lag, a reasonable approximation of the average lag in the fertilizer sector is three years; that is, if a decision to invest in a new fertilizer plant is taken in early 1980, the plant can be expected to be in operation in early 1983.

If a static model is not deemed appropriate by the planner, how many time periods should be specified? The answer depends on the expected rate of growth of demand for end products. If demand is projected to grow very slowly—say, at 2–3 percent a year—a two-period model may be sufficient to draw up a reasonably efficient investment program for the medium term. On the other hand, if demand grows fast—and in developing countries annual rates of

5. In terms of the computations involved in the planning models, it does not make much difference whether ten or fifteen demand regions are decided upon.

growth of over 10 percent are not unusual—this phenomenon needs to be incorporated into the planning model, so that the initial investment decisions are made against the background of a rapidly growing market. As will be explained later, the presence of economies of scale can, under such conditions, justify the installation of temporary overcapacity. In that event, four or five time periods of three years each may be a more appropriate model specification.

Formulating an Investment Program

Once the scope of the planning problem in the fertilizer sector has been specified, the next planning task is to formulate an efficient and internally consistent strategy for investment, production, foreign trade, and distribution. Several problems have to be addressed during this phase; they often involve issues that are highly interdependent and thus must be evaluated simultaneously. Among these issues are site selection, the scaling of capacity, the timing of capacity expansion, and the transport pattern for raw materials, intermediate products, and fertilizer material; also, there are problems associated with selecting the appropriate feedstock, production process, and type of fertilizer material.

Site selection

If more than one potential site has been specified in the planning problem, a decision must be made about the site or sites where the capacity will actually be installed. Several factors affect this decision. First, investment cost, as well as operating cost, may differ among potential sites. Second, each potential site has different implications regarding the transport cost for both raw materials and final products; in the case of a nonintegrated plant, there may be different implications for intermediate products as well. Third, the trade-off between transport cost and economies of scale will have to be determined when decisions are made about the appropriate plant site.

Clearly, evaluating the impact of these factors on site selection can involve cumbersome calculations. This is true particularly if fertilizer demand is heavily dispersed geographically and if it will grow rapidly over time. In that case, the selection of the appropriate plant site cannot be viewed as a static planning problem; rather, the whole lifetime of the plant must be taken into consideration. This raises the possibility of trade-offs over time, since a specific site may be the most efficient, even though during the initial years more attractive alternatives seem to exist.

The question of site selection is interdependent chiefly with the question of whether economies of scale are present in fertilizer production. This latter question raises difficult planning problems concerning the selection of the appropriate scale and timing of new capacity.

Capacity scaling

Most activities within the fertilizer sector exhibit economies of scale in some form or other. This implies that the scale at which each of these activities is carried out directly influences the structure of production costs. Hence, selecting the appropriate scale is vitally important in designing an efficient investment program.

Typically, the relation between the investment cost and the installed capacity can be represented by a curve, as shown in figure 10. When capacity is doubled from X_1 to X_2, the investment cost in-

Figure 10. The Investment Cost Function

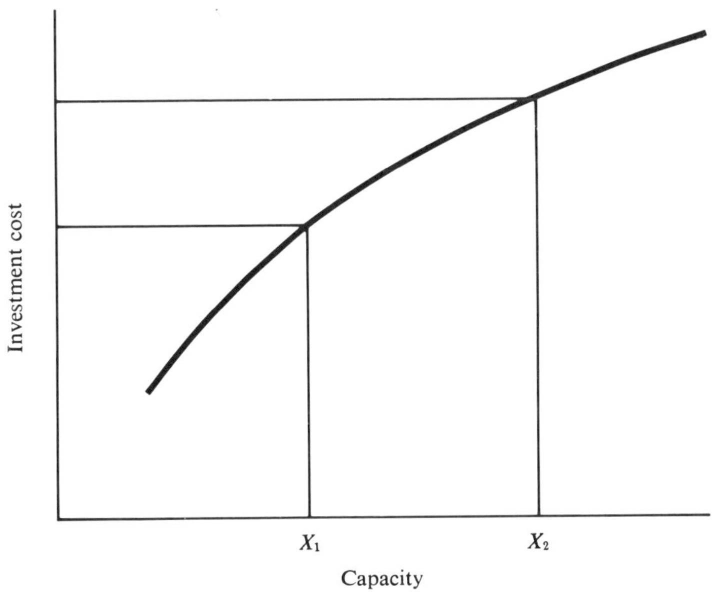

creases, but it does not double. Algebraically, this relationship can be represented by an exponential function of the general form:

$$I = aC^b,$$

where I is total investment, C is plant capacity, a is a constant, and b is the constant elasticity. The parameter b will be less than unity when there are economies of scale, and larger than unity when there are diseconomies of scale. In the chemical sector, the so-called six-tenth rule is often used to approximate capital requirements; in such cases, 0.6 is the value assigned to the parameter b.

The planning problems associated with the capacity-scaling decision can be described, focusing first on the static case. To simplify the example, it is assumed that the decision to be made is about the optimal scale of a fertilizer plant that faces a given, regionally disaggregated market. The possibility of market growth over time is explicitly ignored for the moment. The main planning questions are the following:

- How many plants should be constructed?
- Where should they be located?
- Which plant scales should be selected?

For this static capacity-scaling decision, the trade-off between transport cost and economies of scale is the crucial determinant. In the presence of economies of scale, a few large plants are preferred to many small productive units because of production cost advantages. With the former structure, however, the distribution costs would be higher if the market is geographically dispersed. It is conceivable that distribution costs for certain remote markets would be so high that the cost advantages of a large plant would be eliminated, and that such regions could be better supplied from either imports from abroad or other domestic plants. But caution should be exercised in reaching this judgment, as the following simple numerical example may make clear.

Assume a country that is broken down into two regions, A and B. In region A, the market for a specific fertilizer is 50 units; in region B, the market for the same product is 100 units. In terms of the previously stated questions, the planning problems are the following: Should domestic production be recommended? If so, should two plants be constructed—one in region A and the other in region B? Or should there be just one plant—either in region A or in region B? Furthermore, should the total capacity to be constructed equal the total market demand? Or should one or both regions be supplied through imports from abroad? To answer these questions, information is needed on production cost per unit at various capacity levels, the import price, and transport cost.

Let the production costs vary with scale so that, at a production level of 50 units, the per unit production cost is 110; at 100 units, it is 100; and at 150 units, it is 90. The transport cost between A and B is 10 per unit. The delivered price of the imported product in A is 95 per unit, and in B it is 105.

A simple set of calculations shows that the least-cost solution to the problem is to establish a plant in B that produces 150 units and serves the entire domestic market. Although total costs of meeting domestic demand under this program are lower than under any other alternative, the delivered cost of the product in region A is higher than could be achieved through imports if full-cost pricing were practiced.[6] In this case, region A loses all the cost advantages of larger scale production because of the transport cost between A and B. In contrast, region B reaps the full advantage of its plant having access to the market of region A. To guarantee continued access, it may therefore be to region B's advantage to sell its product at less than full price to region A.

This exceedingly simple example can be made more complex by specifying the problem more realistically. There may be several competing fertilizer products or modes of transport; there may be some question about the availability of infrastructure, the location of raw materials, or the manufacture of intermediates. With these additional specifications, detailed hand calculations become increasingly more difficult, and some efficient screening device becomes necessary to evaluate the alternatives. Such a device becomes even more urgent if the element of time is brought into the picture.

The timing of capacity expansion

If demand for a given fertilizer product is projected to grow over time, and if the domestic production of the fertilizer is contemplated, the selection of the appropriate scale of production is closely related to the timing at which capacity expansion should take place. Since

6. Imports in A have a delivered cost of 95, whereas production in B involves a delivered cost in A of 100 (production cost of 90 at a scale of 150 units, plus 10 for transport cost).

a larger plant is normally preferred to a smaller plant in the presence of economies of scale, all other factors being the same, it may pay to postpone construction of a plant until the size of the market has reached a certain level.[7] If the market continues to grow, the construction of the plant could conceivably be postponed until some technological maximum becomes feasible and diseconomies of scale begin to appear. It is possible, however, that long before this point the size of the domestic market would have permitted domestic production to take place at a scale that results in production costs below import prices. In that case, the planning problem is to decide on the most efficient timing of capacity construction. This decision has to be made on the basis of a comparison between, on the one hand, the present value of the total cost saving that can be made by an earlier and smaller plant in relation to import cost and, on the other hand, the saving of a later and larger plant.

A further possibility is that it may be profitable to install a plant that will initially have some excess capacity. As the market grows, capacity utilization will gradually increase so that, eventually, lower production costs per unit can be achieved than would be the case with a smaller plant. Clearly, the rate of growth of demand, the extent of the scale economies, and the appropriate rate of interest at which future costs and benefits ought to be discounted play the determining role in this decisionmaking process.

The transport problem

Transport cost constitutes the major mitigating factor to centralizing economic activity that exhibits economies of scale. In this context, the transport problem can be defined as one of finding the transport pattern that minimizes the cost of delivering the required quantities of raw materials and intermediate products to the various plant sites, and of fertilizer products to the marketing centers. This is achieved by selecting not only the shortest route but also the least-cost mode of transport among plants, between plants and marketing centers, and between importing points, marketing centers, and plants. Solving the transport problem requires that distances for each mode of transport and rates for each product be correctly

7. In addition, in many developing countries, the technical strength to commission and run several plants starting at the same time is seldom available, thus necessitating phased construction.

specified. The planning models presented in subsequent chapters are well geared to handle the cumbersome calculations required to select the most efficient transport pattern.

The choice of feedstock

Many products in the fertilizer industry can be produced on the basis of several feedstocks. The choice may be among basically different raw materials or products or among different grades of a given product type.

In most cases, the question of feedstock selection will be resolved by comparing the cost of alternative feedstocks. Several problems can arise. First, the comparative cost analysis requires the appropriate pricing of alternative feedstocks. If the feedstock is imported from abroad, the c.i.f. (cost including insurance and freight) import price forms the basis for evaluation. If the raw material is available domestically, the evaluation problem is more difficult because alternative uses—for example, use as an export—should be taken into account.[8] If the raw material is a depletable resource, as will often be the case in fertilizer manufacture, the opportunity cost from the point of view of the entrepreneur may diverge from that of society as a whole.

Other, more indirect problems may arise in the context of feedstock selection. For example, a specific feedstock may produce coproducts or by-products that can be used elsewhere in the economy, whereas alternative feedstocks may not exhibit this feature. This element should obviously be entered into the calculations, because the benefits derived from the sale of by-products can be attributed to the investment program. Second, the use of a particular feedstock may affect a number of economic policy objectives, such as job creation, regional development, or improvement of the environment. These considerations might play a role, for example, in selecting coal as a feedstock for nitrogenous fertilizer production.

So far, the problem of feedstock selection has been discussed as if it could be discussed independently of the other aspects of the

8. Imported phosphate rock is almost invariably beneficiated to a high degree, and its cost is correspondingly high. The advantage of local rock, in this case, would be that it can be used without undue beneficiation and that its cost is correspondingly lower. In such cases, the imported and domestic phosphate rock can be treated as two (substitutable) products.

planning problem. It is not difficult to conceive of circumstances in which this may be an inappropriate approach. To begin with, the comparative cost analysis of alternative feedstocks cannot be carried out unless the location of processing facilities is considered simultaneously. Since the latter will also be influenced by demand factors, the geographical dispersion of demand must be considered as well. In the same vein, if the cost of imported raw materials or intermediate products is a function of the quantity required, the scale of operations of the processing facility must be considered. In turn, different feedstocks may entail different technologies in the processing stage, with different investment requirements and operating costs. Finally, the optimal timing of capacity construction in processing facilities may be affected by the gestation periods required to open mines or to provide adequate transport facilities or infrastructure.

Process selection

If a product that is a candidate for inclusion in the investment program can be produced by more than one process, another dimension is added to the planning problem. When the number of alternative processes is large, this modification of the planning problem can complicate the identification of the optimal program considerably.

The major difficulty of selecting the appropriate production process is that the scale of production often determines which production process is the most attractive. Since the scale of production depends greatly on cost of production and location, among other factors, the choice of process has to be made simultaneously with decisions about other aspects of the investment program. If many products are to be considered at the same time, the selection of production processes may render the planning problem even more complex than it already is. Even using the investment planning models presented in the following chapter, the introduction of alternative production processes greatly increases the difficulty of the planning problem. Thus, the number of alternative processes to be specified in the planning problem should be as limited as possible.

The choice of fertilizer types

Normally, the planning problem should specify a variety of fertilizer products that can be used to meet given nutrient requirements. This specification may or may not be combined with fertilizer recommendations of various degrees of stringency. In practice, at the problem specification stage, fertilizer types are often selected on the basis of technical or agronomic considerations, but that cannot fully account for the interdependencies between supply price, on the one hand, and the various aspects of the planning problem, on the other.

High-analysis fertilizers such as urea are often said to be preferred to lower-analysis fertilizers such as ammonium sulfate because the transport cost per ton of nutrient is lower. Clearly, however, transport cost is not the only element that should be taken into account, and what counts is the total delivered price and agronomic effectiveness of the various products. Circumstances may well exist under which a country would be better off producing its own low-analysis fertilizer material rather than importing high-analysis substitutes. The investigation of this aspect of the program becomes rapidly impossible—particularly if the planning problem involves many products, sites, marketing regions, and so forth—unless an efficient screening device is available. As will be demonstrated, the planning models to be described can be used effectively to address this difficult and, at the same time, crucial problem of fertilizer product choice.

Special problems

The foregoing discussion of decisionmaking problems focused on the major issues related to designing an investment and production strategy. Clearly, in specific situations, other problems can come up that have not been covered so far. For example, a planner may simply want to evaluate the efficiency of an existing industry or, even more specifically, the transport pattern that has evolved over time for fertilizer material. Similarly, a planner may be asked to recommend whether a particular plant should be scrapped, maintained, or modernized. An endless number of area-specific problems can be conceived, and little is served in attempting to enumerate all possibilities. Rather, the next two chapters, which focus specifically on models that can be used to address the planning problems described above, contain guidelines on how to modify the model structure to address specific problems not covered in detail.

8

Planning Models for the Fertilizer Sector

A SERIES OF LINEAR AND MIXED-INTEGER PLANNING MODELS is described in this chapter; those models may be useful in addressing the decisionmaking problems that need to be resolved when formulating an investment and production strategy for the fertilizer sector. The presentation is self-contained, in the sense that prior familiarity with mathematical planning models is not required. The models are presented in order of gradually increasing complexity, from a simple transport model to a full-fledged, dynamic project selection model. Those who are already familiar with such models may wish to skip this chapter and proceed immediately to chapter 9, which starts off with a full statement of the complete model and a list of its variables and parameters.[1]

1. The present chapter follows closely the layout of chapter 3 of volume 1 in this series—David Kendrick and Ardy Stoutjesdijk, *The Planning of Industrial Investment Programs: A Methodology*, The Planning of Investment Programs, ed. Alexander Meeraus and Stoutjesdijk, vol. 1 (Baltimore: Johns Hopkins University Press, 1978) —except when the structure of the fertilizer sector calls for a sector-specific formulation (for example, to account for product substitution on the demand side).

In this chapter, a model that can be used to analyze transport problems relating to the fertilizer sector is presented first. This model can be expanded to include existing production facilities, so that the efficiency of an existing fertilizer sector can be assessed. Next, a series of capacity-expansion models are presented; as new dimensions to the planning problem are gradually added, these models increase in complexity and realism. Toward the conclusion of the chapter, enough background information will have been provided so that one can understand a planning model of the fertilizer sector that is dynamic; covers several potential production sites; explicitly includes the choice of feedstocks, processes, and fertilizer products; and permits the determination of the investment, production, foreign trade, and transport pattern that leads to the least-cost strategy to meet specified fertilizer requirements.

The Transport Problem

Because of the simplicity of the transport model, most textbooks on linear programming begin by describing it. For the fertilizer sector, the transport model has significance beyond its instructive value: transport costs of fertilizer products constitute a significant proportion of total delivered cost of the product to the farmer, and hence they are of considerable importance in determining the least-cost supply pattern.

The transport problem can be described as follows: given a number of plants that can serve a number of markets, which transport pattern will minimize transport costs? Two conditions have to be borne in mind during the solution of this problem. First, no plant can ship more products than it produces (hence, the possibility of inventories is ignored). Second, no market should receive less than it requires (hence, it is assumed that the plants' capacity to produce is sufficient to meet total market requirements).

Let:

i = an individual plant in the set of plants I;
j = an individual marketing sector in the set of marketing centers J;
x_{ij} = the amount of fertilizer shipped from plant i to marketing center j
k_i = the capacity of plant i.

Then, the first building block of the transport model is the following constraint:

(8.1) $$\sum_{j \epsilon J} x_{ij} \leq k_i. \qquad i \epsilon I$$

$$\begin{bmatrix} \textit{Sum of fertilizer} \\ \textit{shipments from} \\ \textit{plant i to all} \\ \textit{marketing centers j} \end{bmatrix} \leq \begin{bmatrix} \textit{Capacity of plant i} \end{bmatrix} \qquad \begin{bmatrix} \textit{For each plant i} \end{bmatrix}$$

In (8.1):

- the symbol ϵ indicates membership in a set;
- the statement $\sum_{j \epsilon J}$ indicates that one should sum over all marketing centers in the set J;
- the symbol $\leq$ indicates less than or equal to;
- the symbols $i \epsilon I$ on the right indicate that there must be a constraint of type (8.1) for each plant i.

Consider a country with two single superphosphate plants and three marketing centers. Then, the set I can be written as $I = \{1, 2\}$ and the set J can be written as $J = \{1, 2, 3\}$, so that (8.1) is written as:

$$x_{11} + x_{12} + x_{13} \leq k_1,$$

$$x_{21} + x_{22} + x_{23} \leq k_2.$$

In other words, the shipments from plant 1 to marketing centers 1, 2, and 3 cannot exceed the capacity of plant 1, and the shipments of plant 2 to marketing centers 1, 2, and 3 cannot exceed the capacity of plant 2.

The second constraint of the transport model stipulates that no marketing center should receive less fertilizer than its specified requirements. Let:

d_j = the fertilizer requirements of marketing center j.

Then, the fertilizer requirement constraint can be written as:

(8.2) $$\sum_{i \epsilon I} x_{ij} \geq d_j. \qquad j \epsilon J$$

$$\begin{bmatrix} \textit{Sum of shipments} \\ \textit{from all plants i} \\ \textit{to each marketing} \\ \textit{center j} \end{bmatrix} \geq \begin{bmatrix} \textit{Fertilizer} \\ \textit{requirement of} \\ \textit{marketing} \\ \textit{center j} \end{bmatrix} \qquad \begin{bmatrix} \textit{For all} \\ \textit{marketing} \\ \textit{centers} \end{bmatrix}$$

In (8.2), the symbol $\geq$ means equal to or larger than. It can be questioned why an inequality sign is specified here rather than an equality sign. Why, indeed, would shipments to any marketing center exceed market requirements? In most cases, shipments to a region would exactly match requirements. Sometimes, however, market requirements can be met by composite products that contain fixed proportions of several elements. Diammonium phosphate (DAP), which contains both nitrogen and phosphorus, provides an example for the fertilizer industry. Unless market requirements to be met by DAP are specified in the same proportion as nutrient content, it is clearly impossible to meet both nitrogen and phosphorus requirements exactly. If the market requirements constraint were specified as an equality, it would not be possible to use DAP to the fullest extent to meet demand; if no other product were available, it might even render the solution of the model infeasible.

For the example given above—that is, a country with two single superphosphate plants and three marketing centers—(8.2) can be written as:

$$x_{11} + x_{21} \geq d_1,$$

$$x_{12} + x_{22} \geq d_2,$$

$$x_{13} + x_{23} \geq d_3.$$

Finally, shipments of fertilizers, x_{ij}, cannot assume negative values. This is formally stated in the model by nonnegativity constraints:

$$x_{ij} \geq 0. \qquad i \in I, \; j \in J \tag{8.3}$$

The objective or criterion of this problem is to minimize transport cost while meeting the constraints (8.1), (8.2), and (8.3). Let:

μ_{ij} = the constant unit transport cost for shipping fertilizer from plant i to marketing center j.

Then, the transport cost of shipment x_{ij} from plant i to marketing center j is equal to:

$$\mu_{ij}x_{ij},$$

and the objective of minimizing total transport cost can be stated as minimizing ξ, where:

(8.4)
$$\xi = \sum_{i \in I} \sum_{j \in J} \mu_{ij} x_{ij}.$$

$$\left[\begin{array}{c}\textit{Total} \\ \textit{transport} \\ \textit{cost}\end{array}\right] = \left[\begin{array}{c}\textit{Sum of the transport} \\ \textit{costs for all shipments} \\ \textit{from all plants } i \textit{ to all} \\ \textit{marketing centers } j\end{array}\right]$$

For the two-plant, three-market example, (8.4) would be written as:

$$\min \xi = (\mu_{11}x_{11} + \mu_{12}x_{12} + \mu_{13}x_{13}) + (\mu_{21}x_{21} + \mu_{22}x_{22} + \mu_{23}x_{23}).$$

In summary, the transport model is to select x_{ij} to minimize total transport costs:

(8.5)
$$\min \xi = \sum_{i \in I} \sum_{j \in J} \mu_{ij} x_{ij},$$

subject to the capacity constraints (8.1), the market requirements (8.2), and the nonnegativity constraints (8.3).

Modeling an Existing Industry

The transport model can be gradually expanded to a model of an existing industry by introducing in turn production cost, multiproduct plants, production processes, intermediate products, interplant shipments, exports, and imports. Finally, a description is given of how product substitution and fertilizer recommendations can be incorporated into the structure of the model. The possibility of capacity expansion is explicitly ignored for the time being.

Production cost

The simplest way to modify the transport model into one that incorporates production cost at plant i is to assume for the time being that production cost per unit of product is constant. Let:

θ_i = the average production cost for a given fertilizer at plant i.

Then, the total production cost for the product at plant i is:

$$\theta_i \sum_{j \in J} x_{ij}.$$

The criterion function of the model must now be modified to include the total production cost at all plants i, as well as the transport cost:

$$\text{(8.6)} \qquad \min \xi = \sum_{i \in I} \sum_{j \in J} \mu_{ij} x_{ij} + \sum_{i \in I} \left(\theta_i \sum_{j \in J} x_{ij} \right),$$

$$\begin{bmatrix} \textit{Total} \\ \textit{cost} \end{bmatrix} = \begin{bmatrix} \textit{Sum of the trans-} \\ \textit{port cost for} \\ \textit{all shipments from} \\ \textit{plants i to all} \\ \textit{marketing centers j} \end{bmatrix} + \begin{bmatrix} \textit{Total production} \\ \textit{cost for all} \\ \textit{plants i} \end{bmatrix}$$

$$= \sum_{i \in I} \sum_{j \in J} x_{ij}(\mu_{ij} + \theta_i).$$

Constraints (8.1), (8.2), and (8.3) remain unchanged.

The simple model above permits one to analyze the trade-off between production and transport costs. If plant 1 has lower production cost than plant 2, it may be able to absorb the transport cost and still deliver the product to a relatively distant market at a lower total cost than plant 2. In that case, because of the cost minimization criterion, shipments from plant 1 to the distant market will be preferred to shipments from plant 2.

A multiproduct model

Normally, more than one fertilizer product is produced in the industry, and thus the model should be generalized to a multiproduct form. This is done simply by adding a subscript c to represent the fertilizer types that can be produced. Let:

C = the set of fertilizers produced in the industry;
x_{cij} = the amount of fertilizer c shipped from plant i to marketing center j.

Then, the model is to select x_{cij} so as to minimize:

$$\text{(8.7)} \qquad \min \xi = \sum_{c \in C} \left(\sum_{i \in I} \sum_{j \in J} \mu_{cij} x_{cij} + \sum_{i \in I} \theta_{ci} \sum_{j \in J} x_{cij} \right),$$

$$\begin{bmatrix} \textit{Total} \\ \textit{cost} \end{bmatrix} = \begin{bmatrix} \textit{Shipment cost} & & \\ \textit{from all plants i} & + & \textit{Production cost} \\ \textit{to all marketing} & & \textit{at all plants i} \\ \textit{centers j} & & \end{bmatrix}$$

subject to the following constraints.

CAPACITY CONSTRAINTS

$$\sum_{j \epsilon J} x_{cij} \leq k_{ci} \qquad c \epsilon C, \; i \epsilon I \tag{8.8}$$

MARKET REQUIREMENTS

$$\sum_{i \epsilon I} x_{cij} \geq d_{cj} \qquad c \epsilon C, \; j \epsilon J \tag{8.9}$$

NONNEGATIVITY CONSTRAINTS

$$x_{cij} \geq 0 \qquad c \epsilon C, \; i \epsilon I, \; j \epsilon J \tag{8.10}$$

Productive units

Until now, plant capacity has been linked to a single fertilizer product. This treatment is unsatisfactory, however, whenever plant capacity can be used to produce more than one product—for example, a bulk-blending plant that can produce a large number of fertilizer mixes of widely varying nutrient content. This possibility can be incorporated into the structure of the model by introducing the notion of productive units that have their capacity expressed in terms of hours of availability or volume of throughput. It now becomes necessary to redefine I as a set of plant locations, with i referring to a particular plant site rather than the plant itself.

To specify the model in this form, let:

z_{ci} = the production of fertilizer c at plant site i;
M = the set of productive units, where m is an individual machine or productive unit in the set;
b_{mci} = the number of units (for example, hours) of capacity used on machine or productive unit m per unit of output of fertilizer c at plant site i.

The model can now be stated as: select x_{cij} and z_{ci} so that the sum of production and shipment costs are minimized. That is:

$$\begin{aligned} \min \xi &= \sum_{c \epsilon C} \Big(\sum_{i \epsilon I} \sum_{j \epsilon J} \mu_{cij} x_{cij} + \sum_{i \epsilon I} \theta_{ci} z_{ci} \Big), \\ &= \sum_{c \epsilon C} \sum_{i \epsilon I} \Big(\sum_{j \epsilon J} \mu_{cij} x_{cij} + \theta_{ci} z_{ci} \Big), \end{aligned} \tag{8.11}$$

subject to a set of constraints.

MATERIAL BALANCE CONSTRAINTS

$$(8.12) \qquad z_{ci} \geq \sum_{j \in J} x_{cij} \qquad c \in C,\ i \in I$$

[Production of fertilizer c at plant site i] ≥ [Shipments of fertilizers c from plant site i to all marketing centers j] [For all fertilizers and all plant sites]

CAPACITY CONSTRAINTS

$$(8.13) \qquad \sum_{c \in C} b_{mci} z_{ci} \leq k_{mi} \qquad m \in M,\ i \in I$$

[Production levels for all fertilizers at plant site i] ≤ [Capacity availability in any productive unit m at plant site i] [For all productive units and all plant sites]

Constraint (8.13) replaces the previous constraint (8.8) and reflects the change in the definition of capacity from a commodity characteristic (k_{ci}) to a machine characteristic (k_{mi}). The coefficient b_{mci} in (8.13) will be positive when a commodity requires a particular productive unit for its production and zero when the productive unit is not required. Finally, two constraints correspond to the previous constraints (8.9) and (8.10). The only difference is that there is an additional nonnegativity constraint for z_{ci}.

MARKET REQUIREMENTS

$$(8.14) \qquad \sum_{i \in I} x_{cij} \geq d_{cj} \qquad c \in C,\ j \in J$$

NONNEGATIVITY CONSTRAINTS

$$(8.15) \qquad x_{ij},\ z_{ci} \geq 0 \qquad i \in I,\ j \in J,\ c \in C$$

A process model

The mathematical formulation of the process model is completed by introducing variable inputs required for the production of fertilizers. To do this, the notion of a productive process must be generalized, from the output of commodity z_{ci} to the activity level of a process z_{pi}, where

z_{pi} = the activity level of process p at plant site i.

This modification of the model permits production methods that create more than one product to be described. For example, carbon dioxide, which is produced as a by-product in the synthesis of ammonia, is required for the production of urea. In addition, the process notation enables one to introduce into the model alternative processes for producing the same good: for example, the use of fuel oil, natural gas, naphtha, or coal for the production of ammonia.

To specify processes, let:

a_{cpi} = the input (−) or output (+) of commodity c by process p at plant site i per unit level of activity of process p.

For example, consider the particular process p for producing the chemical fertilizer single superphosphate. The process has phosphate rock, sulfuric acid, and labor as its main inputs, and electric power and unspecified supplies as its miscellaneous inputs. In such a case, one could have:

a_{cpi} = 1.0 ton	c = single superphosphate
a_{cpi} = −0.6 ton	c = phosphate rock
a_{cpi} = −0.36 ton	c = sulfuric acid
a_{cpi} = −0.4 manhour	c = labor
a_{cpi} = − $0.50	c = miscellaneous material inputs

That is, the process combines 0.6 ton of phosphate rock, 0.36 ton of sulfuric acid, 0.4 manhour, and $0.50 worth of miscellaneous material inputs to produce 1 ton of single superphosphate.

In order to specify a process model, commodities used or produced in the fertilizer industry are divided into five groups: fertilizers that are shipped from plants to markets; intermediate commodities that are either produced within the plant or shipped from other plants; raw materials that are purchased from outside sources; material inputs for which no separate specification is considered necessary, referred to as "miscellaneous material inputs"; and inputs of different types of labor. The latter three categories are considered to be directly variable with output. Accordingly, the set of inputs and outputs C is subdivided into the following subsets:

CF = fertilizer types;
CI = intermediate commodities;

CR = raw materials, miscellaneous material inputs, and labor types.

Since cost is no longer attached to a final commodity, but rather to the various input categories, it is necessary to define:

p_{ci} = the price of input c at plant site i;
u_{ci} = the amount of purchases of input c at plant site i.

Thus:

$$\sum_{c \epsilon CR} p_{ci}u_{ci} = \text{the cost of inputs to plant site } i.$$

With this notation, the process model can specified as: select z_{pi}, x_{cij}, and u_{ci} so as to minimize the sum of total shipment cost and the total cost of raw materials, labor, and miscellaneous material inputs. That is,

$$\text{(8.16)} \qquad \min \xi = \sum_{c \epsilon CF} \sum_{i \epsilon I} \sum_{j \epsilon J} \mu_{cij}x_{cij} + \sum_{c \epsilon CR} p_{ci}u_{ci},$$

subject to the following constraints.

MATERIAL BALANCE CONSTRAINTS ON FERTILIZERS

$$\text{(8.17)} \qquad \sum_{p \epsilon P} a_{cpi}z_{pi} \geq \sum_{j \epsilon J} x_{cij} \qquad c \epsilon CF,\ i \epsilon I$$

[*Production of fertilizer c by all processes p at plant site i*]	$\geq$	[*Shipments of fertilizer c from plant site i to all marketing centers j*]	[*For all fertilizers and all plant sites*]

The typical process p that provides fertilizers can be assigned a coefficient a_{cpi} = 1.0 in the fertilizers, or final commodities, constraint (8.17) because the unit of capacity can be defined arbitrarily in terms of one of the inputs or outputs.

MATERIAL BALANCE CONSTRAINTS ON INTERMEDIATE COMMODITIES

$$\text{(8.18)} \qquad \sum_{p \epsilon P} a_{cpi}z_{pi} \geq 0 \qquad c \epsilon CI,\ i \epsilon I$$

[*Production of intermediate product c by all processes p at plant site i*]	≥ 0	[*For all intermediates and all plant sites*]

The production of fertilizers and some intermediate products (for example, phosphoric acid) requires the use of intermediate products. At least one process p in constraint (8.18) therefore has a negative coefficient a_{cpi}, while at least one process for producing an intermediate good must have a positive coefficient in the intermediate product constraint for the latter to hold. This assumes, for the time being, that there are no interplant shipments of intermediates.

MATERIAL BALANCE CONSTRAINTS ON RAW MATERIALS AND LABOR

(8.19) $$\sum_{p \epsilon P} a_{cpi} z_{pi} + u_{ci} \geq 0 \qquad c \epsilon CR, \; i \epsilon I$$

[Use of raw material c by all processes p at plant site i] + [Purchases of raw materials c at plant site i] ≥ 0 [For all raw materials and all plant sites]

The coefficient a_{cpi} in constraint (8.19) is normally negative, because the production of all intermediate and final products requires raw materials and labor. Purchases of raw materials and hiring of labor u_{ci} therefore have to be positive for the constraint to hold.

CAPACITY CONSTRAINTS

(8.20) $$\sum_{p \epsilon P} b_{mpi} z_{pi} \leq k_{mi} \qquad m \epsilon M, \; i \epsilon I$$

[Total number of units of capacity used in productive unit m for all processes p at plant site i] ≤ [Capacity of productive unit m at plant site i] [For all productive units and all plant sites]

MARKET REQUIREMENTS

(8.21) $$\sum_{i \epsilon I} x_{cij} \geq d_{cj} \qquad c \epsilon CF, \; j \epsilon J$$

NONNEGATIVITY CONSTRAINTS

(8.22) $$x_{cij}, z_{pi}, u_{ci} \geq 0 \qquad i \epsilon I, \; j \epsilon J, \; c \epsilon C, \; p \epsilon P$$

The description of the process model is now complete, although several features of the fertilizer sector are still missing from the model structure: namely, interplant shipments of intermediate products, the possibility of foreign trade in the commodities of the sector that can be traded, and, in particular, the phenomena of fertilizer product substitution and fertilizer use recommendations. These elements are introduced into the model in the next few sections. The remainder of the chapter then focuses on the main subject of this volume—that is, the structure of planning models for expanding capacity in the fertilizer sector.

Interplant shipments

In principle, almost all intermediate products of the fertilizer industry can be shipped among plants, and this possibility should be provided for in the mathematical structure of the model. Two simple changes need to be made to achieve this purpose. First, the balance equation for intermediate products needs to be changed. Second, a transport cost element needs to be added to the objective function. Let:

$x_{cii'}$ = shipments of commodity c from plant site i to plant site i';

$\mu_{cii'}$ = unit cost for transporting commodity c from plant site i to plant site i'.

Then, constraint (8.18) of the process model must be modified to read as follows:

(8.23) $$\sum_{p \epsilon P} a_{cpi} z_{pi} + \sum_{\substack{i' \epsilon I \\ i' \neq i}} (x_{ci'i} - x_{cii'}) \geq 0. \qquad c \epsilon CI, \; i \epsilon I$$

Production of intermediate product c by all processes p at plant site i	+	*Shipments of intermediate product c from all other plant sites minus shipments of intermediate product c to all other plant sites*	≥ 0	*For all intermediate products and all plant sites*

The expression $i' \neq i$ means that only shipments of intermediate products among different plants, not shipments within the same plant, are included.

The change in the objective function of the model requires the addition of transport cost for interplant shipments, so that equation (8.16) now takes the following form:

$$(8.24) \qquad \min \xi = \sum_{c \epsilon CF} \sum_{i \epsilon I} \sum_{j \epsilon J} \mu_{cij} x_{cij} + \sum_{c \epsilon CI} \sum_{i \epsilon I} \sum_{\substack{i' \epsilon I \\ i \neq I}} \mu_{cii} \, x_{cii}$$

$$\begin{bmatrix} \textit{Total} \\ \textit{cost} \end{bmatrix} = \begin{bmatrix} \textit{Transport cost for} \\ \textit{all fertilizers from} \\ \textit{all plant sites to all} \\ \textit{marketing centers} \end{bmatrix} + \begin{bmatrix} \textit{Transport cost for} \\ \textit{all interplant} \\ \textit{shipments of} \\ \textit{intermediates} \end{bmatrix}$$

$$+ \sum_{c \epsilon CR} \sum_{i \epsilon I} p_{ci} u_{ci}.$$

$$+ \begin{bmatrix} \textit{Total cost of raw} \\ \textit{materials, labor,} \\ \textit{and miscellaneous} \\ \textit{material inputs} \\ \textit{at all plant sites} \end{bmatrix}$$

The other elements in the model are not affected by the introduction of interplant shipments of intermediate products.

Foreign trade

The model must now be modified to permit the import of raw materials and the import and export of intermediate products and fertilizer products. In this context, imports and exports refer to shipments from and to areas outside the planning area.

To specify imports and exports, the following new variables and parameters need to be defined:

- v_{ci} = imports of commodity c (raw materials, intermediates, and labor) to plant site i;
- v_{cj} = imports of commodity c (fertilizers) to marketing center j;
- e_{cil} = exports of commodity c from plant site i to export market area l;
- L = set of export markets;
- μ_{ci} = unit transport cost for shipping imported commodity c from the appropriate port of entry to plant site i;
- μ_{cj} = unit transport cost for shipping imported commodity c from the appropriate port of entry to marketing center j;
- μ_{cil} = unit transport cost for shipping commodity c from

plant site i to the appropriate port of exit when the commodity is bound for export market area l;

p^v_{ci} = import price of commodity c at the appropriate port of entry when the commodity is bound for plant site i;

p^v_{cj} = import price of commodity c at the appropriate port of entry when the commodity is bound for marketing center j;

p^e_{cil} = export price of commodity c at the appropriate port of exit when the commodity is bound from plant site i to export market area l.

Exports are labeled by destination l in order to permit the model to include discriminatory pricing and, as explained below, to enable the specification of area-specific limitations to the volume of exports.

The criterion, or objective, function can be simplified by being divided into the following components:

ϕ_ψ = domestic raw materials, miscellaneous material inputs, and labor costs;
ϕ_λ = transport cost;
ϕ_π = import cost;
ϕ_ϵ = export revenues.

Then, the criterion function can be defined as the algebraic (plus and minus) sum of these terms, of which the first three are positive (costs) and the last one is negative (revenues).

The model can now be restated as: select z_{pi} (process levels), x_{cij} (shipments of fertilizers), $x_{cii'}$ (shipments of intermediate goods), e_{cil} (exports), v_{ci} (imports of raw materials, intermediates, and labor), v_{cj} (imports of final goods), and u_{ci} (purchases of domestic inputs), so as to minimize:

$$\min \xi = \phi_\psi + \phi_\lambda + \phi_\pi - \phi_\epsilon, \tag{8.25}$$

where

INPUT COST

$$\phi_\psi = \sum_{c\epsilon CR} \sum_{i\epsilon I} p^d_{ci} u_{ci}, \tag{8.26}$$

$$\left[\textit{Input cost}\right] = \left[\textit{Total cost of domestic raw materials, labor, and miscellaneous material inputs}\right]$$

TRANSPORT COST

(8.27) $$\phi_\lambda = \sum_{c\epsilon CF}\left(\sum_{i\epsilon I}\sum_{j\epsilon J}\mu_{cij}x_{cij} + \sum_{j\epsilon J}\mu_{cj}v_{cj} + \sum_{i\epsilon I}\sum_{l\epsilon L}\mu_{cil}e_{cil}\right) + \sum_{c\epsilon CI}\left(\sum_{i\epsilon I}\sum_{\substack{i'\epsilon I\\ i'\neq i}}\mu_{cii'}x_{cii'} + \sum_{i\epsilon I}\mu_{ci}v_{ci} + \sum_{i\epsilon I}\sum_{l\epsilon L}\mu_{cil}e_{cil}\right) + \sum_{c\epsilon CR}\left(\sum_{i\epsilon I}\mu_{ci}v_{ci}\right),$$

[Transport cost] = [Total cost of transport of fertilizers, intermediates, labor, and raw materials, including domestic transport cost of imports and exports; domestically purchased raw materials are assumed to be priced inclusive of domestic transport cost]

IMPORT COST

(8.28) $$\phi_\pi = \sum_{c\epsilon CF}\sum_{j\epsilon J}p^v_{cj}v_{cj} + \sum_{c\epsilon(CI\cup CR)}\sum_{i\epsilon I}p^v_{ci}v_{ci},$$

[Import cost] = [Total cost of imports of fertilizers and intermediate goods as well as raw materials and labor, where the notation $CI\cup CR$ means the union of the sets CI and CR; that is, the summation is over all commodities that are either intermediate products, raw materials, or labor]

EXPORT REVENUE

(8.29) $$\phi_\epsilon = \sum_{c\epsilon(CF\cup CI)}\sum_{i\epsilon I}\sum_{l\epsilon L}p^e_{cil}e_{cil},$$

[Export revenue] = [Total revenue resulting from exports of fertilizers and intermediate goods]

subject to

MATERIAL BALANCE CONSTRAINTS ON FERTILIZERS

(8.30) $$\sum_{p\epsilon P}a_{cpi}z_{pi} \geq \sum_{j\epsilon J}x_{cij} + \sum_{l\epsilon L}e_{cil} \qquad c\,\epsilon\, CF,\ i\,\epsilon\, I$$

[Production of fertilizer c by all processes p at plant site i] ≥ [Domestic shipments of fertilizer c from plant site i to all marketing centers j] + [Exports of fertilizer c from plant site i to all exporting regions] [For all fertilizers and all plant sites]

MATERIAL BALANCE CONSTRAINTS ON INTERMEDIATE PRODUCTS

$$(8.31)\qquad \sum_{p\epsilon P} a_{cpi}z_{pi} + \sum_{\substack{i'\epsilon I\\ i'\neq i}} x_{ci'i} + v_{ci} \geq \sum_{\substack{i'\epsilon I\\ i'\neq i}} x_{cii'} + \sum_{l\epsilon L} e_{cil} \qquad \begin{matrix} c \,\epsilon\, CI \\ i \,\epsilon\, I \end{matrix}$$

[*Production of intermediate product c at plant site i by all processes p*]	+	[*Shipments of intermediate product c to plant site i from all other plants*]	+	[*Imports of intermediate product c shipped to plant site i*]	≥	[*Shipments of intermediate product c from plant site i to all other plant sites*]	+	[*Exports of intermediate product c to all export regions*]

[*For all intermediate products and all plant sites*]

MATERIAL BALANCE CONSTRAINTS ON RAW MATERIALS, LABOR, AND MISCELLANEOUS MATERIAL INPUTS

$$(8.32)\qquad \sum_{p\epsilon P} a_{cpi}z_{pi} + u_{ci} + v_{ci} \geq 0 \qquad \begin{matrix} c \,\epsilon\, CR \\ i \,\epsilon\, I \end{matrix}$$

[*Use of labor, raw materials, and miscellaneous material inputs c at plant site i by all processes p*]	+	[*Domestic hiring of labor and purchases of raw materials and miscellaneous material inputs c at plant site i*]	+	[*Imports of labor, raw materials, and miscellaneous material inputs c for plant site i*]	≥ 0	[*For all raw materials and all plant sites*]

CAPACITY CONSTRAINTS

$$(8.33)\qquad \sum_{p\epsilon P} b_{mpi}z_{pi} \leq k_{mi} \qquad \begin{matrix} m \,\epsilon\, M \\ i \,\epsilon\, I \end{matrix}$$

[*Capacity required*]	≤	[*Capacity available*]	[*For all productive units and all plant sites*]

MARKET REQUIREMENTS

(8.34) $$\sum_{i \epsilon I} x_{cij} + v_{cj} \geq d_{cj} \qquad c \epsilon CF, \; j \epsilon J$$

Shipments of fertilizer c from all plant sites i to marketing center j	+	*Imports of fertilizer c for marketing center j*	≥	*Requirements of marketing center j for fertilizer c*	*For all fertilizers, and all marketing centers*

EXPORT BOUNDS

(8.35) $$\sum_{i \epsilon I} e_{cil} \leq \bar{e}_{cl} \qquad c \epsilon (CI \cup CF), \; l \epsilon L$$

Exports of commodity c to export area l from all plant sites	≤	*A specified volume of exports of commodity c to export area l*	*For all intermediate products and fertilizers, and all export areas*

Alternative specifications of the export bound are possible; some are indicated in chapter 9. Export bounds are desirable to keep such exports within a realistic range.

NONNEGATIVITY CONSTRAINTS

(8.36) $$z_{pi}, x_{cij}, x_{cii'}, e_{cil}, v_{ci}, v_{cj}, u_{ci} \geq 0. \qquad p \epsilon P, \; i', i \epsilon I, \; c \epsilon C, \; j \epsilon J, \; l \epsilon L$$

By-product sales

Several products of the fertilizer industry can be sold outside the industry as by-products, and this possibility of domestic sales may affect investment decisions. The notations used in the model to denote domestic sales and prices are:

w_{ci} = domestic sales of commodity c as a by-product;
p^d_{ci} = domestic price of commodity c at plant i.

The revenue from the domestic sale of by-products, ϕ_X, should be added to the criterion function (with a negative sign, since it represents a revenue) where:

$$\phi_X = \sum_{c \epsilon CI} \sum_{i \epsilon I} p^d_{ci} w_{ci}. \tag{8.37}$$

Moreover, the material balance constraint for intermediate products (8.31) changes by adding w_{ci} to the right-hand side of the constraint:

$$\sum_{p \epsilon P} a_{cpi} z_{pi} + \sum_{\substack{i' \epsilon I \\ i' \neq i}} x_{ci'i} + v_{ci} \geq \sum_{\substack{i' \epsilon I \\ i' \neq i}} x_{cii'} + \sum_{l \epsilon L} e_{cil} + w_{ci}. \qquad \begin{matrix} c \epsilon CI \\ i \epsilon I \end{matrix} \tag{8.38}$$

Finally, a nonnegativity constraint has to be added for w_{ci}:

$$w_{ci} \geq 0. \qquad \begin{matrix} c \epsilon CI \\ i \epsilon I \end{matrix} \tag{8.39}$$

Product substitution and fertilizer recommendations

Until now, the development of the planning model for the fertilizer sector has followed closely the general industrial planning model. With the introduction of product substitution and fertilizer recommendations, the model structure assumes a form specific to the fertilizer industry.

If fertilizer market requirements are stated in terms of nutrients, a large number of fertilizer types can, in principle, meet market demand. On the other hand, fertilizer recommendations, drawn up by agronomists and soil chemists, tend to limit the scope for choice. In order for these phenomena to be incorporated in the model, the following notations must be introduced:

CQ = the set of all nutrients—usually this set will be restricted to the three primary nutrients (nitrogen, phosphorus, and potassium), although secondary and micronutrients can also be included;

$d_{c'j}$ = requirements of nutrient c' at marketing center j;

$\alpha_{cc'}$ = the content of nutrient c' in fertilizer c;

$\bar{d}_{cj}$ = recommended use of fertilizer c at marketing center j.

The market requirements constraint is now modified as follows:

$$(8.40)\qquad \sum_{i\epsilon I}\sum_{c\epsilon CF} \alpha_{cc'} x_{cij} + \sum_{c\epsilon CF} \alpha_{cc'} v_{cj} \geq d_{c'j}. \qquad \begin{matrix} j \epsilon J \\ c' \epsilon CQ \end{matrix}$$

Quantity of nutrient c′ shipped to marketing center j from all plant sites i	+	*Quantity of nutrient c′ supplied to marketing center j from imports*	≥	*Requirement of nutrient c′ at marketing center j*		*For all marketing centers, and all nutrients*

Moreover, a recommended use constraint is added to the model:

$$(8.41)\qquad \sum_{i\epsilon I} x_{cij} + v_{cj} \geq \bar{d}_{cj}. \qquad \begin{matrix} c \epsilon CF \\ j \epsilon J \end{matrix}$$

Quantity of fertilizer c supplied to marketing center j	≥	*Recom-mended use of fertilizer c at market-ing center j*		*For all fertilizers and all marketing regions*

Recapitulation

The model of an existing industry is now complete. At this point, it might be helpful to give a list of all the symbols used and a statement of the model as it has been developed. First, the symbols are categorized as the sets and indexes, the parameters, and the variables:

Symbol	*Definition*
THE SETS AND INDEXES	
$c \epsilon C$	Commodities used or produced in the fertilizer industry
CF	Fertilizer types
CI	Intermediate products
CQ	Nutrients
CR	Raw materials, miscellaneous material inputs, and labor types
$i, i' \epsilon I$	Plant sites
$j \epsilon J$	Marketing centers
$l \epsilon L$	Export regions
$m \epsilon M$	Productive units
$p \epsilon P$	Processes

Symbol	*Definition*
THE VARIABLES	
z	Process level (production level)
x	Domestic shipments
e	Exports
v	Imports
u	Domestic purchases
w	Domestic sales of by-products
ϕ	Cost groups
ϕ_ψ	Domestic raw materials, miscellaneous material inputs, and labor cost
ϕ_λ	Transport cost
ϕ_π	Import cost
ϕ_ϵ	Export revenue
ϕ_χ	Revenue from domestic sale of by-products
THE PARAMETERS	
a	Process inputs (−) or outputs (+)
b	Number of units of capacity required
k	Initial capacity
d	Market requirements
p^d	Domestic price
p^v	Import price
p^e	Export price
μ	Unit transport cost
α	Nutrient content
$\bar{d}$	Recommended fertilizer use
$\bar{e}$	Export bound

Second, the mathematical structure of the model of an existing industry is described in terms of the constraints and sets as follows.

MATERIAL BALANCE CONSTRAINTS ON FERTILIZERS

$$\sum_{p \epsilon P} a_{cpi} z_{pi} \geq \sum_{j \epsilon J} x_{cij} + \sum_{l \epsilon L} e_{cil} \qquad \begin{matrix} c \epsilon CF \\ i \epsilon I \end{matrix} \tag{8.42}$$

MATERIAL BALANCE CONSTRAINTS ON INTERMEDIATE PRODUCTS

$$\sum_{p \epsilon P} a_{cpi} z_{pi} + \sum_{\substack{i' \epsilon I \\ i' \neq i}} x_{ci'i} + v_{ci} \geq \sum_{\substack{i' \epsilon I \\ i' \neq i}} x_{cii'} + \sum_{l \epsilon L} e_{cil} + w_{ci} \qquad \begin{matrix} c \epsilon CI \\ i \epsilon I \end{matrix} \tag{8.43}$$

MATERIAL BALANCE CONSTRAINTS ON RAW MATERIALS, MISCELLANEOUS MATERIAL INPUTS, AND LABOR TYPES

(8.44) $$\sum_{p \in P} a_{cpi} z_{pi} + u_{ci} + v_{ci} \geq 0 \qquad c \in CR, \; i \in I$$

CAPACITY CONSTRAINTS

(8.45) $$\sum_{p \in P} b_{mpi} z_{pi} \leq k_{mi} \qquad m \in M, \; i \in I$$

MARKET REQUIREMENTS

(8.46) $$\sum_{i \in I} \sum_{c \in CF} \alpha_{cc'} x_{cij} + \sum_{c \in CF} \alpha_{cc'} v_{cj} \geq d_{c'j} \qquad j \in J, \; c' \in CQ$$

RECOMMENDED USE CONSTRAINTS

(8.47) $$\sum_{i \in I} x_{cij} + v_{cj} \geq \bar{d}_{cj} \qquad c \in CF, \; j \in J$$

EXPORT BOUNDS

(8.48) $$\sum_{i \in I} e_{cil} \leq \bar{e}_{cl} \qquad c \in (CI \cup CF), \; l \in L$$

NONNEGATIVITY CONSTRAINTS

(8.49) $$z_{pi}, x_{cij}, x_{cii'}, e_{cil}, v_{ci}, v_{cj}, u_{ci}, w_{ci} \geq 0 \qquad p \in P, \; i', i \in I, \; j \in J, \; c \in C, \; l \in L$$

OBJECTIVE FUNCTION

(8.50) $$\min \xi = \phi_\psi + \phi_\lambda + \phi_\pi - \phi_\epsilon - \phi_\chi$$

where

DOMESTIC INPUT COST

(8.51) $$\phi_\psi = \sum_{c \in CR} \sum_{i \in I} p_{ci}^d u_{ci}$$

TRANSPORT COST

$$(8.52)\quad \phi_\lambda = \sum_{c\in CF}\Big(\sum_{i\in I}\sum_{j\in J}\mu_{cij}x_{cij} + \sum_{j\in J}\mu_{cj}v_{cj} + \sum_{i\in I}\sum_{l\in L}\mu_{cil}e_{cil}\Big) + \sum_{c\in CI}\Big(\sum_{i\in I}\sum_{\substack{i'\in I\\ i'\neq i}}\mu_{cii'}x_{cii'} + \sum_{i\in I}\mu_{ci}v_{ci} + \sum_{i\in I}\sum_{l\in L}\mu_{cil}e_{cil}\Big) + \sum_{c\in CR}\Big(\sum_{i\in I}\mu_{ci}v_{ci}\Big)$$

IMPORT COST

$$(8.53)\quad \phi_\pi = \sum_{c\in CF}\sum_{j\in J}p^v_{cj}v_{cj} + \sum_{c\in(CI\cup CR)}\sum_{i\in I}p^v_{ci}v_{ci}$$

EXPORT REVENUE

$$(8.54)\quad \phi_\epsilon = \sum_{c\in(CF\cup CI)}\sum_{i\in I}\sum_{l\in L}p^e_{cil}e_{cil}$$

REVENUE OF BY-PRODUCT SALES

$$(8.55)\quad \phi_\chi = \sum_{c\in CI}\sum_{i\in I}p^d_{ci}w_{ci}$$

The Static Capacity Planning Model

Planning models that incorporate the possibility of capacity expansion can also be developed. This section treats the capacity planning problem in a situation in which the element of time is not modeled. Such a situation can occur when the planner is asked to draw up an efficient investment plan for capacity expansion in the fertilizer sector for a given year. For example, the planner may be asked in the year 1979 to plan the sector for the year 1985, without having to give details about what happens to the sector during the intervening years, nor having to account for prospective developments beyond 1985. Before the appropriate planning model is discussed, however, the difficulties associated with the presence of economies of scale in fertilizer production should be noted.

The treatment of economies of scale

Economies of scale are exhibited in most activities within the fertilizer sector, especially in the construction cost for new plants.

Figure 11. Linearization of the Investment Cost Function

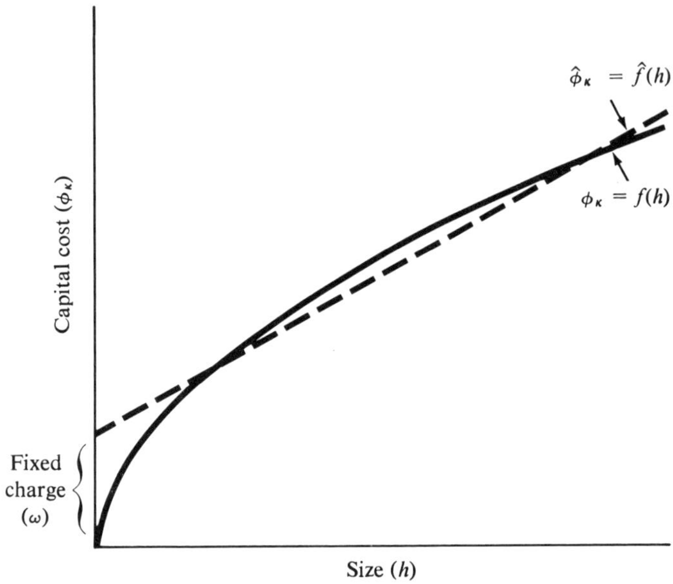

In chapter 7, an example of an investment cost function that incorporates economies of scale was given. Unfortunately, the nonlinearity of that function renders it not directly amenable to treatment in a linear programming model, and a linear approximation needs to be formulated. Figure 11 shows how this linear approximation can be carried out. Algebraically, the linear function can be described as:

$$\hat{\phi}_\kappa = \omega + \nu h, \tag{8.56}$$

where

$\hat{\phi}_\kappa$ = approximate capital cost for a productive unit of size h,
ω = fixed-charge portion of investment cost,
ν = slope of linear portion of investment cost function,
h = size of productive unit to be installed.

The fixed charge, ω, ensures that economies of scale in construction cost will be realized, in the sense that, the larger the capacity constructed, the smaller the incidence of the fixed charge per unit of capacity.

The linear approximation to the investment cost function is not, however, without its problems. At small plant scales, the fit may be very bad; in fact, no observations may exist below some minimum capacity level. Also, beyond a given maximum scale, it is necessary to begin to duplicate facilities and, consequently, to incur the fixed charges again. Therefore, the linear approximation must be specified up to the technical maximum capacity. Between these two extremes, the quality of the linear approximation can vary by productive unit. In some cases, it may be necessary to proceed by iteration or piecewise linear approximation;[2] in many cases, however, it can be assumed that the linear approximation as shown in figure 11 is close enough to the actual investment cost to yield an estimate of investment cost that is within the margin of error that must normally be considered as admissible in estimating capital cost.

When capacity construction is considered in the model, the cost to be incurred for such capacity expansion needs to be included in the objective function. Two complications arise at this point. The first is related to the fixed charge in the capital cost function. The second refers to the fact that, once capacity is constructed, it is available for a certain length of time.

If the capital cost associated with capacity expansion were to be entered into the objective function in the formulation given in (8.56), the fixed charge ω would always be incurred, regardless of whether or not capacity is constructed, because no mechanism is present in the equation that would delete it from total cost. This is in contrast to the variable charge, which is capacity-dependent, so that $\nu h = 0$ whenever h is 0. This problem is solved by introducing a new variable, y, into the function in the following manner:

$$\hat{\phi}_\kappa = \omega y + \nu h. \tag{8.57}$$

Here, y is a variable that can assume only two values, either 1 or 0, where 1 is selected if capacity expansion takes place (so that the fixed charge is incurred), and 0 is selected if no capacity is constructed (so that the fixed charge is deleted). Hence,

$$y = 0 \text{ or } 1. \tag{8.58}$$

2. See Kendrick and Stoutjesdijk, *The Planning of Industrial Investment Programs: A Methodology*, pp. 43–45.

The next question is how to select the appropriate value of y. This requires one additional constraint:

$$h \leq \bar{h}y, \tag{8.59}$$

where

$\bar{h}$ = upper bound on the size of capacity that can be constructed; it may be some arbitrary large number or, if available, a technically defined maximum plant size.

The effect of (8.59) is obvious. Capacity can only be constructed—that is, h can only be a positive number—if $y = 1$. If y is placed at the only other value allowed, $y = 0$, the constraint can only hold if $h = 0$ as well.

The second complication has to do with the fact that capacity, once installed, is available for productive purposes in subsequent years. Even in a static model, this circumstance has to be taken into account, because it affects the way investment cost is charged in the model. Clearly, if the entire investment outlay was charged to the planning year under consideration, it would impose a heavy burden on that year, making it highly unlikely that, in terms of total cost, domestic production would be preferable to imports from abroad. It would appear desirable, therefore, to allocate only a proportion of total investment cost to that year. Based on a device known as the capital recovery factor (CRF), investment cost can be fairly allocated over the years during which the new capacity can be expected to be productive.

The simplest way to explain the significance of the capital recovery factor is to imagine that the newly constructed production capacity is available at a constant annual rental charge. The rental charge can be computed by augmenting the original investment cost by the interest charges attributable to the investment capital incorporated in the production capacity, and by dividing the total by the number of years that constitute the expected productive lifetime of the plant. The formula for calculating the CRF is the same as that for computing an annuity with present value = 1:[3]

$$\sigma_m = \frac{\rho(1+\rho)^{\zeta_m}}{(1+\rho)^{\zeta_m}-1} \tag{8.60}$$

$$= \frac{\rho}{1-(1+\rho)^{-\zeta_m}},$$

3. A complete derivation of the CRF is given in ibid., appendix to chapter 3.

where

σ_m = capital recovery factor for productive unit m,
ρ = discount rate per time interval,
ζ_m = useful life of productive unit m.

The periodical investment charge on a capacity increase is then obtained as follows:

$$\phi_\kappa = \sigma_m(\omega_m y_m + \nu_m h_m). \tag{8.61}$$

The structure of the model

With the description of the 0–1 variables and the capital recovery factor, the most important elements that need to be incorporated into the planning model of an existing industry to transform that model into a capacity planning model have been discussed. Most of the constraints of the previous model remain unaltered. The changes occur in the capacity constraints, the nonnegativity constraints, and the objective function; in addition, the new model contains capacity expansion constraints, and 0–1 or integer constraints.

Until now, the capacity constraint limited the capacity that could be utilized to the amount of the installed capacity. In a planning model that allows capacity expansion, two factors need to be taken into account: first, an increment in capacity is possible; second, during the plan period, a certain amount of capacity may be retired. The new capacity constraint must incorporate both factors. Thus:

$$\sum_{p \in P} b_{mpi} z_{pi} \leq k_{mi} + h_{mi} - s_{mi}. \qquad m \in M, \; i \in I \tag{8.62}$$

$$\left[\begin{array}{c}\textit{Capacity use}\\ \textit{of productive}\\ \textit{unit } m\\ \textit{for all}\\ \textit{processes at}\\ \textit{plant site } i\end{array}\right] \leq \left[\begin{array}{c}\textit{Initial}\\ \textit{capacity of}\\ \textit{productive}\\ \textit{unit } m \textit{ at}\\ \textit{plant site } i\end{array}\right]$$

$$+ \left[\begin{array}{c}\textit{Increment to}\\ \textit{capacity of}\\ \textit{productive}\\ \textit{unit } m \textit{ at}\\ \textit{plant site } i\end{array}\right] - \left[\begin{array}{c}\textit{Capacity}\\ \textit{retirement of}\\ \textit{productive}\\ \textit{unit at}\\ \textit{plant site } i\end{array}\right] \qquad \left[\begin{array}{c}\textit{For all}\\ \textit{productive}\\ \textit{units and}\\ \textit{all plant sites}\end{array}\right]$$

Both k_{mi} and s_{mi} must be exogenously specified; alternatively, k_{mi} can be given in net terms.

As described above, the capacity expansion constraints perform a dual function in the model. First, they force the 0–1 variables y to assume the appropriate value (0 or 1). Second, if there are technical limitations on the magnitude of the capacity expansion, $\bar{h}$ provides a meaningful bound on plant size. Thus, the capacity expansion constraints have the following form:

(8.63) $$h_{mi} \leq \bar{h}_{mi} y_{mi}, \qquad m \in M, \; i \in I$$

[Increment to capacity of productive unit m at plant site i] ≤ [Upper bound on capacity of productive unit m at plant site i] [0–1 investment variable] [For all productive units and all plant sites]

where

(8.64) $$y_{mi} = 0 \text{ or } 1.$$

Two additional nonnegativity constraints are required in the model:

(8.65) $$h_{mi} \geq 0, \qquad i \in I, \; m \in M$$

(8.66) $$y_{mi} \geq 0. \qquad i \in I, \; m \in M$$

To accommodate investment costs, the objective function of the model needs to be modified substantially. As this modification has been discussed extensively above, only the additional element of the objective function is stated here:

(8.67) $$\phi_{\kappa} = \sum_{i \epsilon I} \sum_{m \epsilon M} \sigma_m (\omega_{mi} y_{mi} + \nu_{mi} h_{mi}).$$

[Capital cost charges] = [Capital recovery factor] [Total fixed charge for all productive units at all plant sites + Total variable portion of the capital cost for all productive units at all plant sites]

Recapitulation

The complete static capacity expansion planning model can now be stated. First, the symbols are categorized as the sets and indexes, the parameters, and the variables:

Symbol	*Definition*
THE SETS AND INDEXES	
$c \epsilon C$	Commodities used or produced in the fertilizer industry
CF	Fertilizer types
CI	Intermediate products
CQ	Nutrients
CR	Raw materials, miscellaneous material inputs, and labor types
$i, i' \epsilon I$	Plant sites
$j \epsilon J$	Marketing centers
$l \epsilon L$	Export regions
$m \epsilon M$	Productive units
$p \epsilon P$	Processes
THE VARIABLES	
z	Process level (production level)
x	Domestic shipments
e	Exports
v	Imports
u	Domestic purchases
w	Domestic sales of by-products
y	0–1 investment decisions
h	Capacity expansion
ϕ	Cost groups
ϕ_ψ	Domestic raw materials, miscellaneous material inputs, and labor cost
ϕ_λ	Transport cost
ϕ_κ	Capital cost
ϕ_π	Import cost
ϕ_ϵ	Export revenue
ϕ_χ	Revenue from domestic sale of by-products
THE PARAMETERS	
a	Process inputs (−) or outputs (+)
b	Number of units of capacity required
k	Initial capacity
d	Market requirements

Symbol	*Definition*
THE PARAMETERS (*continued*)	
p^d	Domestic price
p^v	Import price
p^e	Export price
μ	Unit transport cost
α	Nutrient content
s	Retirements of capacity
ρ	Discount rate
σ_m	Capital recovery factor for productive unit m
ω	Fixed-charge portion of investment cost
v	Linear portion of investment cost
$\bar{d}$	Recommended fertilizer use
$\bar{e}$	Export bound
$\bar{h}$	Maximum capacity expansion

Second, the mathematical structure of the static capacity expansion planning model can be described in terms of the constraints and sets as follows.

MATERIAL BALANCE CONSTRAINTS ON FERTILIZERS

$$(8.68) \qquad \sum_{p \in P} a_{cpi} z_{pi} \geq \sum_{j \in J} x_{cij} + \sum_{l \in L} e_{cil} \qquad \begin{array}{l} c \in CF \\ i \in I \end{array}$$

MATERIAL BALANCE CONSTRAINTS ON INTERMEDIATE PRODUCTS

$$(8.69) \qquad \sum_{p \in P} a_{cpi} z_{pi} + \sum_{\substack{i' \in I \\ i' \neq i}} x_{ci'i} + v_{ci} \geq \sum_{\substack{i' \in I \\ i' \neq i}} x_{cii'} + \sum_{l \in L} e_{cil} + w_{ci} \qquad \begin{array}{l} c \in CI \\ i \in I \end{array}$$

MATERIAL BALANCE CONSTRAINTS ON RAW MATERIALS, MISCELLANEOUS MATERIAL INPUTS, AND LABOR TYPES

$$(8.70) \qquad \sum_{p \in P} a_{cpi} z_{pi} + u_{ci} + v_{ci} \geq 0 \qquad \begin{array}{l} c \in CR \\ i \in I \end{array}$$

CAPACITY CONSTRAINTS

$$(8.71) \qquad \sum_{p \in P} b_{mpi} z_{pi} \leq k_{mi} + h_{mi} - s_{mi} \qquad \begin{array}{l} m \in M \\ i \in I \end{array}$$

INVESTMENT CONSTRAINTS

(8.72) $$h_{mi} \leq \bar{h}_{mi} y_{mi} \qquad i \in I,\ m \in M$$

(8.73) $$y_{mi} = 0 \quad \text{or} \quad 1 \qquad i \in I,\ m \in M$$

MARKET REQUIREMENTS

(8.74) $$\sum_{i \in I} \sum_{c \in CF} \alpha_{cc'} x_{cij} + \sum_{c \in CF} \alpha_{cc'} v_{cj} \geq d_{c'j} \qquad j \in J,\ c' \in CQ$$

RECOMMENDED USE CONSTRAINTS

(8.75) $$\sum_{i \in I} x_{cij} + v_{cj} \geq \bar{d}_{cj} \qquad c \in CF,\ j \in J$$

EXPORT BOUNDS

(8.76) $$\sum_{i \in I} e_{cil} \leq \bar{e}_{cl} \qquad c \in (CI \cup CF),\ l \in L$$

NONNEGATIVITY CONSTRAINTS

(8.77) $$z_{pi},\ x_{cij},\ x_{cii'},\ e_{cil},\ v_{ci},\ v_{cj},\ u_{ci},\ w_{ci},\ h_{mi},\ y_{mi} \geq 0 \qquad m \in M,\ p \in P,\ i', i \in I,\ j \in J,\ c \in C,\ l \in L$$

OBJECTIVE FUNCTION

(8.78) $$\min \xi = \phi_\kappa + \phi_\psi + \phi_\lambda + \phi_\pi - \phi_\epsilon - \phi_\chi ,$$

where

CAPITAL COST CHARGES

(8.79) $$\phi_\kappa = \sum_{i \in I} \sum_{m \in M} \sigma_m (\omega_{mi} y_{mi} + \nu_{mi} h_{mi})$$

DOMESTIC INPUT COST

(8.80) $$\phi_\psi = \sum_{c \in CR} \sum_{i \in I} p^d_{ci} u_{ci}$$

TRANSPORT COST

$$(8.81)\quad \phi_\lambda = \sum_{c\epsilon CF}\Big(\sum_{i\epsilon I}\sum_{j\epsilon J}\mu_{cij}x_{cij} + \sum_{j\epsilon J}\mu_{cj}v_{cj} + \sum_{i\epsilon I}\sum_{l\epsilon L}\mu_{cil}e_{cil}\Big)$$
$$+ \sum_{c\epsilon CI}\Big(\sum_{i\epsilon I}\sum_{\substack{i'\epsilon I\\ i'\neq i}}\mu_{cii'}x_{cii'} + \sum_{i\epsilon I}\mu_{ci}v_{ci} + \sum_{i\epsilon I}\sum_{l\epsilon L}\mu_{cil}e_{cil}\Big)$$
$$+ \sum_{c\epsilon CR}\Big(\sum_{i\epsilon I}\mu_{ci}v_{ci}\Big),$$

IMPORT COST

$$(8.82)\quad \phi_\pi = \sum_{c\epsilon CF}\sum_{j\epsilon J}p^v_{cj}v_{cj} + \sum_{c\epsilon(CI\cup CR)}\sum_{i\epsilon I}p^v_{ci}v_{ci}$$

EXPORT REVENUE

$$(8.83)\quad \phi_\epsilon = \sum_{c\epsilon(CF\cup CI)}\sum_{i\epsilon I}\sum_{l\epsilon L}p^e_{cil}e_{cil}$$

REVENUE FROM BY-PRODUCT SALES

$$(8.84)\quad \phi_\chi = \sum_{c\epsilon CI}\sum_{i\epsilon I}p^d_{ci}w_{ci}$$

The Dynamic Capacity Planning Model

Although a static capacity expansion planning model may be the appropriate model in specific circumstances, the element of time will often need to be modeled explicitly in fertilizer sector planning. The presence of economies of scale in fertilizer production, on the one hand, and the likelihood that the demand for fertilizer products is growing over time, on the other hand, result in interdependence that should normally be taken into account in drawing up an efficient investment program for the sector.

Introducing the time element into the model

To introduce time into the model, the subscript t is added to the variables and parameters of the previous model, where:

$t \epsilon T$ = the set of time periods specified in the model.

Each time period t can consist of one or more years. Since the construction period for new investments in the fertilizer sector is often approximately three years, it is convenient to select time periods of three years each, so that investment decisions in period 1 result in operational capacity in period 2, and so on.

The fact that each variable and parameter now has an additional subscript t means that discount rates must be introduced to render costs and benefit streams comparable over time. This would be relatively simple if the model were specified in annual time periods. Consider, for example, a model that covers a nine-year interval, has annual time periods, and has a cost ϕ_t in each year. The discounted cost for the first year would be: $(1 + \rho)^{-1} \phi_t$; for the second year, $(1 + \rho)^{-2} \phi_t$; and for the entire period:

$$\xi = \sum_{t=1}^{9} (1 + \rho)^{-t} \phi_t, \tag{8.85}$$

where

ρ = the annual discount rate,
t = time index.

As was stated above, however, the time periods in the model will usually include more than one year, and that makes the discounting procedure somewhat more difficult. To outline the procedure, assume that the model is specified, not with nine annual planning periods, but with three time periods of three years' duration each. The cost charges for each time period would now be:

$$\begin{aligned} \kappa_1 &= \phi_\tau, & \tau &= 1, 2, 3, \\ \kappa_2 &= \phi_\tau, & \tau &= 4, 5, 6, \\ \kappa_3 &= \phi_\tau, & \tau &= 7, 8, 9, \end{aligned}$$

where

κ_t = the average annual cost for each year during time period t.

Then, (8.85) can be written:

$$\xi = \kappa_1 \sum_{\tau=1}^{3} (1 + \rho)^{-\tau} + \kappa_2 \sum_{\tau=4}^{6} (1 + \rho)^{-\tau} + \kappa_3 \sum_{\tau=7}^{9} (1 + \rho)^{-\tau}, \tag{8.86}$$

where the first term on the right-hand side of (8.86) is the discounted sum of the investment charges during the first three-year period, the second term is the discounted sum of the charges for the second three-year period, and so forth. In its general form, (8.86) can now be rewritten as:

(8.87) $$\xi = \sum_{t=1}^{3} \delta_t \kappa_t,$$

where

$$\delta_t = \sum_{\tau=1+(t-1)\theta}^{\theta} (1+\rho)^{-\tau}$$

$$= \sum_{\tau=1}^{\theta} (1+\rho)^{-\theta(t-1)-\tau},$$

where

θ = the number of years per time period.

The dynamic model

Most of the constraints of the static planning model remain the same in the dynamic specification of the model, except that the subscript t is added to the variables and parameters. For example, the activity level z_{pi} in the dynamic formulation is written as z_{pit}, exports e_{cil} as e_{cilt}, and so forth. In view of the simplicity of this change, the complete dynamic capacity planning model is not restated here; it is described in the next chapter. Since the capacity constraints and the objective function undergo a modification that may require some further explanation, however, that change is described here.

The capacity constraints limit the use of any productive unit in the model to the available capacity. In a dynamic model, it must be taken into account that capacity can be constructed during the planning period, so that at a given point in time capacity use is limited to capacity at the beginning of the planning period, augmented by new capacity constructed during the planning period. The capacity constraints of the dynamic model have the following form:

(8.88) $$\sum_{p \in P} b_{mpi} z_{pit} \leq k_{mi} + \sum_{\substack{\tau \in T \\ \tau \leq t}} (h_{mi\tau} - s_{mi\tau}). \qquad \begin{matrix} i \in I \\ m \in M \\ p \in P \\ t \in T \end{matrix}$$

$$\begin{bmatrix} \textit{Total num-} \\ \textit{ber of units} \\ \textit{of capacity} \\ \textit{used of pro-} \\ \textit{ductive unit} \\ \textit{m for all} \\ \textit{processes p} \\ \textit{at plant} \\ \textit{site i in} \\ \textit{time period t} \end{bmatrix} \leq \begin{bmatrix} \textit{Initial} \\ \textit{capacity} \\ \textit{of produc-} \\ \textit{tive unit m} \\ \textit{at plant} \\ \textit{site i} \end{bmatrix} + \begin{bmatrix} \textit{Capacity} \\ \textit{added during} \\ \textit{previous} \\ \textit{periods in} \\ \textit{the planning} \\ \textit{period minus} \\ \textit{retirements} \\ \textit{during pre-} \\ \textit{vious years} \end{bmatrix} \begin{bmatrix} \textit{For all} \\ \textit{plant sites,} \\ \textit{all productive} \\ \textit{units, all} \\ \textit{processes,} \\ \textit{and all time} \\ \textit{periods} \end{bmatrix}$$

Constraint (8.88) ensures that capacity, once constructed, is carried over into the next time periods of the model and is available for productive purposes. Similarly, it ensures that capacity, once retired, is no longer available in later periods in the model.

The objective function of the dynamic investment planning model, in summary notation, differs from that of the static model because the discount factor is added. That is:

$$\xi = \sum_{t} \delta_t \left(\phi_{\kappa t} + \phi_{\psi t} + \phi_{\lambda t} + \phi_{\pi t} - \phi_{\epsilon t} - \phi_{x t}\right), \tag{8.89}$$

$$\begin{bmatrix} \textit{Total} \\ \textit{cost} \end{bmatrix} = \begin{bmatrix} \textit{Discounted} \\ \textit{sum over} \\ \textit{all time} \\ \textit{periods} \end{bmatrix} \begin{bmatrix} \begin{matrix} \textit{Capi-} \\ \textit{tal} \\ \textit{cost} \end{matrix} + \begin{matrix} \textit{Recur-} \\ \textit{rent} \\ \textit{cost} \end{matrix} + \begin{matrix} \textit{Trans-} \\ \textit{port} \\ \textit{cost} \end{matrix} + \begin{matrix} \textit{Import} \\ \textit{cost} \end{matrix} - \begin{matrix} \textit{Export} \\ \textit{revenue} \end{matrix} - \begin{matrix} \textit{Sales} \\ \textit{of by-} \\ \textit{prod-} \\ \textit{uct} \end{matrix} \end{bmatrix}$$

where

$$\phi_{\kappa t} = \sum_{\substack{\tau \epsilon T \\ \tau \leq t}} \sum_{i \epsilon I} \sum_{m \epsilon M} \sigma_m \left(\omega_{mi\tau} y_{mi\tau} + \nu_{mi\tau} h_{mi\tau}\right). \tag{8.90}$$

$$\begin{bmatrix} \textit{Total} \\ \textit{capital} \\ \textit{cost} \end{bmatrix} = \begin{bmatrix} \textit{Capital} \\ \textit{recovery} \\ \textit{factor} \end{bmatrix} \begin{bmatrix} \begin{matrix} \textit{Fixed} \\ \textit{charge} \end{matrix} + \begin{matrix} \textit{Variable} \\ \textit{charge} \end{matrix} \end{bmatrix}$$

Constraint (8.90) ensures that the investment charges related to capacity constructed during the previous time periods in the model are charged in any time period t.

With these changes and the earlier modifications to the static model, the dynamic investment planning model for the fertilizer sector is fully specified. In the next chapter, a complete description of this model is presented.

9

The Complete Investment Planning Model

A COMPREHENSIVE INVESTMENT PLANNING MODEL for the fertilizer sector is presented in this chapter. The model is dynamic, and it permits the explicit specification of economies of scale in the production of fertilizers and intermediate products. It can incorporate a variety of intermediate and final products, regionally specified fertilizer requirements, alternative production processes, and alternative means of transport. Finally, it permits import and export policies for the sector to be analyzed.

The most exhaustive use of the model is to determine the least-cost investment, production, and trade strategy for the fertilizer sector, over a given planning period and with specified market requirements for fertilizer nutrients. Other uses are also possible. For example, the model can be used to determine the cost implications for the sector of a given investment project or program as compared with alternative project configurations.

With the least-cost objective, the values that minimize the total discounted net cost of meeting market requirements can be selected for the following variables:[1]

- the production levels of fertilizer products and the production process used;
- the production levels of intermediate products and the production process used;
- investments in the sector;
- the shipment of final products from plants to markets and of intermediate products among plants;
- domestic purchases of raw materials, labor, and miscellaneous inputs;
- exports of final and intermediate products within specified bounds;
- imports of intermediate products and raw materials;
- imports of final products to each marketing center in each time period.

The complete model is described in the next section. This is followed by an examination of the size of the model. Then, alternative specifications of the model to suit particular situations and conditions are given. The chapter concludes with a discussion of linking the fertilizer planning model to an agricultural planning model and to other activities.

The Specification of the Model

The complete dynamic investment planning model for the fertilizer sector is described in this section. First, the symbols used in the model are presented. They are categorized as the sets and indexes,[2] the parameters (or exogenous variables),[3] and the (endogenous) variables:

1. Other objectives are, of course, possible; for example, maximizing the rate of return on investments or maximizing the sum of consumers' and producers' surplus.

2. The elements of these sets are explicitly defined in the case study that appears in the second part of this volume.

3. These parameters are specific to both plant location and time. They are plant-location specific to take into account any locational inefficiencies that are unlikely to be remedied during the planning period; they are time specific to take into account any expected improvements in the technology of a particular process at time t (the expectations are those held at the beginning of the planning period). The case study does not take these two considerations into account; hence, the parameters are denoted as a_{cp} and b_{mp}.

Symbol	*Definition*
THE SETS AND INDEXES	
$c \epsilon C$	Commodities used or produced in the fertilizer industry
CF	Fertilizer types
CI	Intermediate products or commodities
CQ	Nutrients
CR	Raw materials, miscellaneous inputs, and labor types
$i, i' \epsilon I$	Plant locations or sites
$j \epsilon J$	Marketing centers
$l \epsilon L$	Export regions
$m \epsilon M$	Productive units[4]
$p \epsilon P$	Production processes[5]
$\tau, t, t' \epsilon T$	Time periods
THE VARIABLES	
z	Process level (production level)
x	Domestic shipments
e	Exports
v	Imports
u	Domestic purchases
w	Domestic sales of by-products
y	0–1 investment decision variable
h	Capacity expansion
ξ	Total discounted net cost

4. The concept of a productive unit is flexible and depends on the level of disaggregation desired. At the aggregate level, a productive unit may be a complete plant or a set of unit operations (for example, crystallization, evaporation, and drying—that is, a subset of the plant). At the micro level, a productive unit may refer to separate pieces of equipment or machinery—that is, a crystallizer or an evaporator or a drier. In such cases, productive units are numbered sequentially; no distinction is made among the processes to which each unit refers. Hence, an evaporator in one process will be denoted by $m = 1$; the same evaporator in another process will be denoted by $m = 2$. A constraint on disaggregation may be the availability of cost data for each individual unit.

5. A production process refers to the production of final or intermediate commodities. Several processes may be available for the production of a single commodity (for example, ammonium nitrate), with each differing in either the inputs used or the unit operations involved. In some cases, the same plant and equipment may be used to produce two final products (for example, monoammonium phosphate and diammonium phosphate); in such cases, the production of each product is referred to as a process.

Symbol	*Definition*
THE VARIABLES (*continued*)	
ϕ	Cost groups
ϕ_κ	Capital cost
ϕ_ψ	Domestic recurrent cost (raw materials, miscellaneous inputs, and labor cost)
ϕ_λ	Transport cost
ϕ_π	Import cost
ϕ_ϵ	Export revenue
ϕ_χ	Revenue from domestic sale of by-products
THE PARAMETERS	
a	Process inputs (−) or outputs (+)
b	Number of units of capacity used
k	Initial capacity
s	Retirements of capacity
d	Market requirements
p^d	Domestic price
p^e	Export price
p^v	Import price
θ	Number of years per time period
ρ	Discount rate per year
δ	Discount factor per time period
σ	Capital recovery factor
σ_m	$\dfrac{\rho\,(1+\rho)^{\zeta_m}}{(1+\rho)^{\zeta_m}-1}$, where ζ_m = life of productive unit m
ω	Fixed-charge portion of investment cost
ν	Linear portion of investment cost
μ	Unit transport cost
α	Nutrient content
$\bar{d}$	Recommended fertilizer use
$\bar{e}$	Export bound
$\bar{h}$	Maximum capacity expansion per time period[6]

The constraints of the model can now be specified, using the notation listed above. A full derivation of the constraints, and a detailed description of their meaning, is given in chapter 8. Here, the constraints are described in conventional summary notation.

6. If the productive unit m is defined as a complete plant producing a commodity c using a process p, then the upper bound on capacity expansion of the plant would depend upon the particular process used. In this case, $\bar{h}_{mit}$ is defined as the maximum of the set of such upper bounds.

MATERIAL BALANCE CONSTRAINTS ON FINAL PRODUCTS

(9.1)
$$\sum_{p \epsilon P} a_{cpi} z_{pit} \geq \sum_{j \epsilon J} x_{cijt} + \sum_{l \epsilon L} e_{cilt} \qquad \begin{array}{l} c \epsilon CF \\ i \epsilon I \\ t \epsilon T \end{array}$$

[Total production of fertilizer c by all processes p at plant site i during time period t] ≥ [Quantity of fertilizer c shipped from plant site i to all market centers j during time period t]

+ [Quantity of fertilizer c exported from plant site i to all export regions during time period t] [For all fertilizers, all plant sites, and all time periods]

MATERIAL BALANCE CONSTRAINTS ON INTERMEDIATE PRODUCTS

(9.2)
$$\sum_{p \epsilon P} a_{cpi} z_{pit} + \sum_{\substack{i' \epsilon I \\ i' \neq i}} x_{ci'it}$$

[Total production of intermediate product c by all processes p at plant site i during time period t] + [Quantity of intermediate product c shipped from plant site i′ to plant site i during time period t]

$$+ v_{cit} \geq \sum_{\substack{i' \epsilon I \\ i' \neq i}} x_{cii't}$$

+ [Quantity of intermediate product c imported to plant site i during time period t] ≥ [Quantity of intermediate product c shipped from plant site i to plant site i′ during time period t]

$$+ \sum_{l \epsilon L} e_{cilt} + w_{cit} \qquad \begin{array}{l} c \epsilon CI \\ i \epsilon I \\ t \epsilon T \end{array}$$

+ [*Quantity of intermediate product c exported from plant site i to all export regions during time period t*] + [*Domestic sales of by-product c at plant site i during time period t*]   [*For all intermediate products, all plant sites, and all time periods*]

MATERIAL BALANCE CONSTRAINTS ON RAW MATERIALS, MISCELLANEOUS INPUTS, AND LABOR TYPES

$$\sum_{p \epsilon P} a_{cpi} z_{pit} + u_{cit} + v_{cit} \geq 0 \qquad c \epsilon CR,\; i \epsilon I,\; t \epsilon T \tag{9.3}$$

[*Raw materials, labor, or miscellaneous inputs used in all processes p at plant i during time period t*] + [*Raw materials, labor, or miscellaneous inputs domestically purchased at plant site i during time period t*]

+ [*Raw materials, labor, or miscellaneous inputs imported to plant site i during time period t*] ≥ 0   [*For all raw material and labor, all plant sites, and all time periods*]

CAPACITY CONSTRAINTS

$$\sum_{p \epsilon P} b_{mpi} z_{pit} \leq k_{mi} + \sum_{\substack{\tau \epsilon T \\ \tau \leqq t}} (h_{mi\tau} - s_{mi\tau}) \qquad m \epsilon M,\; i \epsilon I,\; t \epsilon T \tag{9.4}$$

[*Capacity of productive unit m for all processes p at plant site i during time period t*] ≤ [*Initial capacity of productive unit m at plant site i*]

+ [*Total capacity expansion of productive unit m at plant site i up to time period t*] − [*Total capacity retirement of productive unit m at plant site i up to time period t*]   [*For all productive units, all plant sites, and all time periods*]

MARKET REQUIREMENTS

$$(9.5) \qquad \sum_{c \epsilon CF} \sum_{i \epsilon I} \alpha_{cc'} x_{cijt} + \sum_{c \epsilon CF} \alpha_{cc'} v_{cjt} \geq d_{c'jt} \qquad \begin{matrix} c' \epsilon CQ \\ j \epsilon J \\ t \epsilon T \end{matrix}$$

[Quantity of nutrient c' shipped to marketing center j from all plant sites during time period t] + [Quantity of nutrient c' imported to marketing center j during time period t]

≥ [Requirement of nutrient c' at marketing center j during time period t] [For all nutrients, all marketing regions, and all time periods]

RECOMMENDED USE CONSTRAINTS

$$(9.6) \qquad \sum_{i \epsilon I} x_{cijt} + v_{cjt} \geq \bar{d}_{cjt} \qquad \begin{matrix} c \epsilon CF \\ j \epsilon J \\ t \epsilon T \end{matrix}$$

[Quantity of fertilizer c shipped to marketing center j from all plant sites i during time period t] + [Quantity of fertilizer c imported to marketing center j during time period t]

≥ [Recommended use of fertilizer c at marketing center j during time period t] [For all fertilizers, all marketing regions, and all time periods]

EXPORT CONSTRAINTS

$$(9.7) \qquad \sum_{i \epsilon I} e_{cilt} \leq \bar{e}_{clt} \qquad \begin{matrix} c \epsilon (CF \cup CI) \\ l \epsilon L \\ t \epsilon T \end{matrix}$$

[Quantity of final or intermediate product c exported from all plant sites i to export region l during time period t] ≤ [Maximum quantity of exports of product c to export region l during time period t] [For all fertilizers and intermediate products, all export areas, and all time periods]

CAPACITY EXPANSION CONSTRAINT: MAXIMUM CAPACITY EXPANSION

(9.8) $$h_{mit} \leq \bar{h}_{mit} y_{mit} \qquad m \in M,\ i \in I,\ t \in T$$

[*Increment to capacity of productive unit m at plant site i during time period t*] ≤ [*Upper bound on capacity of productive unit m at plant site i during time period t*]

[0–1 *investment variable*] [*For all productive units, all plant sites, and all time periods*]

CAPACITY EXPANSION CONSTRAINT: ZERO-ONE

(9.9) $$y_{mit} = 0 \quad \text{or} \quad 1 \qquad m \in M,\ i \in I,\ t \in T$$

NONNEGATIVITY CONSTRAINTS

(9.10)

$z_{pit} \geq 0,$		$i \in I$	$t \in T$	$p \in P$
$x_{cijt} \geq 0,$	$c \in CF$	$i \in I$	$t \in T$	$j \in J$
$x_{cii't} \geq 0,$	$c \in CI$	$i \in I$	$t \in T$	$i' \in I$, $i' \neq i$
$v_{cit} \geq 0,$	$c \in (CI \cup CR)$	$i \in I$	$t \in T$	
$v_{cjt} \geq 0,$	$c \in CF$		$t \in T$	$j \in J$
$e_{cilt} \geq 0,$	$c \in (CF \cup CI)$	$i \in I$	$t \in T$	$l \in L$
$u_{cit} \geq 0,$	$c \in CR$	$i \in I$	$t \in T$	
$h_{mit} \geq 0,$		$i \in I$	$t \in T$	$m \in M$
$w_{cit} \geq 0,$	$c \in CI$	$i \in I$	$t \in T$	

OBJECTIVE FUNCTION

(9.11) $$\min \xi = \sum_{t \in T} \delta_t (\phi_{\kappa t} + \phi_{\psi t} + \phi_{\lambda t} + \phi_{\pi t} - \phi_{\epsilon t} - \phi_{\chi t})$$

$$\begin{bmatrix}\textit{Discounted net}\\ \textit{cost}\end{bmatrix} = \begin{bmatrix}\textit{Total capital}\\ \textit{cost during}\\ \textit{time period } t\end{bmatrix} + \begin{bmatrix}\textit{Total domestic}\\ \textit{recurrent cost}\\ \textit{during time}\\ \textit{period } t\end{bmatrix}$$

$$+ \begin{bmatrix}\textit{Total}\\ \textit{transport}\\ \textit{cost during}\\ \textit{time period}\\ t\end{bmatrix} + \begin{bmatrix}\textit{Total}\\ \textit{import cost}\\ \textit{during time}\\ \textit{period } t\end{bmatrix} - \begin{bmatrix}\textit{Total}\\ \textit{export}\\ \textit{revenue}\\ \textit{during time}\\ \textit{period } t\end{bmatrix} - \begin{bmatrix}\textit{Total}\\ \textit{of}\\ \textit{by-product}\\ \textit{sales during}\\ \textit{time period}\\ t\end{bmatrix}$$

where

DISCOUNT FACTOR

(9.12) $$\delta_t = \sum_{\tau=1}^{\theta} (1 + \rho)^{-\theta(t-1)-\tau}$$

CAPITAL COST CHARGES

(9.13) $$\phi_{\kappa t} = \sum_{\substack{\tau \in T\\ \tau \leq t}} \sum_{i \in I} \sum_{m \in M} \sigma_m (\omega_{mi\tau} y_{mi\tau} + \nu_{mi\tau} h_{mi\tau})$$

$$\begin{bmatrix}\textit{Total}\\ \textit{capital cost}\\ \textit{during time}\\ \textit{period } t\end{bmatrix} = \begin{bmatrix}\textit{Capital}\\ \textit{recovery}\\ \textit{factor for}\\ \textit{productive}\\ \textit{unit } m\end{bmatrix} \begin{bmatrix}\textit{Total fixed} & & \textit{Total of the vari-}\\ \textit{charge for all} & & \textit{able portion of the}\\ \textit{productive units} & & \textit{capital cost for all}\\ \textit{installed at all} & + & \textit{productive untis}\\ \textit{plant sites} & & \textit{installed at all}\\ \textit{up to time} & & \textit{plant sites up to}\\ \textit{period } t & & \textit{time period } t\end{bmatrix}$$

where

(9.14) $$\sigma_m = \frac{\rho(1 + \rho)^{\zeta_m}}{(1 + \rho)^{\zeta_m} - 1}$$

DOMESTIC INPUT COST

(9.15)
$$\phi_{\psi t} = \sum_{c \epsilon CR} \sum_{i \epsilon I} p^d_{cit} u_{cit}$$

[Total domestic recurrent cost during time period *t*] = [Cost of domestic raw materials, labor, and miscellaneous inputs purchased at all plant sites during time period *t*]

TRANSPORT COST

(9.16)
$$\phi_{\lambda t} = \sum_{c \epsilon CF} \Big(\sum_{i \epsilon I} \sum_{j \epsilon J} \mu_{cijt} x_{cijt}$$

[Total transport cost during time period *t*] = [Cost of shipping all final products from all plant sites to all domestic markets during time period *t*]

$$+ \sum_{j \epsilon J} \mu_{cjt} v_{cjt} + \sum_{i \epsilon I} \sum_{l \epsilon L} \mu_{cilt} e_{cilt} \Big)$$

\+ [Cost of transporting all imported final products from the border to all domestic markets during time period *t*] + [Cost of transporting all final products exported from all plant sites to the border for all export regions during time period *t*]

$$+ \sum_{c \epsilon CI} \Big(\sum_{i \epsilon I} \sum_{\substack{i' \epsilon I \\ i' \neq i}} \mu_{cii't} x_{cii't} + \sum_{i \epsilon I} \mu_{cit} v_{cit}$$

\+ [Cost of all interplant shipments of all intermediate products during time period *t*] + [Cost of transporting all imported intermediate products from the border to all plant sites during time period *t*]

$$+ \sum_{i \epsilon I} \sum_{l \epsilon L} \mu_{cilt} e_{cilt} \Big) + \sum_{c \epsilon CR} \sum_{i \epsilon I} \mu_{cit} v_{cit}$$

\+ [Cost of transporting all intermediate products exported from all plant sites to all export regions during time period *t*] + [Cost of transporting all imported raw materials and labor to all plant sites during time period *t*]

IMPORT COST

$$\phi_{\pi t} = \sum_{c \in CF} \sum_{j \in J} p^{v}_{cjt} v_{cjt} + \sum_{c \in CI \cup CR} \sum_{i \in I} p^{v}_{cit} v_{cit} \tag{9.17}$$

[*Total import cost during time period t*] = [*Cost of importing all final products sold in all market areas during time period t*] + [*Cost of importing all intermediate products, raw materials, and labor used at all plant sites during time period t*]

EXPORT REVENUE

$$\phi_{et} = \sum_{c \in CF \cup CI} \sum_{i \in I} \sum_{l \in L} p^{e}_{cilt} e_{cilt} \tag{9.18}$$

[*Total export revenue during time period t*] = [*Revenue from the export of all final and intermediate products from all plant sites to all export regions during time period t*]

REVENUE FROM BY-PRODUCT SALES

$$\phi_{\chi t} = \sum_{c \in CI} \sum_{i \in I} p^{d}_{cit} w_{cit} \tag{9.19}$$

[*Total revenue from by-product sales during time period t*] = [*Revenue from domestic by-product sales of commodity c from all plant sites during time period t*]

The Size of the Model

The size of the model cannot be indicated by the mathematical specification of the model; rather, the size depends on the specification of the sets. The sets to be specified are: commodities, C;[7] plant

7. The commodities include final and intermediate products, raw materials, and labor types.

sites, I; domestic marketing regions, J; export market areas, L; nutrients, CQ; productive units, M; production processes, P; and time periods, T.

Clearly, the potential size of the fertilizer planning model is very large. Normally, more than one fertilizer type has to be considered, and more than one plant site may be a plausible candidate for production facilities. To capture the trade-off between economies of scale, on the one hand, and transport cost, on the other, it is desirable to break down the entire market for any plant site into a number of domestic marketing regions and export market areas. Moreover, although the various nutrients are not directly competitive, the existence of multinutrient fertilizers makes it necessary to consider different nutrients simultaneously. Similarly, it may often be necessary to specify various productive units and processes. Finally, to investigate the desirability of constructing temporary overcapacity, so that the advantages of economies of scale can be exploited more fully later, it is necessary to specify several time periods in the model.

Although disaggregation may be desirable, large-scale planning models have a distinct disadvantage: they become extremely expensive to solve, even on modern, high-speed computers. This is particularly the case for models that incorporate economies of scale in the form of 0–1 variables. In the absence of such 0–1 variables, the planning models in this volume reduce to linear programming models. Large models of this type—3,000 to 5,000 constraints—are now routinely solved on large-scale computers, although even they pose serious problems if their structure is complex. Mixed-integer linear programming models of that size can only be solved at reasonable cost if the number of 0–1 variables is limited to a handful, say, 20 to 30. This number is easily reached: one only needs to specify 2 time periods, 5 products, and 2 locations before the number of 0–1 variables reaches 20.

Why does the number of 0–1 variables play such an important role? A more complete explanation of this aspect of the planning problem is given in volume 1 of this series;[8] here, only an intuitive

8. David Kendrick and Ardy Stoutjesdijk, *The Planning of Industrial Investment Programs: A Methodology*, The Planning of Investment Programs, ed. Alexander Meeraus and Stoutjesdijk, vol. 1 (Baltimore: Johns Hopkins University Press, 1978), chapter 8.

explanation is given. Consider, for example, a project planning problem in which the plant site for the production of a given product is to be selected. There are two potential sites, A and B, and four possibilities: plants in both A and B; a plant in A but not in B; a plant in B but not in A; and no plant at all (only imports). Thus, although there are only two 0–1 variables, there are four possible combinations—that is, 2^2. This example can be generalized to the statement that the number of project combinations in a 0–1 investment problem is equal to 2^n, where n is the number of 0–1 variables. If $n = 20$, the number of project combinations is more than 1 million! And each project combination constitutes a separate linear programming problem. Fortunately, procedures have been developed so that it is not necessary to solve each individual linear programming problem; in fact, only a fraction of them is ever solved. These procedures, however, are still sufficiently cumbersome to encourage the user to limit the size of the planning model as much as possible, by carefully specifying the sets and by deleting any decision problems that can be solved or approximated at the outset.

Alternative Specifications of the Constraints

The constraints of the model are specified with sufficient generality to encompass most of the situations that may be considered in planning the fertilizer sector. Some situations may, however, be unique to the specific problem under consideration, and this section addresses such cases. In particular, the constraints discussed here are export constraints, investment constraints, domestic labor constraints, foreign exchange constraints, import constraints, and regional preference constraints. This section is not intended to be exhaustive, and other constraints may be relevant to a particular problem.

Export constraints

The export constraint (9.7) places an upper bound on the export of a given product to a given export market for each time period, for all producing sites taken together. This may not always be the appropriate way to specify the export constraint. Alternative specifications of the export constraint are given below.

TOTAL BY EXPORT MARKET

(9.20) $$\sum_{c \epsilon CF \cup CI} \sum_{i \epsilon I} e_{cilt} \leq \bar{\bar{e}}_{lt} \qquad l \epsilon L, \; t \epsilon T$$

$$\begin{bmatrix} \textit{Quantity of all final} \\ \textit{and intermediate} \\ \textit{commodities exported} \\ \textit{from all plant sites to} \\ \textit{export region } l \textit{ during} \\ \textit{time period } t \end{bmatrix} \leq \begin{bmatrix} \textit{Maximum quantity of} \\ \textit{exports for region } l \\ \textit{during time period } t \end{bmatrix}$$

This constraint limits total exports from all producing locations taken together to each export region during any given time period, without specifying the constraint for each product separately. As a result, the use of constraint (9.20) involves a smaller total number of constraints than (9.7).

TOTAL BY COMMODITY

(9.21) $$\sum_{i \epsilon I} \sum_{l \epsilon L} e_{cilt} \leq \tilde{e}_{ct} \qquad c \epsilon CF \cup CI, \; t \epsilon T$$

$$\begin{bmatrix} \textit{Quantity of final or} \\ \textit{intermediate product } c \\ \textit{exported from all} \\ \textit{plant sites to all} \\ \textit{export regions during} \\ \textit{time period } t \end{bmatrix} \leq \begin{bmatrix} \textit{Maximum quantity of} \\ \textit{exports of final or} \\ \textit{intermediate product} \\ c \textit{ during time period } t \end{bmatrix}$$

It may be desirable to focus on specific commodities rather than on export markets. Constraint (9.21) restricts the total amount of commodity c that can be exported from all plant sites to all export regions during any given time period. It differs from constraint (9.20), which placed an upper bound on the exports to any particular export region. As before, substituting constraint (9.21) for (9.7) decreases the total number of constraints in the model.

TOTAL BY COMMODITY, LOCATION, AND EXPORT REGION

(9.22) $$e_{cilt} \leq \hat{e}_{cilt} \qquad c \epsilon CF \cup CI, \; i \epsilon I, \; l \epsilon L, \; t \epsilon T$$

$$\begin{bmatrix} \textit{Quantity of final or} \\ \textit{intermediate product} \\ c \textit{ exported from plant} \\ \textit{site } i \textit{ to export region} \\ l \textit{ during time period } t \end{bmatrix} \leq \begin{bmatrix} \textit{Maximum quantity of} \\ \textit{commodity } c \textit{ from} \\ \textit{plant site } i \textit{ to export} \\ \textit{region } l \textit{ during time} \\ \textit{period } t \end{bmatrix}$$

This strong constraint restricts the export of a commodity from each producing location to each export region in each time period. The use of constraint (9.22) instead of (9.7) increases the total number of constraints in the model.

AGGREGATE EXPORT CONSTRAINTS

Constraint (9.22) specifies a restriction on the amount of exports for each product, from each plant site, to each export market, and during each time period. It is conceivable that, even though the planner considers this specification the appropriate one, he is interested in knowing which export market, which product, which plant site, or which time period is the most attractive, if a choice has to be made. The simplest way to make such a determination is to formulate an additional constraint which specifies that the arithmetic sum of the individual bounds is larger than a given number. For example, assume that the individual bounds of constraint (9.22) are placed at 10,000 tons, and that there are 2 products, 2 plant sites, 2 export markets, and 2 time periods. This means that there are 16 individual constraints within the constraint set (9.22); in principle, exports could thus total 160,000 tons. If an additional constraint were placed on this total so that exports could amount only to, say, 100,000 tons, the model would be forced to choose product, plant site, export market, and time period for which exports make the greatest contribution to the objective of the model.

The combination of constraint (9.22) with (9.20) would focus on the choice among products and plant sites. A similar purpose would be achieved by restricting the value of $\bar{\bar{e}}_{lt}$:

(9.23) $$\bar{\bar{e}}_{lt} < \sum_{c \epsilon CF \cup CI} \sum_{i \epsilon I} \hat{e}_{cilt}. \qquad l \epsilon L, \; t \epsilon T$$

Maximum quantity of all exports to region l during time period t	<	*Maximum quantity of exports of all final and intermediate products from all plant sites to export region l during time period t*

Similarly, if the planner wants to focus on the most attractive export market or plant site for exports, he can add a constraint of the following form to (9.21):

$$\tilde{e}_{ct} < \sum_{i \epsilon I} \sum_{l \epsilon L} \hat{e}_{cilt}. \qquad (9.24) \qquad c \epsilon CF \cup CI,\ t \epsilon T$$

$$\begin{bmatrix} \textit{Maximum quantity of} \\ \textit{exports of final or} \\ \textit{intermediate product c} \\ \textit{during time period t} \end{bmatrix} < \begin{bmatrix} \textit{Maximum quantity of} \\ \textit{exports of final or} \\ \textit{intermediate product c} \\ \textit{from all plant sites to} \\ \textit{all export regions} \\ \textit{during time period t} \end{bmatrix}$$

Investment constraints

The model specified above does not take into account constraints on investment funds. But there may be situations under which the shortage of capital poses a real constraint, and the optimal program must take this into consideration.

IN EACH TIME PERIOD

$$\phi_{\kappa t} \leq \bar{\phi}_{\kappa t}, \qquad (9.25) \qquad t \epsilon T$$

$$\begin{bmatrix} \textit{Total capital cost dur-} \\ \textit{ing time period t} \end{bmatrix} \leq \begin{bmatrix} \textit{Maximum amount of} \\ \textit{capital available for} \\ \textit{debt servicing during} \\ \textit{time period t} \end{bmatrix}$$

where $\phi_{\kappa t}$ is defined as in (9.13). This constraint restricts the maximum amount of funds available for debt servicing in each time period, $\bar{\phi}_{\kappa t}$, which is given exogenously.

OVER THE PLANNING HORIZON

$$\sum_{t \epsilon T} \delta_t \phi_{\kappa t} \leq \bar{\phi}_{\kappa}, \qquad (9.26)$$

$$\begin{bmatrix} \textit{Present value of total} \\ \textit{capital cost} \end{bmatrix} \leq \begin{bmatrix} \textit{Maximum amount of} \\ \textit{total capital available} \\ \textit{over the relevant} \\ \textit{planning horizon} \end{bmatrix}$$

where δ_t is defined as in (9.12). Here, constraint (9.25) is modified to take into account the entire planning period, and the constraint on capital expenditures is specified as an upper limit that can be incurred over the planning horizon ($\bar{\phi}_{\kappa}$). This figure (given exogenously) is usually specified at the beginning of the planning period in current units of currency; hence, the left-hand side of the constraint incorporates the discount factor.

AGGREGATE CAPITAL CONSTRAINTS

If the planner wishes to investigate in which period it is most attractive to begin to incur periodic capital charges, he can combine constraint (9.25) with a constraint on the value of ϕ_κ:

$$\bar{\phi}_\kappa < \sum_{t \in T} \bar{\phi}_{\kappa t}. \tag{9.27}$$

$$\begin{bmatrix} \textit{Maximum amount of} \\ \textit{total capital available} \\ \textit{over the relevant} \\ \textit{planning horizon} \end{bmatrix} < \begin{bmatrix} \textit{The sum of the maxi-} \\ \textit{mum amount of capi-} \\ \textit{tal available in each} \\ \textit{time period} \end{bmatrix}$$

This will force the model to choose between various time periods.

Domestic labor constraints

The labor requirements of the chemical fertilizer industry are insignificant, as compared with the capital requirements. There may, however, be constraints on highly skilled labor such as managers or plant operators; in particular, these constraints may be location- and time-specific. In other words, if a plant is set up away from urban centers, it may be difficult to obtain the necessary number of managers and plant operators to run the plant at that location during that time period. Such constraints can be introduced into the model.

The elasticity of supply of labor is assumed to be infinite during each time period for each location up to the constraint. The salary or wage rate is thus assumed to be location- and time-specific as before—that is, p^d_{cit}. If the set of labor or skill types is defined by CO, and if subsets are specified: $CO = CO1, CO2, CO3, \ldots$, it is possible to specify skill-specific bounds. For example:

$CO1$ = subset of managers,
$CO2$ = subset of plant operators,
$CO3$ = subset of skilled laborers,
and so on.

This breakdown of labor by type of skill is intended merely to be illustrative; clearly, there is no limit to the extent of disaggregation, except perhaps data availability.

The general constraint can be formulated as:

(9.28) $$u_{cit} \leq \bar{u}_{cit}. \qquad i \in I,\ c \in CO,\ t \in T$$

$$\begin{bmatrix} \text{Total number of} \\ \text{workers of skill class } c \\ \text{at plant site } i \text{ during} \\ \text{time period } t \end{bmatrix} \leq \begin{bmatrix} \text{Maximum number of} \\ \text{workers of skill class } c \\ \text{available at plant} \\ \text{site } i \text{ during time} \\ \text{period } t \end{bmatrix}$$

Generally, these constraints are applicable to the more highly skilled class of workers rather than the unskilled; that is, these constraints may only be relevant for managers and plant operators rather than unskilled labor. Further, equation (9.28) assumes no economies of scale in labor inputs.

Foreign exchange constraints

The model specified above does not consider the possibility of foreign exchange shortage that may be faced by a country and that may thus impose a restriction on the fertilizer sector. It is assumed that this restriction is exogenously imposed by the central planning authority and is hence taken as given by the planner; its value is denoted by the symbol G.

The foreign exchange component of the total cost manifests itself as some proportion (γ_t) of the capital costs ($\phi_{\kappa t}$) in time period t and all of the import costs less export revenues in that time period. The proportion γ_t of capital costs is made time-specific to permit the ratio to alter over time. An approximate value of this ratio is 2:3 for less developed countries, but more accurate values of this fraction can be calculated for each time period. The constraints are given by time periods and over the planning horizon.

IN EACH TIME PERIOD

(9.29) $$\gamma_t \phi_{\kappa t} + \phi_{\pi t} - \phi_{\epsilon t} \leq \bar{G}_t \qquad t \in T$$

$$\begin{bmatrix} \text{Foreign} \\ \text{exchange} \\ \text{component} \\ \text{of capital} \\ \text{cost during} \\ \text{time} \\ \text{period } t \end{bmatrix} + \begin{bmatrix} \text{Import} \\ \text{cost dur-} \\ \text{ing time} \\ \text{period } t \end{bmatrix} - \begin{bmatrix} \text{Export} \\ \text{revenue} \\ \text{during} \\ \text{time} \\ \text{period } t \end{bmatrix} \leq \begin{bmatrix} \text{Maximum} \\ \text{amount of} \\ \text{foreign} \\ \text{exchange} \\ \text{available} \\ \text{during} \\ \text{time} \\ \text{period } t \end{bmatrix}$$

OVER THE PLANNING HORIZON

$$(9.30)\quad \sum_{t\epsilon T} \delta_t(\gamma_t\phi_{\kappa t} + \phi_{\pi t} - \phi_{\epsilon t}) \leq \bar{G}$$

$$\begin{bmatrix} \textit{Present value of the} \\ \textit{foreign exchange} \\ \textit{component of the} \\ \textit{capital cost and net} \\ \textit{import cost} \end{bmatrix} \leq \begin{bmatrix} \textit{Maximum amount of} \\ \textit{foreign exchange} \\ \textit{available over the} \\ \textit{entire planning period} \end{bmatrix}$$

NONBINDING

$$(9.31)\quad \bar{G} < \sum_{t\epsilon T} \bar{G}_t$$

$$\begin{bmatrix} \textit{Maximum amount of} \\ \textit{foreign exchange} \\ \textit{available over the} \\ \textit{entire planning period} \end{bmatrix} < \begin{bmatrix} \textit{Sum of the maximum} \\ \textit{amount of foreign} \\ \textit{exchange available in} \\ \textit{each time period} \end{bmatrix}$$

Constraint (9.31) along with constraints (9.29) and (9.30) ensure that there are nonbinding constraints in some of the time periods.

Import constraints

Import constraints can be added to the system of equations if the central planning authority wishes to restrict the amount of imports and thereby follows a policy of partial or complete import substitution in the fertilizer sector. Constraints can also be imposed on the imports of intermediate products and raw materials, particularly if the central authority wishes to emphasize self-sufficiency in the production of intermediate products and complete exploitation of the locally available raw materials. Hence, the following constraints may be needed to test the effects of import licensing.

FINAL PRODUCTS: TOTAL BY COMMODITY AND MARKET LOCATION

$$(9.32)\quad v_{cjt} \leq \bar{v}_{cjt} \qquad c \epsilon CF,\ j \epsilon J,\ t \epsilon T$$

$$\begin{bmatrix} \textit{Quantity of imports} \\ \textit{of final product c at} \\ \textit{marketing center j} \\ \textit{during time period t} \end{bmatrix} \leq \begin{bmatrix} \textit{Maximum allowable} \\ \textit{imports of final} \\ \textit{product c to market-} \\ \textit{ing center j during} \\ \textit{time period t} \end{bmatrix}$$

FINAL PRODUCTS: TOTAL BY MARKETING CENTER

(9.33) $$\sum_{c \in CF} v_{cjt} \leq \hat{v}_{jt} \qquad j \in J, \quad t \in T$$

[*Quantity of all final products imported to marketing center j during time period t*] ≤ [*Maximum quantity of imports of all final products to marketing center j during time period t*]

FINAL PRODUCTS: TOTAL BY COMMODITY

(9.34) $$\sum_{j \in J} v_{cjt} \leq \tilde{v}_{ct} \qquad c \in CF, \quad t \in T$$

[*Quantity of final product c imported to all marketing centers during time period t*] ≤ [*Maximum quantity of imports of final product c during time period t*]

FINAL PRODUCTS: NONBINDING

To ensure that some of the individual constraints of equation (9.32) are not binding, either constraint (9.32) can be combined with (9.33) and the additional proviso that:

(9.35) $$\bar{\bar{v}}_{jt} < \sum_{c \in CF} \bar{v}_{cjt}. \qquad j \in J, \quad t \in T$$

[*Maximum quantity of imports of all final products to marketing center j during time period t*] < [*Sum of the maximum allowable imports of final product c to marketing center j during time period t*]

or constraint (9.32) can be combined with (9.34) and the proviso that:

(9.36) $$\hat{v}_{ct} < \sum_{j \in J} \bar{v}_{cjt}. \qquad c \in CF, \quad t \in T$$

[*Maximum quantity of imports of final product c during time period t*] < [*Sum of the maximum allowable imports of final product c to marketing center j during time period t*]

Constraints on intermediate products and raw materials must be specified with care to ensure that the solution of the program remains feasible. The constraints are similar to those on final products and they are listed below.

INTERMEDIATE PRODUCTS, RAW MATERIALS, AND LABOR: TOTAL BY INPUT AND PLANT SITE

$$v_{cit} \leq \bar{v}_{cit} \qquad c \in CI \cup CR, \; i \in I, \; t \in T \tag{9.37}$$

INTERMEDIATE PRODUCTS, RAW MATERIALS, AND LABOR: TOTAL BY INPUT

$$\sum_{i \in I} v_{cit} \leq \tilde{v}_{ct} \qquad c \in CI \cup CR, \; t \in T \tag{9.38}$$

INTERMEDIATE PRODUCTS, RAW MATERIALS, AND LABOR: NONBINDING

$$\tilde{v}_{ct} < \sum_{i \in I} \bar{v}_{cit} \qquad c \in CI \cup CR, \; t \in T \tag{9.39}$$

Regional preference constraints

Regional preferences may be incorporated if, for example, the central authority has a strong commitment to "balanced regional growth" or to "income redistribution," and if that authority wishes to achieve those commitments by building projects or plants in one region of the country rather than another. Further, whether the economic system under consideration is capitalist or socialist, it is inevitable that various regional and industrial groups will create demands for departures from economic efficiency. With the help of regional preference constraints, the cost of satisfying such pressure groups can be estimated. With better knowledge of the magnitude of the costs involved, it should be possible to reduce, though not eliminate, the emotional aspect of political decisions about plant site and timing. Under such situations, the relevant constraints can be added to the system of equations already presented.

AT LEAST ONE PLANT

The central authority may, for some political or perceived economic reason, desire that a fertilizer plant be built in a particular location. Such a preference can be expressed by:

$$\sum_{m \in M} \sum_{t \in T} y_{mit} \geq 1, \qquad i \in IN \tag{9.40}$$

where IN, the set of chosen plant sites, is a subset of I. According to this constraint, at least one plant must be built in the chosen location IN during any time period. In this case, the temporal dimension is not important to the central authority, so long as at least one plant is erected in the desired location.

As an example, consider the case of 2 plants and 3 time periods—that is $M = 2$, $T = 3$; then, constraint (9.40) can be written as:

$$\sum_{m=1}^{2} \sum_{t=1}^{3} y_{mit} \geq 1, \qquad i \epsilon IN \tag{9.41}$$

that is,

$$y_{1i1} + y_{1i2} + y_{1i3} + y_{2i1} + y_{2i2} + y_{2i3} \geq 1. \qquad i \epsilon IN$$

Assume further that there is only one desired location—that is, $IN = 1$. If more than one location is desired, there will be an equation like (9.41) for each location. Since the y variables can take on only 0 or 1 values, equation (9.41) permits all the y's to take the value 1, but it insists that at least one y be equal to 1.

AT MOST ONE PLANT

Analogous to constraint (9.40) is one that can reflect the central authority's preference to consider at most one potential location. This can be expressed by:

$$\sum_{m \epsilon M} \sum_{t \epsilon T} y_{mit} \leq 1. \qquad i \epsilon IN \tag{9.42}$$

Such a situation may arise if the central authority believes that, in the interest of regional balance or income distribution, location k should be avoided as a potential plant site if possible. In this case, the central authority exhibits some flexibility, in the sense that the location k should be avoided only if it is possible to do so; if it is not, then only one plant may be built there.

If the authority has definite negative feelings about such a location, then the constraint can be rewritten as:

$$\sum_{m \epsilon M} \sum_{t \epsilon T} y_{mit} = 0. \qquad i \epsilon IN \tag{9.43}$$

Alternative Formulations of the Objective Function

In theory, it is possible to modify the objective function of the model stated in equations (9.11) through (9.19) from a cost-minimizing objective to one that either maximizes profits or maximizes the sum of producers' and consumers' surplus. These latter two objectives require that the model be specified in terms of demand that is responsive to price rather than fixed demands. Although both methods of specification have been employed in linear programming models, there is as yet no computational experience with the use of investment planning models involving 0–1 variables.[9]

Linking the Fertilizer Sector Model to an Agricultural Model

The principal limitation of the sector planning methodology presented in this volume is its partial equilibrium nature; that is, the environment in which the fertilizer sector is supposed to function is exogenously specified, even though significant interdependencies with other sectors—primarily, the agricultural sector—are likely to exist. Clearly, it would be of considerable importance to relate the fertilizer sector model formally to a model of the agricultural sector. From the perspective of the fertilizer sector model, such a linkage would imply that the demand for fertilizer material or nutrients is no longer given; in turn, the agricultural model would not need to be specified with given supply prices for fertilizer types.

In theory, the link between the two models is not difficult to construct. The objective function of the fertilizer model is simply deleted, and the market requirements constraint is replaced by a model of the agricultural sector that generates the market demand for fertilizer types on the basis of the relative contribution each fertilizer type makes to the objective function of the agricultural model. This requires specifying agricultural production technologies that explicitly incorporate fertilizer use, and that show the physical yield from the use of each fertilizer on each crop in each region; such response schedules of physical yield are required for each combination of agricultural inputs that is deemed appropriate.

In practice, linking the two models may run into formidable

9. For a description of the mathematical structure of these alternative formulations, as well as a discussion of their computational problems, see Kendrick and Stoutjesdijk, *The Planning of Industrial Investment Programs: A Methodology*, chapter 7.

difficulties. First, the data requirements are great; in particular, it may be impossible to specify the set of agricultural production technologies accurately. Second, even if it were possible to obtain all the information required, it is far from certain that this system of models could be solved, even on modern, high-speed computers. It is difficult enough to solve the fertilizer model alone; to link this model to a detailed agricultural sector model, in the hope of obtaining a simultaneous solution to the entire system, is probably outside the realm of current technical possibilities.

For the time being, therefore, it would appear that less formal links between the two sector models have to be attempted; the most promising of these may be to adopt an iterative procedure. First, the fertilizer sector model is solved on the basis of varying sets of market requirements by region in terms of nutrients. This gives a supply price schedule for fertilizer nutrients at a range of output levels. Next, the agricultural sector model is solved on the basis of a selection of such supply prices for nutrients by region, resulting in a demand schedule for fertilizers. Provided the marginal product of fertilizer use is decreasing, or the production cost of fertilizers is falling at a declining rate, this procedure must eventually permit a market equilibrium to be identified. The procedure may be extremely time-consuming, however, and therefore costly.

Links with Other Activities

Apart from the agricultural sector, the fertilizer sector may have technological relations with other sectors in the economy. For example, the fertilizer sector requires intermediate products such as sulfuric acid that are extensively used in other industrial activities. Thus, the investment program should be designed so that it covers the possibility of either sales or purchases of intermediate products to or from other sectors. Such intersectoral transactions can apply to fertilizer products as well as intermediate products; for example, ammonium nitrate is used as an explosive in mining operations.

Sometimes the fertilizer industry produces by-products that are of value in other sectors; for example, phosphate rock can have a high iron content that needs to be lowered before the rock can be used in fertilizer manufacture. The resulting by-product—magnetite—can be sold to a local iron and steel industry. In turn, other sectors may produce by-products that are important to the fertilizer sector, either as intermediate or as final products. An example of the former is carbon dioxide, which is important in the manufacture of urea; an example of the latter is basic slag, a by-product of the iron and steel industry and a phosphatic fertilizer in its own right (Thomas slag).

The formal modeling of these intersectoral links is not difficult as long as demand (in the case of sales from the fertilizer sector) and supply (in the case of purchases by the fertilizer sector) can be exogenously specified. Moreover, except in the case of sales of final and intermediate products from the fertilizer sector, prices have to be stated explicitly. If these conditions are not fulfilled, the same linkage problems are encountered as in the case of the agricultural sector.

To introduce these links with other sectors into the mathematical structure of the fertilizer model, the following notation is introduced:

w = domestic sales of by-products, and of final products for nonagricultural use;

u = domestic purchases of by-products, or of fertilizers produced outside the fertilizer sector itself.

$\phi_{\eta t}$ = total cost of purchases from outside the fertilizer industry during time period t.

With this notation, several constraints and the objective function of the model can be modified as follows.

MATERIAL BALANCE CONSTRAINTS ON FERTILIZERS

$$(9.44) \qquad \sum_{p \in P} a_{cpi} z_{pit} + u_{cit} \geq \sum_{j \in J} x_{cijt} + \sum_{l \in L} e_{cilt} + w_{cit} \qquad c \in CF,\ i \in I,\ t \in T$$

$$\begin{bmatrix} \textit{Total production} \\ \textit{of fertilizer} \\ \textit{product c from} \\ \textit{all processes at} \\ \textit{plant site i} \\ \textit{during time} \\ \textit{period t} \end{bmatrix} + \begin{bmatrix} \textit{Domestic pur-} \\ \textit{chases of ferti-} \\ \textit{lizer c from} \\ \textit{outside the} \\ \textit{fertilizer indus-} \\ \textit{try via plant} \\ \textit{site i during} \\ \textit{time period } t^{10} \end{bmatrix} \geq \begin{bmatrix} \textit{Quantity of} \\ \textit{fertilizer c} \\ \textit{shipped to all} \\ \textit{market areas} \\ \textit{from plant} \\ \textit{site i during} \\ \textit{time period t} \end{bmatrix}$$

10. Fertilizer produced as a by-product by another industrial sector is not necessarily produced at one of the plant sites specified for fertilizer production. Instead of introducing new sites, it can be assumed that such fertilizer is shipped to the consuming region via the nearest fertilizer production site.

+ [*Quantity of fertilizer c exported from plant site i to all export regions during time period t*] + [*Quantity of fertilizer c sold outside the agricultural sector from plant site i during time period t*] [*For all fertilizers, all plant sites, and all time periods*]

MATERIAL BALANCE CONSTRAINTS ON INTERMEDIATE PRODUCTS

(9.45) $$\sum_{p \epsilon P} a_{cpi} z_{pit} + \sum_{\substack{i' \epsilon I \\ i' \neq i}} x_{ci'it}$$

[*Total production of intermediate product c from all processes at plant site i during time period t*] + [*Quantity of intermediate product c shipped from plant site i′ to plant site i during time period t*]

$$+ m_{cit} + u_{cit} \geq \sum_{\substack{i' \epsilon I \\ i' \neq i}} x_{cii't}$$

+ [*Quantity of intermediate product c imported to plant site i during time period t*] + [*Domestic purchases of intermediate product c from outside the fertilizer industry, at plant site i, during time period t*] ≥ [*Quantity of intermediate product c shipped from plant site i to plant site i′ during time period t*]

$$+ \sum_{l \epsilon L} e_{cilt} + w_{cit} \qquad c \epsilon CI, \quad i \epsilon I, \quad t \epsilon T$$

+ [*Quantity of intermediate product c exported from plant site i to all export regions during time period t*] + [*Quantity of intermediate product c domestically sold outside the fertilizer sector from plant site i during time period t*] [*For all intermediate products, all plant sites, and all time periods*]

NONNEGATIVITY CONSTRAINTS

Add to (9.10):

(9.46) $w_{cit} \geq 0 \qquad c \in (CF \cup CI) \qquad i \in I \qquad t \in T$

$u_{cit} \geq 0 \qquad c \in (CF \cup CI) \qquad i \in I \qquad t \in T$

OBJECTIVE FUNCTION

(44) $$\min \xi = \sum_{t \in T} \delta_t(\phi_{\kappa t} + \phi_{\psi t} + \phi_{\lambda t} + \phi_{\pi t} + \phi_{\eta t} - \phi_{\epsilon t} - \phi_{\chi t}),$$

[Discounted net cost] = [Total capital cost during time period t] + [Total recurrent cost during time period t] + [Total transport cost during time period t]

+ [Total import cost during time period t] + [Total cost of purchases from outside the fertilizer industry during time period t] − [Total export revenue during time period t] − [Total revenue from sales outside the fertilizer sector during time period t]

where

$$\phi_{\eta t} = \sum_{c \in (CF \cup CI)} \sum_{i \in I} p^d_{cit} u_{cit},$$

[Total cost of purchases from outside the fertilizer industry during time period t] = [Cost of purchases from outside the fertilizer sector of fertilizers and intermediate products during time period t]

and

$$\phi_{\chi t} = \sum_{c \in (CF \cup CI)} \sum_{i \in I} p^d_{cit} w_{cit}.$$

[Total revenue from by-product sales during time period t] = [Revenue from sales of final and intermediate products of the fertilizer industry for use in nonagricultural sectors during time period t]

Conclusion

This presentation of the fertilizer sector model and the model's possible variants has not been exhaustive; rather, it was attempted to demonstrate that the basic model can be modified to suit many different situations.

PART TWO

The Egyptian Fertilizer Sector: A Case Study

10

The Fertilizer Sector in Egypt

THE PRESENT STRUCTURE AND DEVELOPMENT POTENTIAL of the Egyptian fertilizer sector is evaluated in this case study, using several planning models. The primary purpose of the study is to demonstrate that these planning models can be useful analytical tools, and to show that the results described have considerable operational relevance. An attempt has been made, in collaboration with Egyptian sector specialists, to obtain a reasonably accurate statistical representation of the fertilizer sector at the present time. Moreover, the sector's development potential is considered in the light of forecasts of demand and prices consistent with those made by Egyptian planners and fertilizer sector specialists.[1]

The written account of the case study does not explicitly address the difficulties associated with solving the planning models. Mixed-integer programming models are usually difficult to solve; they require sophisticated analysts, as well as computer software and hard-

1. Acknowledgements in connection with the case study are incorporated in the preface to the volume.

ware. The *User's Guide* in this series is designed to address this aspect of the proposed planning methodology.

The case study is organized in the following way. First, a concise description of the fertilizer sector and its role in Egypt is given. Next, the present structure of the sector—including the existing production pattern of the various fertilizer plants in the country, as well as the transporting and importing of raw materials, intermediate products, and fertilizer materials—is analyzed. This analysis is carried out against the background of regionally specified fertilizer use. The third chapter in the case study is perhaps the most important. Given that fertilizer use will continue to increase from present levels, and that existing production capacity is not sufficient to meet even current demand, Egyptian planners are faced with the question: What is the best policy for Egypt to adopt in order to meet future fertilizer demand requirements? Would it be preferable to import fertilizers, to produce them domestically, or both? If some fertilizers are to be imported, which ones should be imported? Which locations should be preferred for fertilizer production? At what scale should fertilizer production take place? Which feedstocks should be used? What is the least-cost transport pattern for both imported and domestically produced fertilizers? Should intermediate products be shipped between plants? A dynamic, mixed-integer planning model of the Egyptian fertilizer industry is used to address these questions, from the point of view of the sectoral planner.[2] In the final chapter of the study, a number of policy experiments are described, to illustrate the impact of various government policies in the areas of fertilizer production, importation, distribution, and pricing on the structure of the fertilizer sector in Egypt.

The Demand for Fertilizers

The construction of the Aswan High Dam effectively marked the end of Egypt's traditional form of irrigation—that is, the seasonal flooding of the Nile. The immediate effect was a significant increase in the demand for chemical fertilizer. Since the turn of the century,

2. This qualification is quite important, since the type of models discussed in this volume are not primarily designed to analyze investments from the point of view of the individual enterprise.

Table 1. *Actual Use of Fertilizer Nutrients in Egypt, 1951–52 to 1974–75*
(thousands of metric tons of nutrients)

Year	*Nitrogenous fertilizers*	*Phosphatic fertilizers*	*Potassic fertilizers*	*Total fertilizer nutrients used*
1951–52	110	27	0.0	137.0
1955–56	114	21	0.0	135.0
1956–57	102	24	0.0	126.0
1957–58	132	27	0.6	159.6
1958–59	137	27	0.8	164.8
1959–60	172	33	1.9	206.9
1960–61	181	34	2.0	217.0
1961–62	186	38	0.9	224.9
1962–63	204	39	1.0	244.0
1963–64	227	43	1.0	271.0
1964–65	253	45	0.6	298.6
1965–66	280	53	0.4	333.4
1966–67	264	44	0.6	308.6
1967–68	259	38	1.5	298.5
1968–69	275	51	1.4	327.4
1969–70	330	57	1.4	388.4
1970–71	299	56	1.8	356.8
1971–72	327	66	1.5	394.5
1972–73	372	65	3.2	440.2
1973–74	n.a.	n.a.	n.a.	n.a.
1974–75	403	74	n.a.	n.a.

n.a. = data not available.
Source: Compiled from unpublished data provided by the General Organization of Agricultural and Cooperative Credit.

Egypt has been importing fertilizer from Chile in the form of natural sodium nitrate. By 1960, the consumption of fertilizer per acre of cultivated land surpassed all developing countries except Taiwan and South Korea. In 1972–73, by far the greatest demand was for nitrogenous fertilizers (84.5 percent of total nutrient demand), followed by phosphatic fertilizers (14.8 percent of total demand); potassic fertilizers represented only 0.7 percent of total demand. Table 1 shows how fertilizer demand has changed over time.

Nitrogenous fertilizers are applied to almost all crops in Egypt; about 90 percent of these fertilizers are used for rice, wheat, maize, cotton, millet, and vegetables. Phosphatic fertilizers have been used in Egyptian agriculture since the early 1930s. They are used mainly for three crops: berseem (Egyptian clover), which accounts for about 33 percent of total consumption; cotton, 32 percent; and rice, 24 percent. The remainder is used for other crops such as sugarcane, beans, sesame, onions, flux, and ground nuts. Potassic fertilizers are used only for fruits, potatoes, and vegetables. Total consumption of potassic fertilizers is very small compared with the other two types, and it tends to fluctuate from year to year; since 1972–73, consumption has averaged around 3,000 metric tons a year.

Fertilizer application rates

The fertilizer application rate is the quantity of fertilizers applied to a unit of land being cultivated with a certain crop. In Egypt, three different rates are identified: actual, assigned or recommended, and economic. The actual rate represents the quantity of fertilizer actually applied by the farmer. The major variables determining this rate are the individual farmer's intuitive judgment, his financial position, and the availability of the appropriate fertilizer. Table 2 shows how this actual rate has changed over time. The general trend is toward increasing rates of application; from 1966 to 1968 and from 1970 to 1971, however, the absolute level of fertilizers used per feddan declined.[3]

The assigned or recommended rate is drawn up by the Ministry of Agriculture for different crops in the different regions of the country. These rates are based on experimental studies undertaken by the ministry's soil chemists, and they take into consideration the various climatic, regional, and soil conditions for different crops. They were put into effect in 1960–61 and are subject to annual revisions, which are determined in great part by the total supply of fertilizers. The present trend is toward increasing the recommended rates.[4] Nitrogenous fertilizers have recommended rates that differ by geographical region for several crops, including wheat, maize, millet, cotton, onions, and sugarcane. For other crops, the rates differ according to the responsiveness of different regions to nitrogenous fertilizer. Phosphatic fertilizers have recommended rates that differ according to the crop rather than the region, whereas potassic fertilizers do not have any recommended rates.

3. A feddan is equal to 1.038 acres.
4. All fertilizer distribution is based on these rates.

Table 2. *Fertilizer Application Rate per Cropped Feddan in Egypt, 1955–56 to 1971–72*

Year	*Total fertilizer nutrients used*[a] *(thousands of metric tons)*	*Total cropped area (thousands of feddans)*	*Fertilizer nutrients used per cropped feddan (kilograms)*
1955–56	135.0	9,962	13.6
1956–57	126.0	10,100	12.5
1957–58	159.6	10,089	15.8
1958–59	164.8	10,289	16.0
1959–60	206.9	10,370	20.0
1960–61	217.0	9,974	21.8
1961–62	224.9	10,366	21.7
1962–63	244.0	10,358	23.6
1963–64	271.0	10,377	26.1
1964–65	298.6	10,261	29.1
1965–66	333.4	10,487	31.8
1966–67	308.6	10,462	29.5
1967–68	298.5	10,742	27.8
1968–69	327.4	10,732	30.5
1969–70	388.4	10,733	36.2
1970–71	356.8	10,700	33.3
1971–72	394.5	10,799	36.5

a. Nitrogen, phosphorus, and potassium.

The Institute of National Planning has been working on the concept of an economic rate of fertilizer use, which takes into account the economic as well as the technological aspects of fertilizer application. In general, this rate is higher than the recommended one.

The projected demand for fertilizers

The objective of the national agricultural policy is to increase agricultural production by 1982 to 150 percent of the 1972 production, primarily through improvements in agricultural technology, including further increases in fertilizer use. Correspondingly, a new set of planned fertilizer application rates has been announced. These rates, which are based upon several considerations, recommend different levels of application for various crops. It is intended that these targets will be attained by 1980 and will remain reasonably stable thereafter. The Ministry of Agriculture has projected the demand for fertilizers on the basis of these planned fertilizing rates and the planned or projected cropping pattern.

The cropping pattern in Egypt is determined by several factors, of which the most important are available land and water. The pattern that has emerged is the triennial rotation system—that is, a three-year rotation of crops. The crops are grown in a sequence according to the seasons. There are three basic seasons: the winter season, when crops are cultivated during October and November and are harvested during April and May; the summer season, when crops are cultivated from March to June and are harvested from August to October; and the Nili season, when crops are cultivated from the second half of June to the end of July and are harvested from October to December. The importance of the Nili season has declined, however, because of the completion of the Aswan High Dam, which has provided more water for the summer season.

Table 3. *Estimated and Projected Use of Nitrogenous Fertilizer Nutrients for Various Crops, 1973–85*
(thousands of metric tons)

Crop	*1973*	*1974*	*1975*	*1976*	*1977*	*1982*	*1985*
Barley	3.5	3.2	3.5	4.0	4.0	6.5	6.9
Cotton	69.3	69.3	74.3	74.3	79.2	82.5	80.0
Flax	2.6	2.5	2.7	2.8	3.0	2.9	2.5
Fruits	22.0	23.0	24.8	26.0	27.5	32.3	34.9
Legumes	3.9	4.0	4.4	4.5	4.8	5.5	5.7
Maize	86.8	85.3	94.3	91.7	98.6	116.3	120.0
Millet	23.1	21.9	22.6	22.2	23.6	33.5	34.4
Oilseeds	3.0	3.2	3.7	4.1	4.6	5.5	5.7
Onions	5.0	5.1	6.0	6.1	6.2	7.0	8.0
Rice	40.5	40.5	43.1	43.2	45.7	48.3	50.9
Sugarcane	22.9	24.1	25.7	26.7	29.5	30.4	31.9
Vegetables	37.9	38.9	39.8	41.2	41.9	53.1	54.9
Wheat	54.7	54.8	59.1	59.1	64.0	75.0	76.2
Others	5.5	4.8	4.9	4.8	5.0	7.3	1.5
Total	380.7	380.6	408.9	410.2	437.6	506.1	513.5

Note: Years refer to cropping years.

Source: Ministry of Agriculture, quoted in R. Hassan and others, *An Economic Study of Problems and Prospects of Fertilizers' Utilization, Production, and Marketing in the Arab Republic of Egypt* (Cairo: Institute of National Planning, 1973).

Table 4. *Estimated and Projected Use of Phosphatic Fertilizer Nutrients for Various Crops, 1973–85*
(thousands of metric tons)

Crop	*1973*	*1974*	*1975*	*1976*	*1977*	*1982*	*1985*
Cotton	24.8	24.8	24.8	37.1	37.1	37.1	36.0
Flax	0.7	0.7	0.7	1.1	1.1	1.1	0.9
Fodder	48.4	48.4	48.2	71.6	71.0	72.5	72.4
Fruits	4.5	4.7	9.8	10.2	10.6	12.3	13.3
Legumes	7.2	7.5	7.7	7.9	8.0	12.4	12.8
Oilseeds	2.7	2.8	4.5	5.0	5.2	7.8	8.1
Onions	1.0	1.0	1.1	1.2	1.2	1.3	1.5
Rice	18.4	18.4	18.5	27.7	27.8	28.6	30.2
Vegetables	12.2	12.6	12.8	26.6	27.1	34.3	35.4
Others	1.7	1.5	1.4	2.7	2.6	3.6	0.8
Total	121.6	122.4	129.5	191.1	191.7	211.0	211.4

Note: Years refer to cropping years.
Source: Ministry of Agriculture, quoted in Hassan and others, *An Economic Study of Problems and Prospects.*

The cropping pattern is also related to the area upon which the demand projections are based. Because of the increase of nonagricultural uses of land, the total agricultural land has declined by 60,000 feddans over the past few years. Legislative measures have been instituted to prevent further loss. Moreover, land reclamation programs have been instituted to increase the area of new land to be put under cultivation. The planned increase is from about 480,000 feddans in 1972 to about 668,000 by 1977.

Based on the above considerations, the ministry has projected the demand for fertilizers for the period 1976–85. These projections are presented in tables 3, 4, and 5.

Over the period 1973–85, nitrogenous fertilizers are projected to retain their dominant position and, in terms of nutrients, their use is expected to increase at an average annual rate of 2.5 percent. At the same time, the use of phosphatic fertilizers, in terms of nutrients, is projected to increase by 4.7 percent a year. The implied rate of growth in potassic fertilizer use is highest—that is, 8.1 percent a year. In that case, however, the base-year estimate for total use is so low that, in spite of the high growth rate, projected 1985 usage is still relatively small. Four crops—namely, wheat, maize, rice, and

Table 5. *Estimated and Projected Use of Potassic Fertilizer Nutrients for Vegetables and Fruits, 1973–85*
(thousands of metric tons)

Crop	*1973*	*1974*	*1975*	*1976*	*1977*	*1980*	*1985*
Fruits	1.1	1.1	1.2	1.2	1.7	1.9	2.1
Vegetables	2.0	2.0	2.1	2.1	4.3	5.5	5.7
Total	3.1	3.1	3.3	3.3	6.0	7.4	7.8

Note: Years refer to cropping years.
Source: Ministry of Agriculture, quoted in Hassan and others, *An Economic Study of Problems and Prospects*.

cotton—account for about two-thirds of the total nitrogen requirement. Sugarcane, vegetables, and fruits account for another one-fifth. Thus, the projections do not entail any significant change in the consumption pattern of fertilizers. The increase in the consumption of potassic fertilizers results primarily from the increase in the area for vegetables and fruits, which are the only sources of demand for such fertilizers. In addition, the completion of the Aswan High Dam has given rise to an increase in the use of such fertilizers; the reason is that it has deprived the soils of the richness of the Nile "silt" or "alluva," which was naturally rich in potash. Thus, chemical fertilizers must now substitute for the natural ones.

The Domestic Production of Fertilizers

Only nitrogenous and phosphatic fertilizers are produced domestically in Egypt; there is no production of potassic fertilizers, and the relatively small potash demand is met entirely by imports. In 1975, there were three nitrogenous fertilizer plants and four phosphatic fertilizer plants in operation. The products and the technology used varied according to plant location.

The nitrogen fertilizer industry

Nitrogen fertilizer production began in Egypt in 1951 when the El Nasr Company for Fertilizers and Chemicals produced its initial output of 83,000 tons of calcium nitrate (15.5 percent nitrogen). Until 1961, this continued to be the only nitrogenous fertilizer produced in Egypt. Although this product is well suited to the high acidity of Egyptian soils, its low nitrogen content means that the transport cost per ton of nutrient is high. It also requires large amounts of inert matter, and it is highly subject to leaching.

During the 1950s, imports of calcium ammonium nitrates increased rapidly, and in 1954 it was decided to produce these fertilizers domestically. Calcium ammonium nitrate has a higher nitrogen content (ranging from 20 to 33.5 percent nitrogen) than calcium nitrate, and it is resistant to leaching. In 1963, the company's plant at Suez began producing ammonium sulfate. These three types of fertilizers are the only nitrogenous fertilizers produced in Egypt, as is shown in table 6. They are produced domestically at four plants, as described below.

THE EL NASR COMPANY FOR FERTILIZERS AND CHEMICALS AT SUEZ. The El Nasr Company plant at Suez began producing calcium nitrate (15.5 percent nitrogen) in 1951 and reached a peak level of 275,000 tons in 1963–64. In 1963, this company began producing ammonium sulfate (20.6 percent nitrogen) at an initial experimental output of 365 tons and reached a level of 98,300 tons in 1966–67. The 1967 war with Israel led to a reduction in the production of calcium nitrate and ammonium sulfate to 140,000 tons and 46,600 tons, respectively, in 1967–68. In the following year, production was further reduced to 111,000 tons of calcium nitrate and 32,000 tons of ammonium sulfate. Both plants were completely shut down on March 9, 1969.

The ammonia production at the complex utilizes the partial oxidation process, using the refinery gas supplied by the Suez refineries; the gas reforming unit was added in 1958. In addition, the plant has six units producing nitric acid (55 percent concentration) from ammonia oxidation. Five of these units require 8,250 tons a year of ammonia and the sixth, installed in 1958, requires 13,860 tons a year. Calcium nitrate is produced using the direct process;[5] two lines are used, each producing 125,000 tons a year. Construction was begun on the unit in 1946, and the plant was ready in 1950; it is completely manual. The damage to this plant caused by the 1967 war was scheduled to be repaired by mid-1976, after which production was expected to resume.

5. That is, the direct reaction of limestone with nitric acid.

Table 6. *Domestic Production of Nitrogenous Fertilizers by Type and Producing Unit, 1962–63 to 1974–75*
(tons)

Year	*Calcium nitrate: 15.5 percent; El Nasr Co., Suez*	*Ammonium sulfate: 20.6 percent*			*Calcium ammonium nitrate*				
		El Nasr Co., Suez	*El Nasr Co., Helwan*	*Total*	*20.5 percent; KIMA Co., Aswan*	*26 percent; KIMA Co., Aswan, and El Nasr Co., Helwan*	*31 percent; KIMA Co., Aswan*	*33.5 percent; El Nasr Co., Helwan*	*Total*
1962–63	267,000	365	0	365	320,819	0	0	0	320,819
1963–64	275,026	64,500	0	64,500	417,010	0	0	0	417,010
1964–65	270,655	79,994	3,837	83,831	96,619	266,123	0	0	362,742
1965–66	266,789	83,887	3,593	87,480	0	379,509	0	0	379,509
1966–67	262,813	98,352	3,914	102,266	0	394,143	0	0	394,143
1967–68	140,276	46,611	4,434	51,054	0	437,937	0	0	437,937
1968–69	111,251	32,124	4,624	36,748	0	0	370,538	0	370,538
1969–70	0	0	4,500	4,500	0	0	377,107	0	377,107
1970–71	0	0	4,200	4,200	0	0	379,564	0	379,564
1971–72	0	0	6,800	6,800	0	400,000[a]	400,255	38,000[a]	838,255
1972–74[b]	n.a.	n.a.	n.a.	n.a.	n.a.	n.a.	n.a.	n.a.	n.a.
1974–75	0	0	8,000	8,000	0	0	347,000	90,000	437,000

Source: Compiled from the records of General Organization for Chemical Industries.
a. Production of El Nasr Company for Coke and Chemicals at Helwan.
b. Data for 1972–74 are not available.

Ammonium sulfate is no longer being produced at Suez, and the original sulfuric acid plant, which was built in 1962, has been sold to the Abu Zaabal Fertilizer Company and moved to Abu Zaabal. In 1976, the ammonium sulfate plant was still damaged as a result of the 1973 war with Israel, but repairs, which should take about two to three months, were expected to be made in the near future. No ammonium sulfate will be produced, however, until a new source of sulfuric acid is available, either from a new plant or in the form of shipments from another plant location.

In 1964, the El Nasr Company at Suez began to expand the fertilizer complex by adding new units for the production of calcium ammonium nitrate, ammonia, and nitric acid. Construction was completed in 1967 but, because of the war in that year, production never began. These units were subsequently disbanded and transferred to a new location at Talkha.

The refinery gas required for ammonia production is obtained from the Suez refineries, which process crude oil from the Sinai and other oil fields. In 1967, the crude from the Sinai was preferred because it yielded the most desirable composition of refinery gas. This composition, however, depends upon the depth from which the crude is extracted. Since 1967, the Sinai oil fields have been exploited by the Israelis, and thus oil will have to be extracted from a greater depth than before; this will affect the composition of the refinery gas used for ammonia. This factor, among others, has led some to consider using natural gas, rather than refinery gas, as the input into the existing plant. This natural gas will have to be piped in either from the Red Sea wells (pipe length, 300 kilometers) or from Helwan which receives it from the Western Desert.

THE EGYPTIAN CHEMICAL INDUSTRIES (KIMA) AT ASWAN. The location of the Suez plant and the increasing demand for fertilizers in the late 1950s posed certain problems. The Suez refineries supplied all their gases to the existing calcium nitrate plant and could not accommodate a greater capacity. Appreciable reserves of natural gas had not been discovered. It was therefore decided to carry out an old plan for electrifying the Aswan Dam and to use an electrolytic process to obtain the required hydrogen.[6] The construction of the plant,

6. In 1937, at the initiative of the government, the English Electric Company submitted a proposal to electrify the dam for 6.9 million Egyptian pounds. The project, which only needed the approval of the Parliament, was shelved.

KIMA, was well coordinated with the electrification of the dam, and it started producing calcium ammonium nitrate (20.5 percent nitrogen) in 1960 at an initial rate of 75,000 tons a year. This was increased to 417,000 tons a year in 1964. In response to the increasing demand for high-analysis fertilizers, the 20.5 percent variety was abandoned in favor of the 26 percent form, and in 1968 the plant started producing a fertilizer with an even higher concentration—namely, calcium ammonium nitrate of 31 percent nitrogen.

The ammonia required to manufacture this high-analysis fertilizer is produced from electrically generated hydrogen. The water electrolysis plant is claimed to be the largest in the world. In recent years, this plant has been undergoing renovation; some of the electrolysis units were replaced by new ones in 1974, whereas others have been renewed by replacing some parts. The long-term plans at KIMA are to replace all units with new ones. The newer units are more efficient than the old ones (each new unit replaces two old ones and has a lifetime that is 50 percent longer than the old ones).[7] There are four units for ammonia production with a total throughput of 150,000 tons a year. Part of this ammonia is utilized in the manufacture of nitric acid (265,000 tons a year), and the remainder is used in the production of prilled calcium ammonium nitrate (363,000 tons a year). Given the dry climate of the region, it appears possible that the calcium ammonium nitrate can be upgraded from 31 percent nitrogen to 33.5 percent nitrogen.

The large quantities of water required to produce hydrogen are obtained from the Nile, and the water is demineralized on the site by resins and ion exchange. The electricity is obtained from the Aswan Dam, the nitrogen (for ammonia production) is obtained from the atmosphere using an air-liquefication plant, and the limestone (used in calcium ammonium nitrate) is obtained from quarries owned by KIMA.[8]

THE EL NASR COMPANY FOR COKE AT HELWAN. The El Nasr Company for Coke was established in 1960 to produce coke and small amounts

7. There are very low economies of scale in this process of ammonia production.

8. In addition to fertilizers, ferrosilicone alloys are also produced at KIMA. This location was chosen because of the availability of cheap electricity (1 million kilowatt hours). The required iron scraps are obtained from Cairo factories and the coke from Helwan. Some of this product is sent back to the steel complex at Helwan and the remainder is exported.

of other chemicals. Initially, the coke plant was intended to serve the forging and power requirements of the Helwan iron and steel complex. In 1964, however, the company began using part of the by-product gas to produce ammonium sulfate (20.1 percent nitrogen). Then, in 1971, the company started producing calcium ammonium nitrate, initially at a concentration of 26 percent nitrogen, and later at 33.5 percent.

At present, ammonia is produced by the partial oxidation of coke-oven gas at the rate of 42,000 tons a year. This is less than the design capacity of 56,000 tons a year because of bottlenecks in the coke-gas plant and in the cracking department (that is, in the production of hydrogen for ammonia synthesis). Thus, only two out of the three ammonia streams are in operation. There are plans to pipe natural gas to this location from the Abu Gharahib fields in order either to convert the present process of ammonia production to one using natural gas or to permit capacity expansion of ammonia.[9] The calcium ammonium nitrate (33.5 percent nitrogen) is produced at a rate of 90,000 tons a year, which is less than the design capacity because of the bottlenecks mentioned above. The amount of ammonium sulfate produced is only 8,000 tons a year, and it is obtained as a by-product of the scrubbing of coke gas with sulfuric acid.

The major raw material that drives this complex is the coal used in the coke plant, which is independently operated. The coal is imported primarily from the Soviet Union, but Poland, Australia, and Czechoslovakia serve as other sources. The fertilizer complex then buys the coke gas from the coke plant.

THE EL NASR COMPANY FOR FERTILIZERS AND CHEMICALS AT TALKHA. The El Nasr Company for Fertilizers and Chemicals at Talkha began producing calcium ammonium nitrate in July 1975; it thus represents the most recent nitrogen fertilizer complex in Egypt. The units involved were initially erected at Suez as an extension to the existing complex there. Because of the war in 1967, however, production of calcium ammonium nitrate was interrupted, and the entire set of units (that is, the ammonia, nitric acid, and calcium ammonium nitrate plants) was dismantled and moved to Talkha. Construction was completed in early 1975, and the production of calcium ammonium nitrate commenced soon after.

9. The economics of this conversion to natural gas are discussed in chapter 13. It is shown that this conversion process would be an uneconomical proposition.

The ammonia is produced by the partial oxidation of natural gas. At present, this is the only location in Egypt that uses natural gas in ammonia manufacture. The plant requires a liquid-air plant from which nitrogen and oxygen are obtained, and its design capacity of 400 tons a day has already been attained. Part of the ammonia is oxidized to produce nitric acid (55 percent concentration). There are three such units, each producing nitric acid at a rate of 350 tons a day. A fourth unit will be attached to the ammonia-urea complex being built at Talkha (known as Talkha II).

The remainder of the ammonia, along with the nitric acid, is utilized to make calcium ammonium nitrate at the rate of 600 to 800 tons a day. This is less than the rated design capacity of 1,000 tons a day because of caking problems encountered in the storage department and bottlenecks in the transportation sector. The nitrogen content of the calcium ammonium nitrate was initially 26 percent; by the end of 1975, however, this was raised to 31 percent, and it is hoped to raise this even further to 33.5 percent.

The phosphate fertilizer industry

The phosphate fertilizer industry in Egypt grew out of both the strong domestic demand resulting from the cultivation of beans and clover and the abundant domestic supply of phosphate rock. Some of this rock was initially applied directly to the soil in areas with sufficient soil acidity. Later, as more deposits were discovered, most of the rock was exported to Japan, and by 1936 total exports of phosphate rock had reached 500,000 tons. In that year, Egypt began exploiting her natural advantage in producing superphosphates. The output of the industry has shown an upward trend at an average annual growth rate of about 8.8 percent; the annual changes in output are shown in table 7. In the late 1950s, the output was sufficient to meet domestic demand and permit some exports. From 1961 to 1966, however, imports were needed to meet domestic demand; after that period, imports of superphosphate ceased, and Egypt reemerged as an exporter, mainly to the Arab countries.

THE EL NASR PHOSPHATE COMPANY AT KAFR EL ZAYAAT. The first superphosphate factory in Egypt was established in 1937 at Kafr El Zayaat with an annual capacity of 25,000 tons. This capacity was expanded in 1949, 1956, and 1964, until it reached a level of 200,000 tons of single superphosphate a year.

Table 7. *Annual Output of Phosphatic Fertilizers and Percent Change in Output from Year to Year, 1950–71*[a]

Year	Output of superphosphate: 15 percent P_2O_5	Percent change from year to year
1950	69,283	—
1951	88,486	2.7
1952	106,136	19.9
1953	66,723	−37.1
1954	107,900	61.7
1955	137,050	25.1
1956	156,516	15.9
1957	177,474	11.9
1958	178,630	2.0
1959	167,410	−5.7
1960	189,620	12.6
1961	179,779	−5.2
1962	171,000	−4.9
1963	158,000	−7.6
1964	216,205	36.8
1965	258,609	19.6
1966	271,016	4.8
1967	265,000	−2.2
1968	309,000	16.6
1969	344,000	11.3
1970	447,000	29.9
1971	522,000	16.8

— = not applicable.

Source: For the period 1950–60: Ministry of Agriculture, *Monthly Bulletin of Agricultural Economics and Statistics*, various issues. For the period 1961–70: Public Agency for General Mobilization and Statistics, *Annual Book for General Statistics*, various issues. For 1971: General Organization of Chemical Industries, unpublished data.

a. Excluding ground rock phosphate.

All the superphosphate produced at Kafr El Zayaat has a nutrient content of 15.5 percent P_2O_5; it is in powdered form and is produced using the conventional den method described in chapter 4. Initial production of the required sulfuric acid was accomplished using imported pyrites, but the subsequent expansion of the sulfuric acid plant utilized elemental sulfur. The total annual sulfuric acid production now stands at 100,000 tons.

THE EL NASR PHOSPHATE COMPANY AT ABU ZAABAL. The second

superphosphate plant in Egypt was erected at Abu Zaabal in 1948. Like the factory at Kafr El Zayaat, it produces powdered single superphosphate with a nutrient content of 15.5 percent P_2O_5 using the den method. Its capacity is 200,000 tons a year. Four sulfuric acid plants, yielding a total annual output of 150,000 tons, are located at this site. Three of these plants produce acid using pyrites; the most recent one, however, uses elemental sulfur.

Future expansion under consideration at this site includes a new sulfuric acid unit producing 100,000 tons a year, a phosphoric acid plant with a capacity of 60,000 tons a year, and a superphosphate plant with a capacity of 200,000 tons a year. The phosphoric acid is to be used in the production of enriched superphosphate and, later, triple superphosphate. Some thought is being given to the production of monoammonium phosphate, diammonium phosphate, and ammonium sulfate using ammonia from Talkha.[10]

THE EL NASR PHOSPHATE COMPANY AT ASSIOUT. The most recent superphosphate plant operates at Assiout. It started production in 1969 and produces granular single superphosphate (15.5 percent P_2O_5) using the den method. The design capacity of this plant is 200,000 tons a year, and a capacity expansion of an equivalent amount is planned for the future. Unlike the other two factories, it produces sulfuric acid from imported elemental sulfur. The amount of sulfuric acid that can be produced at this location is 80,000 tons a year and, to accommodate the future expansion of single superphosphate, a capacity expansion of 80,000 tons a year of sulfuric acid is planned.[11]

Raw Materials for Fertilizer Production

The major raw materials required in fertilizer production in Egypt are pyrites, elemental sulfur, phosphate rock, and natural gas. Of these, pyrites and sulfur, which are used in the production of the intermediate product sulfuric acid, are imported. No deposits of sulfur or usable pyrites are known to exist in Egypt. Pyrites are ob-

10. These plans are evaluated in chapter 13. It is shown there that the most efficient project would be the erection of a new phosphoric acid plant and the production of powdered triple superphosphate.

11. These plans are also evaluated in chapter 13. Capacity expansion at this location turns out to be uneconomical because of the low phosphorus demand in the surrounding governorates.

tained from Cyprus, Yugoslavia, and the Soviet Union; sulfur is imported from the United States, Poland, and Iraq. Substantial reserves of phosphate rock and natural gas do, however, exist in Egypt.

Phosphate rock reserves

Considerable deposits of phosphate rock are located in Egypt, but rock production is small and therefore Egypt plays a relatively minor role in the world trade of phosphate rock. The largest known deposit is at Abu Tartur in the Kharga region of the Western Desert. An estimated deposit of 987 million tons of phosphate rock has been identified, and an unknown large quantity of rock is thought to exist in parts of the area not yet surveyed. Of the reserves surveyed, 525 million tons of rock at a grade of 28 to 30 percent P_2O_5 can be mined. These reserves, however, lie about 100 meters below the surface and will have to be mined underground. In order to exploit the rock, its iron content must be reduced; it contains 4.3 to 4.9 percent iron in the form of pyrites and 0.7 to 1.7 percent in the form of aluminum oxide.[12] It is assumed that reduction is possible, and thus production is expected to commence in 1980–81.

Another deposit exists at West Sebeya, where a mine owned by the Abu Zaabal Fertilizer Company is producing 100,000 tons of rock a year. In the same area, there is another deposit of 150 million tons of 20 to 21 percent P_2O_5 grade rock with an iron content of 2 to 3 percent. By 1980–81, an annual production of 120,000 tons of P_2O_5 is expected.

At East Sebeya, 150,000 to 200,000 tons of rock are being produced for local consumption. The P_2O_5 content of this rock is 28 to 29 percent. A new project currently under construction is expected to reach an output of 1 million tons of rock in two stages. The first stage is to produce 300,000 tons of 30 percent P_2O_5 rock in 1980–81, and the second stage will produce the rest.

Several medium grade (20 to 30 percent P_2O_5) deposits of commercial significance lie in the Eastern Desert. The deposits near the Safaya port have been mined for many years, especially for exports. By 1980, all mines in this area are expected to be depleted. Further south are the Qusayr deposits, which have also been mined for several years. When these mines are also depleted (around 1980),

12. The pyrites exist in the form of impurities that cannot be used as a raw material in sulfuric acid production because of separation problems.

production will shift to Abu Shigela, where the reserves are estimated to be equivalent to about 40 million tons of upgraded 30 percent P_2O_5 rock. This rock will be used mainly for exports. South of Safaya, at Hamrawein, is another extensive deposit of 1.3 million tons of rock. It is to be beneficiated to 600,000 tons of 32 to 33 percent P_2O_5 to supply the domestic and export needs of Egypt.

Natural gas reserves

In conjunction with Ente Nazionale Idrocarburi (ENI) of Italy, the Egyptian General Petroleum Corporation (EGPC) has developed a natural gas field (92.8 percent methane) at Abu Madi, about 40 kilometers north of Talkha. The identified recoverable reserves are estimated to be between 30 billion and 40 billion cubic meters. The anticipated daily consumption is 26 million cubic meters, which should give the identified reserves a life of at least thirty years. Additional reserves may be identified as the drilling continues. The gas is now used for the Talkha I and II plants and for a local power station and township.

Two other major gas discoveries have been made in the Delta area. The first field, at Abu Kir, is located in the sea about ten miles offshore. It has reserves that are currently estimated to be around 22 billion cubic meters, although more reserves are likely to be proven in this area in the near future. The gas has a methane content (by volume) of 94 percent and, like the Abu Madi gas, is free of sulfur. This gas will be used for the ammonia-urea complex due in Abu Kir in 1978–79. The second gas field, at Abu Gharahib, has known recoverable reserves of 40 billion cubic meters. This gas is expected to be piped to Helwan and Cairo.

The Transport of Fertilizers

Egyptian fertilizers are either produced domestically or imported. They must then be transported from plants or ports of landing to the main stations in the various governorates; this is the first activity in the distribution system required to feed the sectional stores or the stores of the agricultural cooperative societies. The various products are transported to the governorates as follows:

- the calcium ammonium nitrate produced at the KIMA plant at Aswan covers the needs of the Upper Egypt governorates excluding Giza;
- the calcium ammonium nitrate produced at the El Nasr plant

at Helwan covers the needs of Giza, Fayoum, Menoufia, and Kalubia governorates;

- the single superphosphate produced at the Abu Zaabal factory covers the needs of Kalubia, Suez, Fayoum, Sharkia, and parts of Dakahalia and Menoufia governorates;
- the single superphosphate produced at Kafr El Zayaat is transported to Alexandria, Behera, Gharbia, Kafr El Sheikh, Damietta, and parts of Dakahalia and Menoufia governorates;
- the single superphosphate from the Assiout plant covers the needs of the Upper Egypt governorates excluding Giza;
- all imported nitrogenous fertilizers are distributed to Lower Egypt excluding the governorates of Menoufia and Kalubia;
- all imported potash fertilizers are distributed to all the relevant governorates of Egypt.

The rule that guides decisions about the distribution of fertilizers is simple: the output produced at any plant is transported to an agricultural area on the sole basis of its proximity to that plant. Fertilizers are transported either by lorries, by railways, or by river transport, as is shown in table 8. Clearly, the predominant mode of trans-

Table 8. *The Transport of Fertilizers by Governorates Covered and Mode of Transport*

Type of fertilizer	*Governorates covered*	*Mode of transport*
Imported		
Nitrogenous fertilizers	Lower Egypt excluding Menoufia and Kalubia	Lorries
Potash fertilizers	All relevant governorates	Lorries and railways
Domestically produced		
CAN from KIMA plant at Aswan	Upper Egypt excluding Giza	Inland waterways and railways
CAN from El Nasr plant at Helwan	Giza, Fayoum, Menoufia, and Kalubia	Lorries
SSP from Abu Zaabal plant	Kalubia, Suez, Giza, Fayoum, Sharkia, and parts of Dakahalia and Menoufia	Lorries
SSP from Kafr El Zayaat plant	Alexandria, Behera, Gharbia, Kafr El Sheikh, Damietta, and parts of Dakahalia and Menoufia	Lorries and railways
SSP from Assiout plant	Upper Egypt excluding Giza	Lorries and railways

port is by lorries. In 1972, 93.3 percent of all fertilizer material transported was shipped by lorries, 5 percent by rail, and only 1.7 percent by river transport.

The main reasons why lorries dominate as the mode of transport of fertilizers are that they are fast and are considered to be the safest mode, thereby minimizing losses. In addition, they present a direct mode of transport from the factory or port to the governorates; thus, loading and unloading need to be undertaken only once rather than twice as in the case of river and rail transport. Rail transport is currently handicapped by the shortage of wagons in Egypt. Although river transport is the cheapest mode, there are few ports and few facilities for loading and unloading.

The Prices of Fertilizers

Fertilizer prices in Egypt have been controlled by the government since 1960. These prices are determined by Ministerial Orders of the Ministry of Industry in collaboration with the Ministry of Agriculture and the Agricultural Prices Balancing Fund. Fertilizer prices are fixed at all levels, and the retail prices are unified across the country. No distinction is made between domestically produced and imported fertilizers.

The pricing policy for domestically produced fertilizers

Basically, there are three levels of prices: the "ex factory" price, the wholesale price, and the retail price.

The ex factory price is the price paid by the Agricultural Cooperative Credit Organization—that is, the Credit Bank—to the local producer of the fertilizer. This price varies from factory to factory and thus assures a differential return for the same product: for example, table 9 illustrates the different prices for single superphosphate (15 percent, P_2O_5).

The second stage is the wholesale price, which is the price of delivered fertilizers at the central stores of the governorates. The fertilizers are delivered by the Credit Bank to the central stores that belong to the various cooperative societies. The commercial margin at this stage varies from 0.3 percent of the consumer price for ammonium sulfate to 6.5 percent for calcium ammonium nitrate. In

Table 9. *Average Total Cost, Ex Factory Price, and Net Return for Selected Fertilizers, 1971–72*

Plant and product	*Average total cost (Egyptian pounds per ton)*[a]	*Ex factory price (Egyptian pounds per ton)*	*Net return (percent)*
Kafr El Zayaat: SSP 15 percent	10.536	12.998	23.0
Assiout: SSP 15 percent	10.744	12.725	18.0
Abu Zaabal: SSP 15 percent	12.529	12.914	3.0
Aswan: CAN 31 percent	30.396	36.024	18.5
Helwan: CAN 33.5 percent	69.553	34.144	−50.9
Helwan: ammonium sulfate 20.6 percent	33.746	27.076	−6.67

Source: The General Organization of Chemical Industries.
a. Includes raw materials and direct costs, wages, depreciation, indirect costs, marketing and administrative costs.

addition to this margin, since 1965 a treasury tax has been imposed on fertilizer sales. It is a specific tax of 1 Egyptian pound for each ton of fertilizer product; it thus charges lower concentrate fertilizers a higher tax rate. This tax is added to the wholesale price.

The final stage is the retail price, which is divided into two components. The first component is the retail price to consumers (or farmers) who are members of the cooperative societies. The second component is the retail price to nonmembers. The price paid by the nonmembers is 5.26 percent above that paid by the members.

The levels of prices for the various domestically produced fertilizers in 1971–72 are shown in table 10.

The pricing policy for imported fertilizers

The price of imported fertilizers delivered to the stores of the Credit Bank in the governorates is made up of the import price (c.i.f.); the transport cost to the stores; customs duties; the cost of unloading, storing, and packaging; and the commission of the Credit Bank. Since the prices of the domestic and imported fertilizers are equalized, the difference between the retail price and the delivered price of the imported fertilizers accrues to the Agricultural

Table 10. *Prices and Margins of Distribution of the Locally Produced Fertilizers, 1971–72*
(Egyptian pounds per ton)

Type of fertilizer	*Ex factory sales price*	*Transport cost*	*Package*	*Taxes*	*Price of delivery at the central stores*	*Whole-sale margin*	*Retail sales price to the cooperative members*	*Retail margin*	*Retail sales price to nonmembers*
Superphosphate: 15 percent									
Powdered, in jute sack	10.950	1.800	—	1.000	13.750	1.117	14.867	0.783	15.650
Powdered, in polyethylene sack	11.550	1.800	—	1.000	14.350	1.185	15.535	0.765	16.300
Powdered, in jute and polyethylene sack	11.450	1.800	—	1.000	14.250	1.140	15.340	0.810	16.200
Granular, in jute sack	11.050	1.800	—	1.000	13.850	0.900	14.750	1.000	15.740
Granular, in polyethylene sack	11.650	1.800	—	1.000	14.450	1.130	15.580	0.830	16.400
Granular, in jute and polyethylene sack	11.550	1.800	—	1.000	14.350	1.130	15.480	0.830	16.300
Calcium nitrate:									
15.5 percent	20.800	1.800	—	1.000	33.600	1.150	24.750	1.250	26.000
Ammonium sulfate:									
20.6 percent	21.700	1.800	3.000	1.000	27.500	0.100	27.600	1.400	29.000
Calcium ammonium nitrate:									
26 percent	29.502	1.800	—	1.000	32.333	2.333	34.635	1.500	36.135
Calcium ammonium nitrate:									
31 percent	35.300	2.000	—	1.000	38.300	1.871	40.171	2.629	42.800
Calcium ammonium nitrate:									
33.5 percent	39.300	1.800	—	1.000	42.100	1.400	43.500	2.240	45.740

— = not applicable.
Source: General Organization for Industrialization.

Table 11. *Prices and Margins of Distribution for Imported Fertilizers, 1970–71*
(Egyptian pounds per ton)

Type of fertilizer	*Price (cost and freight)*	*Price of imported fertilizer at the stores of the Credit Bank*	*Retail sales price to the cooperative members*	*Retail price to nonmembers*
Urea: 46 percent	20.930	30.170	60.800	64.000
Ammonium sulfate:				
20.6 percent	7.780	13.880	27.600	29.000
Ammonium nitrate:				
33.5 percent	17.490	24.311	43.600	45.840
Potassium chloride:				
60 percent	—	22.700	24.750	26.000
Calcium ammonium nitrate:				
26 percent	16.619	20.782	33.300	35.800
Nitro-ammonium sulfate:				
26 percent	18.368	21.541	33.200	35.000
Potassium sulfate:				
20.5 percent	—	32.700	24.750	26.000
Ammonium sulfate:				
20.6 percent	23.179	27.870	27.600	29.000
Compound fertilizers	32.800	45.873	41.800	44.000
Single superphosphate	10.320	17.120	12.875	13.500

— = not applicable.
Source: Agricultural Prices Balancing Fund.

Prices Balancing Fund. Table 11 indicates such prices for imports in 1970–71. In the case of some fertilizers, such as potassium sulfate and single superphosphate, the retail price is below the delivered price. Such products are subsidized from the Balancing Fund.

The prices of different fertilizers

The prices of nitrogenous fertilizers have been determined and changed by a series of six Ministerial Orders since 1960, as shown in table 12. The last order, which was in 1968, determined the prices of calcium ammonium nitrate 31 percent at 39.71 Egyptian pounds a ton and calcium ammonium nitrate 33.5 percent at 43.6 Egyptian pounds a ton.

Phosphatic fertilizer prices have been determined by nine Minis-

Table 12. *Cooperative Sales Prices of Nitrogenous Fertilizers as Determined by Ministerial Orders, 1960–72*
(Egyptian pounds per ton)

Year	*Ministerial Order number*	*Chilean sodium nitrate*	*Calcium nitrate: 15.5 percent*	*Ammonium sulfate: 20.5 percent*	*Calcium ammonium nitrate: 20.5 percent*	*Calcium ammonium nitrate: 26 percent*	*Calcium ammonium nitrate: 31 percent*	*Calcium ammonium nitrate: 33.5 percent*	*Ammonium nitrosulfate: 26 percent*	*Urea: 46 percent*	*Compound fertilizers 25–10–0*
1960	245	24.700	23.750	26.600	26.600	33.300	—	—	34.200	—	—
1961	—	23.750	23.750	26.600	—	—	—	—	34.200	—	—
1962	542	23.750	23.750	26.600	26.600	—	—	—	32.300	—	—
1963	—	23.750	23.750	26.600	26.600	—	—	—	32.300	—	—
1964	1,316	—	23.750	26.600	26.600	33.300	—	—	32.300	60.800	40.800
1965	437	—	24.750	27.600	27.600	33.300	—	—	32.300	60.800	—
1966	—	—	24.750	27.600	27.600	33.300	—	—	32.300	60.800	—
1967	—	—	24.750	27.600	27.600	33.300	—	—	32.300	60.800	—
1968	99	—	24.750	27.600	27.600	33.300	39.710	—	32.300	60.800	—
1968	134	—	—	—	—	—	—	43.600	—	—	—
1969	—	—	24.750	27.600	27.600	33.300	39.710	43.600	32.300	60.800	—
1970	—	—	24.750	27.600	27.600	33.300	39.710	43.600	32.300	60.800	—
1971	—	—	24.750	27.600	27.600	33.300	39.710	43.600	32.300	60.800	—
1972	—	—	24.750	27.600	27.600	33.300	39.710	43.600	32.300	60.800	—

— = not applicable.
Note: Sales price includes treasury tax beginning in 1965.
Source: General Organization of Chemical Industries.

Table 13. *Cooperative Sales Prices of Phosphatic Fertilizers as Determined by Ministerial Orders, 1960–72*
(Egyptian pounds per ton)

Year	*Ministerial Order number*	*Concentration of* P_2O_5	*Superphosphate: powdered, in jute sack*	*Superphosphate: granulated, in polyethylene sack*	*Superphosphate: granulated, in jute and polyethylene sack*	*Superphosphate: powdered, in jute and polyethylene sack*
1960	1,087	18 percent	13.300	—	—	—
	—	15 percent	10.515	—	—	—
	642	15 percent	10.450	—	—	—
1961–62	—	18 percent	13.300	—	—	—
1963	—	15 percent	10.450	—	—	—
1963	458	15 percent	11.875	—	—	—
1964	1,276	16 percent	12.160	—	—	—
	—	15 percent	11.875	—	—	—
	1,316	17 percent	12.920	—	—	—
1965–66	—	16 percent	12.160	—	—	—
1967	—	17 percent	12.920	—	—	—
	—	15 percent	11.875	—	—	—
1968	143	15 percent	11.875	—	—	—
1969–70	596	15 percent	11.875	12.920	12.4785	12.274
1971	330	15 percent	13.9175	14.630	14.535	15.440
1972	40	15 percent	14.8675	15.580	15.485	15.390

— = not applicable.
Note: Sales price includes Treasury tax.
Source: General Organization of Chemical Industries.

terial Orders issues since 1960, as shown in table 13. The last order, which was issued in 1972, determined the prices of powdered and granulated single superphosphate in jute and polyethylene bags at an average of 15 Egyptian pounds a ton.

The potash fertilizer price has been set by only two Ministerial Orders at 23.75 Egyptian pounds a ton for potassium sulfate and potassium chloride; the price level has remained unchanged since 1960. These fertilizers are not produced domestically and are thus imported; no treasury tax has been imposed on them.

The Import of Fertilizers

Egypt has always imported fertilizers to supplement its domestic production. Over time, as the consumption pattern changed, so did the import pattern. At the turn of the century, Egypt imported only sodium nitrate (from Chile); since then, it has imported different types of nitrogenous, phosphatic, and potash fertilizers. During World Wars I and II, trade blockades reduced imports substantially. By the second war, Egypt had become a heavy user of fertilizers, and thus the war had a major impact on the country's agricultural productivity. After that period, as fertilizer use increased, imports increased significantly despite large expansions in domestic production. At present, fertilizer imports are confined to nitrogenous and potash fertilizers; phosphatic fertilizer imports were stopped in 1966–67. Since no raw materials for potash fertilizers are available locally, imports will continue to be the sole source of supply.

Import policy

Egypt has not had a well-defined policy for importing fertilizers. Import targets are included in the five-year fertilizer plan, but they do not materialize and are subject to continuous change. The common practice has been to adopt annual plans that are influenced by several factors including variations in domestic output, consumption requirements, and available foreign exchange that can be allocated to fertilizer imports.

Estimates of import quantities are based on the difference between domestic output and consumption and on the availability of foreign exchange. These estimates are worked out by the General Organization for the Agricultural Prices Balancing Fund (previously known as the Fertilizer Subsidizing Fund). The Fund then submits its estimates to the Treasury for allocation of the necessary foreign exchange. The Treasury considers these estimates in the light of its foreign exchange budget and determines the import quota, which is classified according to type of payment (free currency, payment agreements, credit facilities). The Fund then coordinates the transactions between the different public trade agencies, which submit their preliminary tenders concerning specific quantities of different types of fertilizers, prices, and payment conditions. A special committee—consisting of representatives of the Fund, the Credit Bank, trade companies, and representatives of foreign agencies—selects the most suitable offers according to price considerations and terms of shipment. The payment conditions and credits are put at the trade companies' disposal for implementation. Thereafter, the companies assume full responsibility for obtaining the fertilizers with certain specifications and according to a time schedule. These imports are required to be shipped by Egyptian vessels.

In the past few years, imported types of fertilizers were confined to ammonium sulfate (21 percent), calcium ammonium nitrate (20.5 percent, 26 percent, and 33 percent), urea (46 percent), and potassium chloride (60 percent). Recent trends have shown an emphasis on imports of higher analysis fertilizers.

As a result of the present import policy, the prices paid for fertilizers of the same type and concentration differ, even in the same year, according to the exporting country and the payment arrangements. This policy is also responsible for excess imports that have caused bottlenecks in unloading, transportation, and distribution in some years and shortages of imported quantities in others.

The import sources are numerous. In the past ten years, the main countries exporting fertilizers to Egypt have been Italy, Rumania, Belgium, Kuwait, Poland, the Netherlands, Bulgaria, the Soviet Union, Switzerland, France, the German Democratic Republic, the Federal Republic of Germany, and Lebanon. Most of the nitrogenous fertilizer imports—about 75 percent on the average—have been from free-exchange countries. This percentage increased steadily from about 68 percent in 1959–60 to 95 percent in 1969–70, and then decreased to about 58 percent in 1971–72. Most of the phosphatic fertilizer imports were also from free-exchange countries; these imports ceased in 1966–67. Yugoslavia, which was a major source of the phosphatic fertilizer imports in 1961–62, was the only socialist country to export these fertilizers to Egypt. Potash fertilizer imports started in 1964–65 at a very low level, and from only three countries: France, Italy, and the German Democratic Republic. East Germany has been the sole source of potash imports in the past few years.

Conclusion

This chapter has provided a brief, conventional description of the fertilizer sector in Egypt. Although the chapter has given some insight into the past growth and the present structure of the fertilizer sector and has described the role the government plays in pricing and importing fertilizer materials, neither the type of information provided nor the organization of that information are immediately useful for a planning model. In some respects, considerably greater detail is required; in others, entire categories of data are unnecessary. This will become clear when several planning models of the Egyptian fertilizer sector are presented in the next few chapters.

11

An Analysis of the Egyptian Fertilizer Sector in 1975

THE STRUCTURE OF THE EGYPTIAN FERTILIZER SECTOR in the year 1975 is analyzed in this chapter.[1] For that purpose, a simple mathematical model of the sector, closely following the model of an existing industry developed in chapter 8 above, will be formulated.

Before the analytical framework is described and the numerical information given, however, the scope and purpose of the analysis will be summarized. Initially, a model that is excessively restrictive in terms of alternative choices will be formulated; several of these restrictions will be successively dropped or relaxed in the course of the analysis so that their individual impact can be assessed. The starting point of the analysis is actual recorded use of fertilizer material by type in each of the twenty governorates of Egypt in 1975.[2] By definition, the supply of these fertilizers must have originated either from domestic production facilities in 1975 or from imports. The model is

1. The date 1975 refers to the "fertilizer year," which runs from July 1974 to June 1975.

2. Potassic fertilizers are not included in this analysis because their use in Egypt is limited, and no scope for their domestic production appears to exist.

free to select the least-cost supply pattern—either from alternative domestic supply sources for the same product, or by importing. Domestic supplies are, however, subject to capacity constraints that are initially defined in terms of the actual production levels achieved in 1975. Fertilizer materials can be transported from supply sources to the various marketing centers (assumed to be the major town in each governorate) by waterway, road, or rail; in accordance with the actual situation, however, it is first assumed that all final products are transported by lorry, and that all raw materials are transported by barge and, if necessary, lorry. With this specification, the model can be used to select the least-cost supply and shipment pattern for fertilizers in 1975; the model will determine whether a fertilizer should be imported or produced domestically, given the existing production facilities and their location.

If this determination were the only objective, however, the planning model would hardly be required, because these questions can be answered by inspecting the original data; that is, an analysis of marginal production cost in domestic plants, import price, and transport cost would be sufficient to arrive at the same answers. The value of the model will be in its ability to carry out a number of experiments by slightly varying the restrictions. In a short period of time, it can obtain a great number of detailed numerical results, presented in a systematic and uniform way, thus facilitating comparisons. Then, the following refinements can be made to the model: drop the restriction on interplant shipments of intermediate products, relax the capacity constraints to allow 100 percent capacity utilization, and investigate the implications of greater flexibility in fertilizer use by specifying nutrient requirements rather than requirements by fertilizer type. The static analysis of these questions will indicate how the operation of the fertilizer sector can be improved in the short run. Given the simplified nature of the model, conclusions along these lines are only tentative and indicative; all require further, more detailed analysis. In this regard, the model serves as a device to generate particular options that deserve further study, not as a device that produces firm recommendations for action.

The Structure of the 1975 Model

In this section, a detailed description is given of the 1975 model of the Egyptian fertilizer sector.

The demand for fertilizers

Egypt is divided into twenty governorates; these have been considered as separate demand regions in this and subsequent models in order to capture the importance of spatial aspects of the structure of the fertilizer sector. The major city in each governorate is designated as the marketing center for that demand region, and it serves as the reference point for calculating transport distances between sources of fertilizer supply and the demand region. The twenty governorates and their marketing centers are the following:

Governorate	*Marketing center*
Alexandria	Alexandria
Behera	Demanhur
Gharbia	Tanta
Kafr El Sheikh	Kafr El Sheikh
Dakahlia	El Mansura
Damietta	Damietta
Sharkia	Zagazig
Ismailia	Ismailia
Suez	Suez
Menoufia	Shibin El Kom
Kalubia	Benha
Giza	Giza
Beni Suef	Beni Suef
Fayoum	El Fayoum
Minia	El Minia
Assiout	Assiout
New Valley	El Kharga
Sohag	Sohag
Quena	Quena
Aswan	Aswan

The map indicates the geographical location of these governorates and marketing centers.

An estimate of the level of fertilizer use by type is given for each demand region in table 14. This table, therefore, also gives a comprehensive listing of all relevant fertilizer types in 1975.

The basic condition to be fulfilled in this model is that the sum of shipments of fertilizer material to each demand region, from domestic supply sources and imports, equals fertilizer use in each region. In this initial version of the model, no room is left for choice; that is, the

Table 14. *Consumption of Fertilizers by Demand Region and Fertilizer Type, 1974–75*
(thousands of tons)

Demand region	*Calcium ammonium nitrate: 26 percent*	*Calcium ammonium nitrate: 31 percent*	*Calcium ammonium nitrate: 33.5 percent*	*Ammonium sulfate*	*Urea*	*Single super-phosphate: 15.5 percent*	*Com-pound 1: 25–5.5–0*	*Com-pound 2: 30–10–0*	*Di-ammonium phosphate*
Alexandria	0	0	5	3	1	8	0	0.0	0.0
Behera	1	0	25	90	35	64	1	0.1	0.1
Gharbia	0	0	17	60	28	57	1	0.2	0.1
Kafr El Sheikh	1	0	10	45	22	25	2	0.2	0.0
Dakahlia	1	0	26	60	20	52	1	0.0	0.0
Damietta	0	0	2	15	8	5	0	0.0	0.0
Sharkia	1	0	31	50	28	43	1	0.1	0.0
Ismailia	0	0	4	6	2	4	0	0.0	0.0
Suez	0	0	1	0	0	1	0	0.0	0.0
Menoufia	0	0	24	21	30	33	2	0.1	0.1
Kalubia	0	0	25	16	7	22	1	0.0	0.1
Giza	0	0	40	6	2	14	1	0.1	0.0
Beni Suef	1	0	15	1	20	13	3	0.0	0.0
Fayoum	1	0	20	6	20	17	1	0.0	0.0
Minia	2	15	35	1	41	50	3	0.2	0.1
Assiout	1	20	26	1	27	35	5	0.1	0.0
New Valley	0	0	0	0	1	1	0	0.0	0.0
Sohag	0	65	3	0	7	20	1	0.0	0.0
Quena	0	95	2	0	3	8	0	0.0	0.0
Aswan	0	40	0	0	0	8	0	0.0	0.0
Total	9	235	311	381	302	480	23	1.1	0.5

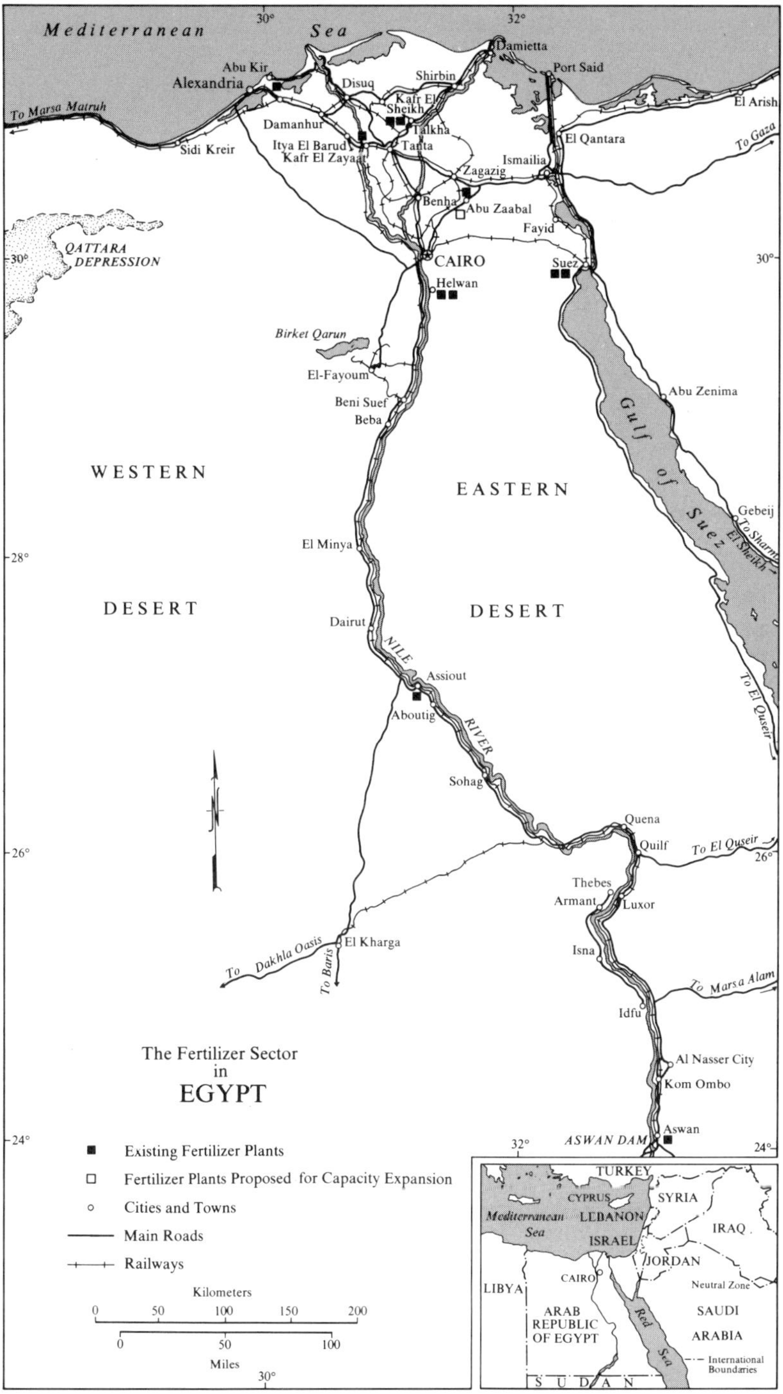
The Fertilizer Sector
in
EGYPT
Existing Fertilizer Plants
Fertilizer Plants Proposed for Capacity Expansion
Cities and Towns
Main Roads
Railways
Kilometers
0 50 100 150 200
0 50 100
Miles
Mediterranean Sea
WESTERN DESERT
EASTERN DESERT
QATTARA DEPRESSION
Gulf of Suez
NILE RIVER
Birket Qarun
Alexandria
Abu Kir
Disuq
Shirbin
Damietta
Port Said
Kafr El Sheikh
Talkha
Damanhur
Itya El Barud
Kafr El Zayaat
Tanta
Zagazig
Ismailia
El Qantara
El Arish
To Gaza
To Marsa Matruh
Sidi Kreir
Benha
Abu Zaabal
Fayid
CAIRO
Suez
Helwan
El-Fayoum
Beni Suef
Beba
Abu Zenima
Gebeij
To Sharm El Sheikh
El Minya
Dairut
Assiout
Aboutig
To El Quseir
Sohag
Quena
Quilf
Thebes
Armant
Luxor
Isna
Idfu
To Marsa Alam
Al Nasser City
Kom Ombo
Aswan
ASWAN DAM
El Kharga
To Dakhla Oasis
To Baris
30°
32°
28°
26°
24°
TURKEY
CYPRUS
SYRIA
Mediterranean Sea
LEBANON
ISRAEL
IRAQ
JORDAN
CAIRO
LIBYA
Neutral Zone
ARAB REPUBLIC OF EGYPT
SAUDI ARABIA
Red Sea
International Boundaries
SUDAN

recorded composition of fertilizer use has to be reproduced exactly. Later, this condition will be relaxed and the only stipulation will be that the required quantity of nitrogen and phosphate nutrient is supplied, regardless of the material used. The initial conditions can be stated mathematically as follows:

$$\sum_{i \in I} x_{cij} + v_{cj} \geq \bar{d}_{cj}, \qquad c \in CF, \quad j \in J \tag{11.1}$$

where

x_{cij} = the shipment of fertilizer c from domestic plant i to demand region j, where $\sum_{i \in I}$ means that such shipments for all plants in the set I should be summed;
v_{cj} = the imports of fertilizer c for demand region j;
$\bar{d}_{cj}$ = the actual use of fertilizer c in demand region j.

The statements on the right refer to the set coverage: CF denotes the set of fertilizers; $j \in J$ means that constraint (11.1) needs to be specified for every demand region.

The supply of fertilizers

The fertilizers used in 1975 were supplied from domestic production facilities or from imports. To model the possible supply from imports for the purpose of this planning model (in which fertilizer types used are strictly specified), one simply needs to specify the import possibility for each fertilizer product actually used in 1975 and the location of all relevant ports. In this case, all imports are assumed to have entered Egypt through Alexandria. To model the possible supply from domestic production facilities, one needs to specify the location of production facilities, the production capacities of all productive units at each site, and the technological coefficients that describe the transformation of raw materials to intermediates and of either or both into particular final products. The technological coefficients can be broken into two categories: input-output coefficients giving the detailed material input requirements per unit of output of the various processes in the model, and the capacity required in each productive unit as a ratio of the design capacity. As was described in chapter 8, it is often possible to distinguish a category of miscellaneous inputs that can be combined into a cost figure per ton of output, and that do not need to be specified separately. The main criterion for inclusion into this category is that the input in question can be expected to be available in the relevant quantity range at a given price.

In table 15, the location of plants in operation in 1975 is given, together with the design capacity of each productive unit and the process in use during that year. Input-output coefficients are given in table 16. Labor requirements in intermediate and final product manufacture are not included among the basic data for reasons that will be explained shortly.

Modeling the supply side

The basic technological relationships that describe the supply side in the model are conveniently specified in three sets of material balance constraints—for final products, for intermediate products, and for raw materials and miscellaneous inputs—and in a set of capacity constraints.

MATERIAL BALANCE CONSTRAINTS ON FINAL PRODUCTS

$$\sum_{p \epsilon P} a_{cp} z_{pi} \geq \sum_{j \epsilon J} x_{cij} \qquad c \epsilon CF, \; i \epsilon I \tag{11.2}$$

The right-hand side of this constraint corresponds closely to one of the terms in constraint (11.1) and represents the sum of the shipments of product c (a fertilizer type) from plant location i to all marketing centers j. The expression on the left-hand side denotes the production of final product c by all processes p at plant location i. The typical process p that provides final products can be assigned a coefficient $a_{cp} = 1.0$.

MATERIAL BALANCE CONSTRAINTS ON INTERMEDIATE PRODUCTS

$$\sum_{p \epsilon P} a_{cp} z_{pi} \geq 0 \qquad c \epsilon CI, \; i \epsilon I \tag{11.3}$$

This constraint states that the production of intermediate product c at plant location i with process p should at least equal total use of intermediate product c at plant location i. CI is the set of intermediate products.

Since final products, and some intermediate products, require intermediate products in their production, at least one of the input-output coefficients associated with process p in constraint (11.3) will have a negative sign. For the constraint to hold, therefore, at least one process p in (11.3) will need to have a positive sign denoting the

Table 15. *Design Capacity of Plants by Plant Location and Productive Unit*[a]
(tons per day)

Plant location	*Sulfuric acid: sulfur*	*Sulfuric acid: pyrites*	*Nitric acid: ammonia oxidation*	*Ammonia: water electrolysis*	*Ammonia: coke-oven gas*	*Ammonium sulfate: by-product of coke-oven plant*	*Single superphosphate: den method*	*Calcium ammonium nitrate: 31 percent and 33.5 percent*
Aswan	—	—	800	450	—	—	—	1,100
Helwan	—	—	282	—	172[b]	24	—	364
Kafr El Zayaat	200	50	—	—	—	—	600	—
Assiout	250	—	—	—	—	—	600	—
Abu Zaabal	242	227	—	—	—	—	600	—

— = not applicable.
Source: Plant managers.
a. The design capacity of a productive unit is the production level that in principle can be reached. In reality, this production level is rarely achieved, and in most cases it was found that actual production in Egypt in 1975 was lower than design capacity.
b. At Helwan, ammonia is used to produce nitric acid; ammonium sulfate is a direct by-product of the coke-oven plant associated with the steel works at Helwan.

Table 16. *Input-Output Coefficients*[a]
(tons of input per ton of output, unless otherwise noted)

Inputs	*Sulfuric acid: sulfur*	*Sulfuric acid: pyrites*	*Nitric acid: ammonia oxidation*	*Ammonia: water electrolysis*	*Ammonia: coke-oven gas*	*Ammonium sulfate: by-product of coke-oven plant*	*Single superphosphate: den method*	*Calcium ammonium nitrate: 31 percent*	*Calcium ammonium nitrate: 33.5 percent*
Major inputs									
Electricity[b]	—	—	—	−12.0	—	—	—	—	—
Coke-oven gas[c]	—	—	—	—	−2.0	—	−0.62	—	—
Phosphate rock:									
30 percent P_2O_5	—	—	—	—	—	—	—	—	—
Pyrites	—	−0.826	—	—	—	—	—	—	—
Sulfur	−0.334	—	—	—	—	—	—	—	—
Sulfuric acid	1.0	1.0	—	—	—	−0.76	−0.41	—	—
Ammonia	—	—	−0.292	1.0	1.0	−0.26	—	−0.20	−0.21
Nitric acid	—	—	1.0	—	—	—	—	−0.71	−0.76
Ammonium sulfate	—	—	—	—	—	1.0	—	—	—
Single superphosphate	—	—	—	—	—	—	1.0	—	—
Calcium ammonium nitrate:									
31 percent	—	—	—	—	—	—	—	1.0	—
Calcium ammonium nitrate:									
33.5 percent	—	—	—	—	—	—	—	—	1.00
Limestone	—	—	—	—	—	—	—	−0.12	−0.04

(Table continues on the following page)

Table 16 (*continued*)

Inputs	*Sulfuric acid: sulfur*	*Sulfuric acid: pyrites*	*Nitric acid: ammonia oxidation*	*Ammonia: water electrolysis*	*Ammonia: coke-oven gas*	*Ammonium sulfate: by-product of coke-oven plant*	*Single superphosphate: den method*	*Calcium ammonium nitrate: 31 percent*	*Calcium ammonium nitrate: 33.5 percent*
Miscellaneous inputs									
Electricity[d]	−50.0	−75.0	−231.0	−1,960.0	−19.0	−14.0	—	—	—
Blast-furnace gas[e]	—	—	—	−609.0	—	—	—	—	—
Bags[f]	—	—	—	—	−22.0	−22.0	—	−23.0	−23.0
Cooling water[e]	−20.0	−20.0	−0.6	−700.0	−17.0	−6.0	—	−49.0	−49.0
Steam	—	—	—	−4.0	—	—	—	−0.4	−0.5

— = not applicable.
a. Material input requirements per unit of output of the various processes in the model.
b. Megawatt hours per ton of output.
c. Thousand cubic meters per ton of output.
d. Kilowatt hours per ton of output.
e. Cubic meters per ton of output.
f. Units per ton of output.

production of an intermediate product. The latter statement applies only in the case of the particular specification of the intermediate product material balance constraint. Once interplant shipments, or imports of intermediates, are allowed, it is no longer necessary for a particular plant to produce its own intermediates. Imports of intermediate products did not occur in 1975, and they are highly unlikely to be efficient in the near future; therefore, they are not considered in the context of the static model. Interplant shipments did not occur in 1975 either; the case for such shipments is less clear-cut, however, and will therefore be analyzed below.

MATERIAL BALANCE CONSTRAINTS ON RAW MATERIALS AND MISCELLANEOUS INPUTS

$$\sum_{p \epsilon P} a_{cp}\, z_{pi} + u_{ci} + v_{ci} \geq 0 \qquad c \epsilon CR \quad i \epsilon I \tag{11.4}$$

The use of raw material or miscellaneous material input c in process p at plant location i is at least equal to the sum of the amounts of input c purchased domestically and imported from abroad. In this set of constraints, the coefficient a will usually be negative. CR is the set of raw materials and miscellaneous material inputs.

Miscellaneous inputs normally are not imported. The coefficient a_{cp} for miscellaneous inputs can be either expressed in physical terms (for example, cubic meters of cooling water per ton of output) or lumped together in a value term (dollars per ton of output). In this case, the former version is employed to facilitate using the model to check the consistency of data at the plant level; these data include specific requirements for some of the individual miscellaneous inputs by plant.

CAPACITY CONSTRAINTS

$$\sum_{p \epsilon P} b_{mp}\, z_{pi} \leq k_{mi} \qquad i \epsilon I \quad m \epsilon M \tag{11.5}$$

In (11.5), b_{mp} denotes the number of units of capacity used on productive unit m per unit of output of process p at plant location i. The constraint simply states that the total amount of capacity used cannot exceed the available capacity of productive unit m at plant location i. M correspondingly stands for the set of productive units.

As shown in table 14, actual production levels of the various productive units in the Egyptian fertilizer industry were generally below the design capacities in 1975; the rate of capacity utilization was reportedly between 70 and 100 percent. In the initial version of the static model, in which the situation in 1975 is reconstructed, the value of k_{mi} in the capacity constraint (11.5) is placed at a level that might have been attained for each productive unit at each plant site for that year. In other words, if that volume of output could be produced efficiently at each location, the model is free to select it; the model may, however, select a lower volume of output if this is preferable, given the overall objective. In a variant of this specification, it is assumed that there were no technical reasons why capacity utilization could not reach 100 percent, and the implications that this would have had for the performance of the sector are indicated.

NONNEGATIVITY CONSTRAINTS

$$x_{cij},\ v_{cj},\ z_{pi},\ u_{ci} \geq 0 \qquad c \in C,\ i \in I,\ j \in J,\ p \in P \tag{11.6}$$

The objective function

The preceding constraints state that a given pattern of fertilizer use by demand region and by fertilizer type should be met by either imports or domestic production. The latter requires that raw materials be transformed to intermediate and final products—this is governed by well-defined input-output coefficients—and that installed capacity be utilized at specific rates. Only some raw materials can be imported, and no imports or interplant shipments of intermediate products can take place. Some fertilizer types (CAN 26 percent, urea, diammonium phosphate, and two compounds) had to be imported because no domestic production facilities existed in 1975; others (CAN 31 percent, CAN 33.5 percent, single superphosphate, and ammonium sulfate) were either purchased from domestic sources or imported.

The selection from among the various alternatives specified is based on cost information incorporated in the objective function, in which a unit cost is specified for each of the activities in the model.

The objective function includes the following cost categories, the sum of which is to be minimized:

$$\min \xi = \phi_{\psi} + \phi_{\lambda} + \phi_{\pi}, \tag{11.7}$$

where

ϕ_ψ = recurrent cost, including the cost of domestic raw materials;

ϕ_λ = domestic transport cost;

ϕ_π = import cost.

Two cost categories do not need to be considered in this exercise. First, capital cost does not enter the picture, because it can be considered as sunk cost (that is, a cost already incurred) in 1975, reflecting decisions that were taken previously. Whether or not installed capacity should be used is a short-term decision that may affect total benefits; cost associated with the equipment itself, irrespective of whether or not it is used, is the same whatever short-term decisions are taken, and this cost category can therefore be ignored by the sectoral planner. A similar argument applies to labor cost. In Egypt, the labor force associated with a fertilizer plant is fixed, and closely monitored by the central government. Only if production is halted entirely, and the plant is scrapped, can this cost category be considered as variable. Since the plants were in operation in 1975, labor cost can be ignored in the model. Labor cost can be added separately to the other cost categories, if total production cost is desired.

RECURRENT COST

The recurrent cost included here is that incurred for purchasing local raw materials and miscellaneous material inputs included in the set *CR*. Several raw materials can be purchased locally:

- Electricity, which is used in ammonia production at Aswan in the water-electrolysis process.
- Coke-oven gas, which is used in ammonia production at Helwan. The gas is obtained from the coke plant attached to the fertilizer and iron and steel complexes.
- Phosphate rock, which is used in the production of SSP at Abu Zaabal, Assiout, and Kafr El Zayaat. The rock is obtained primarily from the Sebeya mines and each plant pays a different delivered price for the rock. These differences arise because of transport cost, part or full ownership of the mines, and special agreements.
- Limestone, which is used in the production of CAN at Helwan and Aswan. Helwan obtains its limestone from mines close to the

Table 17. *Prices of Raw Materials from Domestic Sources by Plant Location, 1975*
(Egyptian pounds)

Plant location	*Limestone (per ton)*	*Coke-oven gas (per cubic meter)*	*Electricity (per megawatt hour)*	*Phosphate rock (per ton)*	*Sulfuric acid (per ton)*
Helwan	1.2	16	—	—	3
Aswan	1.2	—	1	—	—
Assiout	—	—	—	3.5	—
Kafr El Zayaat	—	—	—	5.0	—
Abu Zaabal	—	—	—	4.0	—

— = not applicable.

complex and Aswan's supply comes from quarries belonging to the complex, about forty-five kilometers from the plant.

- Sulfuric acid, which strictly speaking is an intermediate product produced by the fertilizer complex. This is true in all cases except one—at Helwan it is a by-product of the coke plant and is used to produce 8,000 tons of ammonium sulfate a year. For the purposes of this study, therefore, sulfuric acid is treated as a raw material, but only in the production of ammonium sulfate at Helwan.

The prices assumed for raw materials from domestic sources, at the different plant sites, are given in table 17.

The miscellaneous material inputs include electricity (except at Aswan), boiler feed water, cooling water, pressurized steam, and bags.[3] The prices assumed to reflect the 1975 situation are given in table 18.

The detailed statement in the objective function for this cost category is:

$$\phi_\psi = \sum_{c \epsilon CR} \sum_{i \epsilon I} p^d_{ci}\, u_{ci}, \tag{11.8}$$

3. The amount of high pressure steam is aggregated over the pressures used in the plant. Although this is a fairly crude approximation, the procedure should not significantly bias the results because the cost of steam is only a small part of the total operating cost. The bags are 50 kilogram polyethylene.

Table 18. *Prices of Miscellaneous Inputs, 1975*
(Egyptian pounds)

Miscellaneous input	*Price*
Electricity (per kilowatt hour)	0.007
Blast-furnace gas (per cubic meter)	0.0075
Cooling water (per cubic meter)	0.031
Pressurized steam (per ton)	1.25
Bags (per bag)	0.28

where p^d_{ci} is the purchase price for each raw material and miscellaneous output.

TRANSPORT COST

Three modes of transportation are possible: road, rail, and waterway. The bulk of Egyptian fertilizer, however, is transported by lorries. Specifically, the following assumptions have been made:

- all shipments of final products from plants to the marketing centers are undertaken by lorry;
- all imports of final products from the port of entry to the marketing centers are transported by lorry;
- the transport of all raw materials to the plants is undertaken by barge or by barge and lorries where appropriate.

The rate schedules for each mode of transportation were obtained in consultation with the General Organization for Industrialization:

Transport mode	*Rate schedule (Egyptian pounds per ton)*
Road transport	0.5 + 0.0144 × distance in kilometers
Waterway transport	1.0 + 0.003 × distance in kilometers

Each rate schedule has both a fixed and a variable cost. The fixed cost includes the costs of loading, unloading, and handling.

The distances involved in transporting the various products are presented in tables 19 and 20. Table 19 represents the road distance from each plant to each marketing center in the relevant governorate,

Table 19. *Road distances from Plants and Alexandria (for Imports) to Marketing Centers for Final Products*
(kilometers)

Marketing center	*Kafr El Zayaat*	*Abu Zaabal*	*Helwan*	*Assiout*	*Aswan*	*Alex-andria*
Alexandria	119	210	244	607	1,135	—
Demanhur	42	50	184	547	1,065	600
Tanta	20	65	122	485	1,003	166
Kafr El Sheikh	20	105	162	525	1,043	161
El Mansura	58	138	152	515	1,033	224
Damietta	131	216	233	596	1,114	283
Zagazig	78	60	110	473	991	256
Ismailia	241	142	173	536	1,054	381
Suez	246	224	178	541	1,059	386
Shibin El Kom	33	154	109	472	990	157
Benha	66	97	76	439	957	190
Giza	133	48	9	372	890	287
Beni Suef	248	163	105	257	775	359
El Fayoum	230	145	88	308	826	341
El Minia	372	288	230	132	650	384
Assiout	504	420	362	—	518	616
El Kharga	703	619	561	199	519	815
Sohag	603	519	461	99	419	715
Quena	746	662	604	242	276	858
Aswan	1,022	938	880	518	—	1,134

as well as the distance from Alexandria, through which imports are assumed to enter Egypt. Table 20 presents the distances covered by imports of raw materials from Alexandria to the plants. These imports are transported by barge either directly to the plant or, in some cases, to a point a few kilometers away from the plant, with the remaining distance being covered by lorries. This takes into account cases—such as at Kafr El Zayaat—where the canal does not go all the way to the plant site and the products must be unloaded a few kilometers away and then transported by lorries.

Transport cost is represented in the objective function in the following way:

(11.9)

$$\phi_\lambda = \sum_{c \epsilon CF} \left(\sum_{i \epsilon I} \sum_{j \epsilon J} \mu_{cij} \, x_{cij} + \sum_{j \epsilon J} \mu_{cj} \, v_{cj} \right) + \sum_{c \epsilon CR} \sum_{i \epsilon I} \mu_{ci} \, v_{ci}.$$

The first block stands for the transport cost for all domestically

Table 20. *Distances from Alexandria to Plant Locations for Imports of Raw Materials*
(kilometers)

Plant location	*Distance by waterway*	*Distance by road*	*Total distance*
Kafr El Zayaat	104	6	110
Abu Zaabal	210	0.1	210.1
Helwan	183	—	183
Assiout	583	—	583
Aswan	1,087	10	1,097

Table 21. *Prices of Imports, 1975*
(U.S. dollars per ton)

Product	*Average c.i.f. import price*
Pyrites	17.5
Sulfur	55
Calcium ammonium nitrate: 26 percent	75
Calcium ammonium nitrate: 31 percent	90
Calcium ammonium nitrate: 33.5 percent	100
Urea: 46 percent	150
Ammonium sulfate: 20.1 percent	75
Diammonium phosphate: 18–46–0	175
Compound 1: 25–5.5–0	100
Compound 2: 30–10–0	130

produced and imported fertilizers; the second block stands for the transport cost associated with the domestic shipment of imported raw materials. The transport cost for domestic raw materials and miscellaneous inputs is assumed to be included in the supply price at the plant site.

IMPORT COST

The final component of the objective function covers the import cost of fertilizers and raw materials. Average c.i.f. import prices for 1975 are given in table 21 for all relevant products.

The import cost in the objective function can be specified as:

$$\phi_\pi = \sum_{c \epsilon CF} \sum_{j \epsilon J} p^v_{cj} \, v_{cj} + \sum_{c \epsilon CR} \sum_{i \epsilon I} p^v_{ci} \, v_{ci}. \tag{11.10}$$

Recapitulation

Before the results obtained with the 1975 model of the Egyptian fertilizer sector are considered, the more conventional formal statement of the model will be given. First, the symbols are categorized and defined.

Symbol	*Definition*
THE SETS AND INDEXES	
$i \epsilon I$	Plant locations
	Aswan
	Helwan
	Kafr El Zayaat
	Assiout
	Abu Zaabal
$j \epsilon J$	Demand regions
	Alexandria
	Behera
	Gharbia
	Kafr El Sheikh
	Dakahlia
	Damietta
	Sharkia
	Ismailia
	Suez
	Menoufia
	Kalubia
	Giza
	Beni Suef
	Fayoum
	Minia
	Assiout
	New Valley
	Sohag
	Quena
	Aswan
$m \epsilon M$	Productive units
	Sulfuric acid: sulfur
	Sulfuric acid: pyrites
	Nitric acid
	Ammonia: water electrolysis

Symbol	*Definition*
THE SETS AND INDEXES (*continued*)	
	Ammonia: coke-oven gas
	Calcium ammonium nitrate
	Ammonium sulfate
	Single superphosphate: 15.5 percent
$p\epsilon P$	Processes
	Sulfuric acid: sulfur
	Sulfuric acid: pyrites
	Nitric acid
	Ammonia: water electrolysis
	Ammonia: coke-oven gas
	Ammonium sulfate
	Single superphosphate: 15.5 percent
	Calcium ammonium nitrate: 31 percent
	Calcium ammonium nitrate: 33.5 percent
$c\epsilon CF$	Fertilizers
	Calcium ammonium nitrate: 26 percent
	Calcium ammonium nitrate: 31 percent
	Calcium ammonium nitrate: 33.5 percent
	Single superphosphate: 15.5 percent
	Ammonium sulfate
	Urea
	Diammonium phosphate
	Compound 1: 25–5.5–0
	Compound 2: 30–10–0
$c\epsilon CI$	Intermediate products
	Ammonia
	Nitric acid
	Sulfuric acid
$c\epsilon CR$	Raw materials and miscellaneous inputs
	Coke-oven gas
	Phosphate rock
	Limestone
	Sulfuric acid: Helwan
	Elemental sulfur
	Pyrites
	Electricity
	Blast-furnace gas
	Cooling water
	Steam
	Bags
THE VARIABLES	
z	Process level (production level)
x	Domestic shipment activity
v	Imports
u	Domestic raw material purchases

Symbol	*Definition*
THE VARIABLES (*continued*)	
ξ	Total cost
ϕ_ψ	Domestic recurrent cost
ϕ_λ	Transport cost
ϕ_π	Import cost
THE PARAMETERS	
a	Input (−) or output (+) coefficient
b	Capacity utilization coefficient
k	Initial capacity
p^d	Domestic price
p^v	Import price (c.i.f.)
$\bar{d}$	Actual consumption of fertilizer in 1975
μ	Transport cost

Second, the constraints of the model are specified.

MARKET REQUIREMENTS

(11.11) $$\sum_{i \in I} x_{cij} + v_{cj} \geq \bar{d}_{cj} \qquad c \in CF,\ j \in J$$

MATERIAL BALANCE CONSTRAINTS ON FINAL PRODUCTS

(11.12) $$\sum_{p \in P} a_{cp}\, z_{pi} \geq \sum_{j \in J} x_{cij} \qquad c \in CF,\ i \in I$$

MATERIAL BALANCE CONSTRAINTS ON INTERMEDIATE PRODUCTS

(11.13) $$\sum_{p \in P} a_{cp}\, z_{pi} \geq 0 \qquad c \in CI,\ i \in I$$

MATERIAL BALANCE CONSTRAINTS ON RAW MATERIALS AND MISCELLANEOUS INPUTS

(11.14) $$\sum_{p \in P} a_{cp}\, z_{pi} + u_{ci} + v_{ci} \geq 0 \qquad c \in CR,\ i \in I$$

CAPACITY CONSTRAINTS

(11.15) $$\sum_{p \in P} b_{mp}\, z_{pi} \leq k_{mi} \qquad i \in I,\ m \in M$$

NONNEGATIVITY CONSTRAINTS

(11.16) $$x_{cij},\ v_{cj},\ z_{pi},\ u_{ci} \geq 0 \qquad c \in C,\ i \in I,\ j \in J,\ p \in P$$

THE OBJECTIVE FUNCTION

$$\min \xi = \phi_\psi + \phi_\lambda + \phi_\pi \tag{11.17}$$

DOMESTIC RECURRENT COST

$$\phi_\psi = \sum_{c \epsilon CR} \sum_{i \epsilon I} p^d_{ci}\, u_{ci} \tag{11.18}$$

TRANSPORT COST

$$\phi_\lambda = \sum_{c \epsilon CF} \left(\sum_{i \epsilon I} \sum_{j \epsilon J} \mu_{cij}\, x_{cij} + \sum_{j \epsilon J} \mu_{cj}\, v_{cj} \right) + \sum_{c \epsilon CR} \sum_{i \epsilon I} \mu_{ci}\, v_{ci} \tag{11.19}$$

IMPORT COST

$$\phi_\pi = \sum_{c \epsilon CF} \sum_{j \epsilon J} p^v_{cj}\, v_{cj} + \sum_{c \epsilon CR} \sum_{i \epsilon I} p^v_{ci}\, v_{ci} \tag{11.20}$$

Results of the Basic 1975 Model: Solution 1

Planning models like those presented in this volume typically produce a wealth of numerical results. Some of the results are in quantitative terms, and they concern the level of production of final and intermediate products at each location and for each productive unit, the quantity of product imported, the quantity of product shipped from each point of supply (domestic production site or point of entry for imports), the number of ton-kilometers for each mode of transport, and the quantity of domestic raw materials and miscellaneous inputs used at each site. In addition, a variety of results are obtained in value terms, relating to operating cost, cost of domestic raw materials, import cost, and domestic transport cost. In combination with this financial information, shadow prices derived from the model's solution can be put to a number of uses, as will be explained later. Additional categories of results can be achieved using either the less restrictive versions of the model described in subsequent sections of this chapter, or, in particular, the dynamic models described in chapter 12.

Until recently, the sheer magnitude and detail of the results were a severe obstacle to the analyst. Using modern data management systems and a computer, however, the analyst can obtain the desired information in tabular form that is easily assimilated. Among other things, these systems permit the analyst to concentrate on well-defined areas of interest. That is obviously important in the case of multifaceted planning problems such as in the fertilizer sector since the sector planner, the plant manager, the agronomist, the engineer, and the farmer are all likely to be interested in different aspects of the solution.

In this presentation of the results, it is clearly impossible to cater to all of these diverse needs. But that would not appear to be necessary in any case, for what is of interest is the type of results obtained rather than the complete and detailed numerical results as they apply to Egypt. At the same time, it is impossible to avoid empirical results altogether. In what follows, only the numerical output that is needed to convey a flavor of the nature of the results obtained is presented. Greater detail is found in a document that was produced specifically for Egyptian planners and sector specialists at the World Bank, in the course of conducting the present study.[4]

Production and imports

If actual production and import levels of fertilizer products in 1975 are compared with those obtained by means of the model, there appears to be close correspondence in most cases. This is not too surprising, given the restrictive conditions under which the model was solved. Several products for which no domestic production facilities existed were consumed in 1975; obviously, to meet the demand requirements, these products needed to be imported in the appropriate quantities. Whenever domestic production facilities exist, they are used rather than imports to meet demand requirements; given that neither labor nor capital cost is taken into account in the static model, and that almost all domestic production facilities have a transport cost advantage over imports, this result is also fairly straightforward.

Nevertheless, some interesting discrepancies between the original data and the model's solution appeared. For example, in the case of

4. Armeane M. Choksi, Alexander Meeraus, and Ardy Stoutjesdijk, "A Planning Study of the Egyptian Fertilizer Sector," Staff Working Paper, no. 269 (Washington, D.C.: World Bank, July 1977).

the fertilizer plant at Aswan, it was found that the plant management's estimate of the production level in 1975 was substantially above that obtained with the model. Upon inspection, it appeared that the model's result was the logical consequence of the fertilizer demand estimate made by the Ministry of Agriculture; that is, the plant was producing exactly the amount of product the ministry claimed was used in 1975. Part of the discrepancy might possibly be explained by inventory build-up.[5] It would appear, however, that there is a basic inconsistency in the data: either demand was underestimated or production levels were overestimated. Since the estimated production level was close to design capacity, even though extensive repairs were carried out on the plant's equipment in 1975, it would seem that the major source for the discrepancy is an erroneous production estimate at Aswan.

A comparatively minor discrepancy was found in the case of the phosphatic fertilizer plant at Assiout, where again the reported production level was above that obtained with the model. At that time, the only competitor, at Abu Zaabal, was producing at full capacity, as the plant claimed. But the reported level of demand could not possibly permit both plants to be working at full capacity, unless large inventories were built up. Since Abu Zaabal had lower marginal cost of production (derived from the shadow price information in the solution) than Assiout—an advantage that was apparently not eliminated by a possible transport advantage that the latter might have had with respect to the markets—Abu Zaabal produced at full capacity in the model while Assiout did not.

Some aggregate results

To provide a basis for comparing subsequent versions of the model, described in the next few sections, some of the important overall results obtained thus far are summarized in table 22. As was explained above, neither capital cost nor labor cost is considered in the model. Moreover, in line with what actually happened in 1975, it is assumed that no interplant shipments of intermediates took place, and that road transport dominated.

5. Exports of fertilizer material were not reported to have taken place in 1975.

Table 22. *Summary of Aggregate Results of the 1975 Model*

Variable	*Numerical results*	*Percent distribution*
Demand/supply of fertilizers (thousands of tons)		
Domestic supply	805.7	46.3
Imports	936.1	53.7
Total fertilizer requirements	1,741.8	100.0
Cost categories (millions of Egyptian pounds)		
Operating cost[a]	8.1	13.8
Domestic raw materials cost[b]	3.7	6.3
Transport cost	5.9	10.0
Import cost[c]	41.1	69.9
Total cost	58.8	100.0
Transport requirements (millions of ton-kilometers)		
Waterway	19.5	5.4
Road	337.7	94.6
Total transport requirements	357.2	100.0

a. These refer to the cost of the total use of electricity (excluding Aswan), blast-furnace gas, cooling water, steam, and bags at all plants in the sector.
b. These are the costs of limestone, coal gas, electricity (at Aswan only), phosphate rock, and sulfuric acid (at Helwan only) used in the sector.
c. Imports are evaluated at the official exchange rate.

Introducing Interplant Shipments: Solution 2

According to available data, no interplant shipments of intermediate products occurred in Egypt in 1975. This section analyzes whether such interplant shipments might have been efficient in those cases where capacity constraints did not restrict them from taking place. For that purpose, the model needs to be modified in several respects.

First, a plant need not produce the intermediate products it requires; it may purchase such products from other domestic plants. This possibility can be incorporated in the material balance constraint for intermediate products as follows:

$$(11.21) \qquad \sum_{p \in P} a_{cpi}\, z_{pi} + \sum_{\substack{i' \in I \\ i' \neq i}} (x_{ci'i} - x_{cii'}) \geq 0. \qquad c \in CI \quad i \in I$$

Table 23. *Interplant Distances for Shipments of Intermediate Products*
(kilometers)

Plant location	*Kafr El Zayaat*	*Abu Zaabal*	*Helwan*	*Assiout*	*Aswan*
Kafr El Zayaat	—	85	230	479	983
Abu Zaabal	85	—	61	420	924
Helwan	230	61	—	400	900
Assiout	479	420	400	—	504
Aswan	983	924	904	504	—

— = not applicable.

The difference between this formulation of the constraint and that in (11.3) is the second term on the left-hand side, which stands for shipments of intermediate product c from all other plant locations i' to plant location i, minus the shipments of intermediate product c from plant location i to all other plant locations i'.

Second, the objective function needs to be modified so that cost considerations can be brought to bear upon the choice. Transport cost is the only component of the objective function that needs to be altered; it is now formulated as follows:

$$\phi_\lambda = \sum_{c \in CF} \left(\sum_{i \in I} \sum_{j \in J} \mu_{cij} \, x_{cij} + \sum_{j \in J} \mu_{cj} \, v_{cj} \right) + \sum_{c \in CI} \sum_{i \in I} \sum_{\substack{i' \in I \\ i' \neq i}} \mu_{cii'} \, x_{cii'} + \sum_{c \in CR} \sum_{i \in I} \mu_{ci} \, v_{ci}, \tag{11.22}$$

where the third term represents the transport cost for interplant shipments of intermediate product.

Third, this new version of the model requires a distance table with the transport distances among the relevant plant sites and a rate structure that can be assumed for interplant shipments. The interplant distances are given in table 23. It is assumed that interplant shipments take place by rail and that the applicable rate schedule (in Egyptian pounds per ton) is:

$$\text{Rail transport} = 0.5 + 0.03 \times \text{km}.$$

With these three modifications, the option of interplant shipments of intermediate products can be analyzed. The import of final products is not affected, and the sector remains equally dependent on imports from abroad for fertilizer material. The production of ammonia from coke-oven gas at Helwan, however, is sufficiently expensive to make purchase of ammonia from Aswan attractive on the transport cost assumptions. At all plants, both production and shipments of fertilizer materials remain unchanged, but relaxing the interplant shipment constraint increases ammonia production at Aswan by almost 40 percent and brings it to within 10 percent of full-capacity utilization. In terms of the total cost of meeting fertilizer demand in 1975, the cost saving associated with interplant shipments is not negligible—1.4 million Egyptian pounds for 1975 alone, or 2.4 percent of total cost for that year. Even if it is taken into account that no adequate shipment facilities for ammonia exist at Aswan, it might be worth looking into the scope for interplant shipments to Helwan in some more detail. Once the model is converted into a dynamic planning model, however, and once other sources of nitrogenous fertilizer material enter the picture, this possibility may turn out to be less attractive.

Full Capacity Utilization: Solution 3

The 1975 model incorporates a capacity constraint on all productive units in the Egyptian fertilizer industry that is close to actual production levels achieved in that year. To the extent that the objective of the static model is to reproduce what actually happened in 1975, the choice of this capacity constraint is justified. For several reasons, however, it is of interest to assume that the various productive units could have attained capacity utilization rates of 100 percent, if these were efficient. First, by comparing the total cost of meeting fertilizer requirements in 1975 at these two different levels of capacity utilization—actual and full—one can estimate the benefits that could be derived from higher levels of domestic production and compare these with the cost that would have to be incurred to remove the constraints on higher levels of capacity utilization, whether they are import restrictions on spare parts, raw materials, or the like. Second, because several plants compete for the same markets, potentially higher production levels permit some further analysis of the relative efficiency of existing plants, as measured by market penetration.

To introduce this modification, the model structure itself remains basically unchanged; only the numerical value associated with constraint (11.5), k_{mi}, changes. In overall terms, the solution with full capacity utilization costs 2 million Egyptian pounds (or 3.5 percent) less than the original solution, and 600,000 Egyptian pounds (or 1 percent) less than the solution incorporating interplant shipments to meet total fertilizer requirements in 1975. This gain, although not insignificant, is surprisingly small. Several reasons account for this. First, with a few exceptions, rates of capacity utilization in 1975 were not particularly low; only one plant (Helwan) produced below 85 percent of design capacity. Second, for several products, demand constraints prevent all plants from producing at full capacity, and, in fact, the solution of this version of the model permits the relatively efficient plants to be identified easily.[6]

Solution 3 introduces several major changes from Solution 2. In the case of phosphatic fertilizer production, only the plant at Abu Zaabal benefits from the relaxation of the capacity constraint and increases its production and sales, at the expense of both other plants producing single superphosphate. The production of sulfuric acid on the basis of imported pyrites, as opposed to elemental sulfur, is relatively expensive. Consequently, the relaxed capacity constraint shows higher capacity utilization of sulfuric acid production facilities based on elemental sulfur and sharply reduced imports of pyrites. This applies particularly to Kafr El Zayaat, where facilities for both processes are in use.

In nitrogenous fertilizer production, an interesting switch occurs. The plant at Aswan further increases its output of ammonia and, in fact, reaches full capacity utilization. The plant ships 35 percent of total output to Helwan, where it is converted to CAN 33.5 percent. The Helwan plant's shipments of CAN 33.5 percent compete directly with Aswan's own shipments of CAN 31 percent in Middle and Upper Egypt, and result in slightly lower production levels at Aswan than in previous solutions.

6. If demand constraints do not prevent all plants from producing at full capacity, one may want to introduce artificially low demand constraints to gain insight into the relative efficiency of individual plants. Shadow prices on product shipments permit the same analysis.

The Composition of Fertilizer Demand: Solution 4

Until now, the objective of the 1975 model was to find the least-cost pattern of supply to meet specific fertilizer requirements in each of the twenty demand regions, stated in terms of the quantity and types of fertilizer actually used in 1975. The choice was limited to the source of supply. Since several fertilizers are close substitutes, in the sense that they can provide the same major nutrient (or nutrients, in the case of multinutrient fertilizers), it is worth investigating whether the nutrient requirements in Egyptian agriculture are currently being met by the least-cost mix of fertilizer types.[7]

To carry out this investigation, a number of modifications need to be made. First, the set CQ, which is the set of nutrients considered in the study, must be introduced. The set contains two elements c': nitrogen and phosphorus. Second, the nutrient content of all fertilizers in the model, denoted by the coefficient $\alpha_{cc'}$, needs to be specified. With the help of this coefficient, it is possible to express shipments of fertilizer material in terms of nutrient content.

The constraint that specifies market requirements is now written as follows:

$$(11.23) \qquad \sum_{c \epsilon CF} \sum_{i \epsilon I} \alpha_{cc'} \, x_{cij} + \sum_{c \epsilon CF} \alpha_{cc'} \, v_{cj} \geq \bar{d}_{c'j}. \qquad j \epsilon J, \; c' \epsilon CQ$$

The difference between this statement and constraint (11.1) is simply that now a given quantity of nutrients needs to be supplied in each region, $\bar{d}_{c'j}$, rather than a given quantity of fertilizer material. With this modification, the model is free to select the least-cost pattern of fertilizer supply as long as the nutrient requirements are met.

Fairly sizable savings could have been achieved in 1975 if a different combination of fertilizers had been used. In fact, compared with the original solution, the objective function value falls by more than 12 percent, or 7.2 million Egyptian pounds. To identify the changes that take place exclusively as a result of the modified demand con-

7. The degree to which substitution among categories of fertilizers can occur is a point of controversy among experts. Different fertilizers may contain the same major nutrient (N, P, K) or a combination of those; usually, however, they contain widely varying amounts of other elements affecting plant growth. Moreover, there may be important variations in other properties.

straint, the present solution should be compared with Solution 2, which is identical in its specification in all other respects.

No major changes occur in the supply pattern of phosphatic fertilizer. Domestically produced single superphosphate remains competitive with the various multinutrient compounds that can be imported, given the model's price specification. If the compounds do not have to be used, they are no longer imported, with the exception of diammonium phosphate which appears competitive in the coastal demand regions with single superphosphate produced at Kafr El Zayaat. The imported quantity of DAP is small, however.

The more interesting changes occur in the case of nitrogenous fertilizers. In previous solutions, as in actual practice, a wide variety of fertilizer materials in this category are imported. If the model is free to choose the composition of fertilizer supply, the picture changes radically. With the exception of some CAN 26 percent destined for Alexandria, imports are limited to CAN 31 percent, and all other imported nitrogenous fertilizers disappear from the scene. Similarly, domestic production of CAN 31 percent increases to full capacity (at Aswan), and interplant shipments of ammonia from Aswan to Helwan virtually stop. On the basis of the solution, the Aswan plant appears to be a relatively efficient supplier of nitrogen nutrients in Upper Egypt; because of a transport cost disadvantage, however, it cannot compete in other parts of Egypt with the Helwan plant or with imports. As long as part of nitrogen demand is met by fertilizers other than CAN 31 percent, the plant runs into a market constraint. As soon as the constraint on fertilizer type is relaxed, the plant supplies all nitrogen requirements in Upper Egypt. The plant at Helwan is affected by these changes only to the extent that it can no longer purchase surplus ammonia from Aswan and has to produce its own ammonia requirements from coke-oven gas.

Summary

In table 24, a summary of the results is presented. From the statistics provided, it is clear that by far the greatest changes occur when the demand specification is modified. It would appear that efforts to increase capacity utilization in existing facilities cannot be expected to have substantial payoffs. On the other hand, the possibility of moderate interplant shipments of ammonia should be explored.

Table 24. *Summary of Results of the Static Model*
(amounts in millions of Egyptian pounds)

	Solution 1: original		*Solution 2: interplant shipments*		*Solution 3: interplant shipments and full capacity*		*Solution 4: interplant shipments and no fertilizer recommendations*	
Objective function	*Amount*	*Percent*	*Amount*	*Percent*	*Amount*	*Percent*	*Amount*	*Percent*
Transport cost	5.9	10.0	6.9	12.0	7.1	12.5	6.1	11.8
Domestic raw materials cost	3.7	6.3	2.9	5.1	3.1	5.5	4.2	8.1
Operating cost	8.1	13.8	6.5	11.3	6.7	11.8	9.2	17.8
Import cost	41.1	69.9	41.1	71.4	39.8	70.1	32.1	62.2
Total value of objective function	58.8	100.0	57.4	100.0	56.8	100.0	51.6	100.0

Note: Components may not add to totals because of rounding.

12

A Medium-Term Planning Model of the Egyptian Fertilizer Sector

DYNAMIC SECTORWIDE PLANNING MODELS are used in this chapter to analyze possible development strategies for the fertilizer sector in Egypt. For that purpose, the model used in the previous chapter is modified, so that the time dimension is incorporated into the structure of the model, so that investment activities (and concomitant labor hiring) can be undertaken in the sector, and so that the scope for exports can be analyzed. To describe the mathematical structure of this dynamic model, the procedure adopted in chapter 11 is repeated: that is, each set of constraints is explained in detail, and the data input required with the new formulation is indicated. Following this description, the dynamic model is presented in summary form. A computer-readable description of all the sets and all the numerical data used in the dynamic model is given in an appendix to the case study.

The Structure of the Dynamic Model

In many respects, the structure of the dynamic model is similar to that of the static 1975 model. Several of the constraints differ only in the sense that a time subscript is added to variables and parameters.

The demand for fertilizers

The fertilizer demand constraint in the static model evolved from a formulation in which final demand was specified in terms of fertilizer product types with no choice allowed among fertilizer types supplying the same nutrient to one in which final demand in each region was specified in nutrients, so that the model could be used to find the least-cost combination of fertilizers to make up required supply levels. The former formulation of the demand constraints was given in (11.1); the latter, in (11.25).

For the dynamic model, basically the same formulation is used:

$$\sum_{c \epsilon CF} \sum_{i \epsilon I} \alpha_{cc'} x_{cijt} + \sum_{c \epsilon CF} \alpha_{cc'} v_{cjt} \geq \bar{d}_{c'jt}, \qquad c' \epsilon CQ,\; j \epsilon J,\; t \epsilon T \tag{12.1}$$

where the notation has the same meaning as in chapter 11, with the addition of the subscript t referring to the time period. Thus:

$\alpha_{cc'}$ = the percentage of nutrient c' in fertilizer c;
x_{cijt} = the shipment of fertilizer material c from domestic plant site i to marketing center j during time period t;
v_{cjt} = the shipment of imported fertilizer material c to marketing center j during time period t;
$\bar{d}_{c'jt}$ = the required supply of nutrient c' in marketing center j during time period t.

The sets are:

CF = set of fertilizers,
I = set of plant sites,
J = set of governorates,
CQ = set of nutrients,
T = set of time periods.

The set of fertilizers in the dynamic model is larger than that in the 1975 model, so that additional production possibilities can be analyzed. The set now includes the following products (asterisks denote additions to the set as specified for the static model):

$c \epsilon CF$ = Urea
Calcium nitrate*
Calcium ammonium nitrate: 31 percent

Calcium ammonium nitrate: 33.5 percent
Ammonium sulfate
Monoammonium phosphate*
Diammonium phosphate
Single superphosphate
Powdered triple superphosphate*
Granular triple superphosphate*
Nitrophosphate*

The set of plant sites I has been expanded to include the following:

$i \epsilon I$ = Aswan
Helwan
Kafr El Zayaat
Assiout
Suez*
Talkha*
Abu Kir*
Abu Zaabal

Both the set of governorates J and the set of nutrients CQ remain unchanged. The added set of time periods T contains the following elements:

$t \epsilon T$ = 1 = 1979–81
2 = 1982–84
3 = 1985–87.

In addition to (12.1), the dynamic model includes a set of constraints that limit the freedom of choice in the model regarding the type of fertilizers that can meet fertilizer demand, which is expressed in terms of nutrients. In the case of Egypt, this restriction is necessary particularly for urea, the use of which is projected to grow only gradually. This set of constraints has the following form:

$$(12.2) \qquad \sum_{i \epsilon I} \alpha_{cc'} \, x_{cijt} + \alpha_{cc'} \, v_{cjt} \leq \eta_t \, d_{c'jt}, \qquad \begin{array}{l} c = \text{urea} \\ c' = \text{nitrogen} \\ t \epsilon T \\ j \epsilon J \end{array}$$

where

η_t = percentage of nitrogen demand that can be met by the use of urea.

The assumptions regarding demand growth in terms of nutrients were decided upon in close consultation with Egyptian sector specialists—particularly, staff of the Ministry of Agriculture. Demand for nitrogen is expected to grow at an annual rate of 4.6 percent, whereas demand for phosphorus may grow as much as 10.4 percent a year. Representatives of the nitrogenous fertilizer industry disagreed with the projection of nitrogen consumption made by the Ministry of Agriculture, and it was difficult to reconcile that disagreement. In the sensitivity analysis presented later in this chapter, the model has been used to evaluate the implications of a higher growth rate for nitrogen nutrients.

A similar disagreement arose regarding the likely speed of adoption of urea by Egyptian farmers. With two sizable ammonia/urea complexes under construction, it is evident that the industry believes that farmers will switch rapidly from the traditional, low-analysis fertilizers such as calcium ammonium nitrate to the more efficient urea. Experts of the Ministry of Agriculture, however, believe this will not occur rapidly. If constraint set (12.2) is used, explicit restrictions on the use of urea can be incorporated in the model. A compromise between these two positions was reached by postulating the following pattern. During the first time period, 1979–81, no more than 60 percent of all nitrogen requirements should be met by urea. In the period 1982–84, this proportion is increased to 75 percent; in the period 1985–87, 85 percent of nitrogen is supplied by urea. To measure the cost of this possibly less-than-optimal policy, these restrictions are deleted in the sensitivity analysis.

The supply of fertilizers

On the supply side, several modifications have to be made to the 1975 model. As was indicated above, the set of fertilizers to be considered is expanded to include products not produced or imported in 1975. This permits an assessment of whether the product mix currently in use or being produced in Egypt can be improved upon. In particular, the feasibility of the following processes can be investigated: producing fertilizers such as monoammonium phosphate or diammonium phosphate (both high-analysis compounds with rapidly growing international markets) for domestic use as well as exports; converting the existing single superphosphate facilities at Abu Zaabal to one that produces powdered or granular triple superphosphate; and, finally, producing nitrophosphates at Suez—a suggestion made by sector specialists at the World Bank.

Since projects are under construction at Abu Kir and Talkha, and since the Suez site is being considered for another project, the set of plant sites I was similarly expanded. Moreover, to permit exports, the activity e was introduced; so also was the set L, in which each element l represents a port of exit (either Alexandria or Suez).

The material balance constraints now have the following form.

MATERIAL BALANCE CONSTRAINTS ON FINAL PRODUCTS

$$(12.3) \qquad \sum_{p \epsilon P} a_{cpit}\, z_{pit} \geq \sum_{j \epsilon J} x_{cijt} + \sum_{l \epsilon L} e_{cilt} \qquad \begin{matrix} c \epsilon CF \\ i \epsilon I \\ t \epsilon T \end{matrix}$$

The difference between this constraint and the corresponding one in the static model is twofold. First, the subscript t has been added to render activity levels period-specific. Second, the possibility of exports has been incorporated. Thus, the constraint now specifies that the production of fertilizer type c by all processes p at plant site i during time period t should at least equal shipments of fertilizer product c from plant site i to all domestic markets j in time period t, augmented by all exports of that fertilizer type from that plant site in that period.[1]

MATERIAL BALANCE CONSTRAINTS ON INTERMEDIATE PRODUCTS

$$(12.4) \qquad \sum_{p \epsilon P} a_{cpit}\, z_{pit} + \sum_{\substack{i' \epsilon I \\ i' \neq i}} x_{ci'it} + v_{cit} \geq \sum_{\substack{i' \epsilon I \\ i' \neq i}} x_{cii't} + \sum_{l \epsilon L} e_{cilt} \qquad \begin{matrix} c \epsilon CI \\ i \epsilon I \\ t \epsilon T \end{matrix}$$

This constraint states that the production of intermediate product c at plant site i in time period t by all processes p, augmented by shipments from other plants i' and imports, should at least equal shipments of intermediate product c to other plant sites and exports. Compared with the corresponding constraint in the static model, this constraint permits products to be imported, exported, and shipped between plants.

MATERIAL BALANCE CONSTRAINTS ON RAW MATERIALS AND MISCELLANEOUS INPUTS

$$(12.5) \qquad \sum_{p \epsilon P} a_{cpit}\, z_{pit} + u_{cit} + v_{cit} \geq 0 \qquad \begin{matrix} c \epsilon CR \\ i \epsilon I \\ t \epsilon T \end{matrix}$$

1. The export possibility is constrained; the procedure used is described below.

This constraint is simply a restatement of constraint (11.4) in the static model, with the addition of the time subscript t.

MATERIAL BALANCE CONSTRAINTS ON LABOR

For all practical purposes, the labor force associated with fertilizer plants represents a fixed cost to the plant, much the same as equipment cost. There can be no short-term adjustments in the labor force in response to production changes. In the static model, therefore, labor cost did not need to be incorporated. In the dynamic model, in which it is assumed that similar treatment of labor will be imposed upon plants, labor costs should be modeled in the same way as investment cost, in the sense that the labor force is fixed with capacity installed. Thus, the material balance constraint for labor has the following form:

$$(12.6) \qquad u_{cit} - \sum_{\substack{\tau \in T \\ \tau \leq t}} \sum_{m \in M} (\omega_{ci\tau}\, y_{mi\tau} + \nu_{ci\tau}\, h_{mi\tau}) \geq 0. \qquad \begin{matrix} c \in CO \\ i \in I \\ t \in T \end{matrix}$$

In this constraint, the first expression has the familiar meaning of domestic outlays for labor cost, and the second expression indicates how labor costs are generated. The term $y_{mi\tau}$ is a variable that can assume the values 0 or 1 only; if a plant of any size is constructed, it must assume the value 1. (The section below on capacity expansion explains how this is done.) The term $h_{mi\tau}$ denotes the size of the capacity. The coefficients $\omega_{ci\tau}$ and $\nu_{ci\tau}$ are, respectively, a fixed and a variable charge for labor costs. The cost function for labor is estimated on the basis of available information from existing plants; from this it appears that the following function approximates actual labor costs fairly well:

$$LC = 180{,}000\, n + 0.45\, h,$$

where

LC = the total labor cost for the complex in Egyptian pounds per year;

n = an integer variable denoting the number of productive units on the complex;

h = the capacity expansion variable in tons per year of total product (that is, final and intermediate product).

The cost function is therefore made up of both a fixed charge, ω, and a variable cost, ν. The fixed charge is 180,000 Egyptian pounds a year, which is the amount required if a decision is made to build a productive unit. This includes the cost of supervision, administrative personnel, and overhead charges; it gives rise to economies of scale in labor. The variable cost is 0.45 Egyptian pounds a year per ton of capacity of total product. Labor costs are a function of capacity installed rather than size of the investment.

CAPACITY CONSTRAINTS

$$(12.7)\quad \sum_{p \in P} b_{mpit}\, z_{pit} \le k_{mi} + \sum_{\substack{\tau \in T \\ \tau \le t}} \Big[h_{mi\tau} + \sum_{g \in G} (f_{mgi} U_{gi\tau}) \Big] \qquad \begin{array}{r} i \in I \\ m \in M \\ t \in T \end{array}$$

The capacity constraint expresses the condition that the number of capacity units used on productive unit m per unit of output of process p at plant site i in time period t cannot exceed the available capacity. Since the dynamic model explicitly permits the expansion of capacity at any of the sites in the set I, however, it is necessary to take this possibility into account in the capacity constraint. Accordingly, the term $\sum_{\substack{\tau \in T \\ \tau \le t}} h_{mi\tau}$ denotes the amount of capacity constructed at plant site i, in terms of productive unit m, since the beginning of the planning period.

Often, it is possible to specify in advance which investment possibilities need to be considered. If all investment alternatives were incorporated, the number of possibilities that would have to be investigated would be no less than $M \times I \times T$: that is, $16 \times 8 \times 3 = 384$, or a total of 2^{384} project combinations—an astronomically large number. Closer consideration of the set M, however, makes clear at once that the number of alternatives can be reduced considerably by using common sense and knowledge of the local area. The set M contains the following elements:

1. Sulfuric acid: sulfur
2. Sulfuric acid: pyrites
3. Nitric acid
4. Ammonia: water electrolysis
5. Ammonia: coke-oven gas
6. Ammonia: natural gas
7. Ammonia: refinery gas
8. Phosphoric acid
9. Calcium ammonium nitrate
10. Calcium nitrate
11. Ammonium sulfate
12. Urea
13. Ammonium phosphates
14. Single superphosphates
15. Triple superphosphates
16. Nitrophosphates

This list of productive units is dominated by existing plants in the Egyptian fertilizer industry rather than by units that should be considered in light of present-day technology, raw materials available in Egypt, and projected world market prices. In fact, for all practical purposes, elements 2, 4, 5, 7, and 9–11 in the list can be disregarded for new capacity construction at all sites and for all time periods. Construction of ammonia and urea capacity needs to be considered only at Abu Kir and Suez. Finally, construction of nitrophosphate capacity needs to be considered only at Suez. As a result of these judgments, the number of project possibilities can be reduced from 384 to 25 per time period, or a total of 75.

The specific situation in Egypt required that constraint (12.7) incorporate another possibility—that is, the possibility of upgrading existing capacity. For example, the plant at Helwan produces ammonia using a technologically outdated process: coke-oven gas conversion. It is thus of interest to investigate the desirability of upgrading to a natural gas process. Since only part of the unit would need to be replaced, and since it would be of fixed capacity, its capital cost can be estimated in advance—US $20 million.

This conversion possibility is referred to in the third term in the capacity constraint:

$$\sum_{\substack{\tau \in T \\ \tau \leq t}} \sum_{g \in G} (f_{mgi} U_{gi\tau}),$$

where f_{mgi} is the conversion variable, and $U_{gi\tau}$ is a variable that can assume two possible values: 1 if conversion takes place, and 0 if it does not. Because a positive cost is associated with the f variable (to be described below in the treatment of the objective function), U will be forced to assume the value 0 unless the upgrading proves to be advantageous.

Constraint (12.7) requires four additional sets of constraints.

MAXIMUM CAPACITY EXPANSION CONSTRAINTS

$$h_{mit} \leq \bar{h}_{mit}\, y_{mit} \qquad i \in I,\; m \in M,\; t \in T \tag{12.8}$$

MUTUAL EXCLUSIVITY CONSTRAINTS

$$\sum_{t \in T} U_{git} \leq 1 \qquad g \in G,\; i \in I \tag{12.9}$$

INTEGRALITY CONSTRAINTS

(12.10) $$y_{mit} = 0 \text{ or } 1 \qquad i \in I,\ m \in M,\ t \in T$$

(12.11) $$U_{git} = 0 \text{ or } 1 \qquad g \in G,\ i \in I,\ t \in T$$

The maximum capacity constraint (12.8) plays a dual role. First, it states the obvious condition that no capacity can be installed beyond what is technically feasible for a productive unit at a given site. Second, it forces the 0–1 variable y to assume the value 1 in order to enable capacity construction. This is important because, as will be shown shortly, the y variable is associated with the fixed-cost portion of investment cost in the objective function.

The mutual exclusivity constraint (12.9) simply states that capacity conversion can take place only once during the planning period.

Finally, the integrality constraints (12.10) and (12.11) are self-evident.

The treatment of exports

The dynamic model has been formulated using two sets of export constraints. The first one has the following form.

EXPORT CONSTRAINTS BY COMMODITY AND PLANT SITE

(12.12) $$\sum_{l \in L} e_{cilt} \leq \sum_{l \in L} \bar{e}_{cilt} \qquad c \in CF,\ i \in I,\ t \in T$$

This constraint simply states that exports of any particular fertilizer from a given plant site in each time period are limited to an exogenously specified amount. Initially, this limit has been placed at 25,000 tons of product annually. Since many products are produced, or can be produced, at many different sites, this restriction alone would not prevent the model from coming up with an unrealistically high level of total exports. Therefore, constraint set (12.12) has been complemented with a constraint set that limits the total volume of exports to a level far below the sum of the constraints on individual products and sites.

AGGREGATE EXPORT CONSTRAINT

$$\sum_{c \in CF} \sum_{i \in I} \sum_{l \in L} \bar{e}_{cilt} \leq \hat{e}_t \qquad t \in T \tag{12.13}$$

In the base case, the value of $\hat{e}_t$ has arbitrarily been placed at 100,000 tons of material. In addition to limiting the total volume of exports in each time period, (12.13) has another function. By imposing a limit on total exports that is below the sum of the limits imposed on the export of each fertilizer from each production site, the constraint forces the model to select the fertilizer type and production site that is the most efficient for export. If no exports are efficient, (12.13) is redundant.

Nonnegativity constraints on activity levels

The specification of the dynamic model—like that of the 1975 model—includes nonnegativity constraints on all activity levels.

NONNEGATIVITY CONSTRAINTS

$$z_{pit}, x_{cijt}, x_{cii't}, v_{cit}, v_{cjt}, e_{cilt}, u_{cit} \geq 0 \qquad \begin{matrix} c \in C \\ i, i' \in I \\ j \in J \\ l \in L \\ m \in M \\ p \in P \\ t \in T \end{matrix} \tag{12.14}$$

The objective function

The objective function of the dynamic model is formulated in terms similar to those of the static model—that is, as a cost-minimizing function. Since both investment and upgrading activities, as well as exports can be considered in the dynamic model, the formulation of the objective function needs to be expanded. In addition, the time factor needs to be taken into account. Finally, the impact of working capital on total cost needs to be considered.

In summary form, the objective function of the dynamic model is specified as follows:

(12.15)

$$\min \xi = \sum_{t \epsilon T} \delta_t \, (\phi_{\kappa t} + \phi_{\psi t} + \phi_{\lambda t} + \phi_{\mu t} + \phi_{\pi t} - \phi_{\epsilon t}),$$

[*Total discounted cost*] = [*Discount factor*] [*Total capital cost during time period t*] + [*Total domestic recurrent cost during time period t*] + [*Total transport cost during time period t*] + [*Total working capital cost during time period t*] + [*Total import cost during time period t*] − [*Total export revenue during time period t*]

where

(12.16)

$$\delta_t = \sum_{\tau=1}^{\theta} (1 + \rho)^{-\theta(t-1)-\tau}.$$

[*Discount rate*]

A full derivation of the discount rate is given in chapter 8. In this particular application of the model, there are three time periods—namely, 1979–81, 1982–84, and 1985–87. The real discount rate ρ used in the model is 10 percent.

Each of the components of the objective function can now be specified in detail.

CAPITAL COST CHARGES

(12.17)

$$\phi_{\kappa t} = \sum_{\substack{\tau \epsilon T \\ \tau \leq t}}^{t} \Big[\sum_{i \epsilon I} \sum_{m \epsilon M} \sigma_m \, (\omega_{mi\tau} \, y_{mi\tau} + \nu_{mi\tau} \, h_{mi\tau}) + \sum_{i \epsilon I} \sum_{g \epsilon G} \sigma_g \, \omega_{gi\tau} \, U_{gi\tau} \Big],$$

where

(12.18)

$$\sigma_m = \frac{\rho(1 + \rho)^{\zeta_m}}{(1 + \rho)^{\zeta_m} - 1}.$$

[*Capital recovery factor*]

Table 25. *The Investment Cost Functions for the Dynamic Model*

Productive unit	*Fixed charge: ω (millions of U.S. dollars)*	*Variable charge: ν (thousands of U.S. dollars a ton per year)*
Urea	16.7	52.2
Ammonium phosphate	4.5	32.4
Single superphosphate	7.5	25.5
Triple superphosphate	7.0	34.2
Sulfuric acid: elemental sulfur	8.5	33.0
Ammonia: natural gas	47.9	103.8
Phosphoric acid	10.0	57.0
Nitrophosphates	8.0	70.0

The derivation of the capital recovery factor σ_m is also given in chapter 8. With ρ equal to 10 percent, and with the useful life of capacity, ζ_m, placed at an average of fifteen years, the capital recovery factor is equal to 0.1315.

The term $(\omega_{mi\tau}\, y_{mi\tau} + \nu_{mi\tau}\, h_{mi\tau})$ was likewise explained in chapter 8. To recapitulate briefly, ω_{mit} is the fixed element in the linear approximation of the investment cost function; since it is a constant in the objective function, it needs to be eliminated if no capacity is constructed. To that end, it is linked to $y_{mi\tau}$, which is a variable that can assume only the values 0 or 1, where the former is chosen if no capacity is constructed. The variable $h_{mi\tau}$ denotes the capacity scale that is constructed, whereas the coefficient ν_{mit} is the variable portion of the investment cost function. Table 25 gives the value for $\omega_{mi\tau}$ and $\nu_{mi\tau}$ for the productive units that are relevant to the dynamic model.

The investment (or capital) costs used in this study are based on Tennessee Valley Authority estimates for different plant sizes and are given in constant 1975 U.S. dollars. They include U.S. battery limits, auxiliary and support facilities, spare parts, training, start-up, fifteen-day storage for ammonia and phosphoric acid, twenty-day bag storage, and power and steam generation. In addition, the cost of site preparation and off-site facilities needs to be incorporated. This is done by using a site factor of 1.3 for all plant sites in Egypt. This factor is applied to the total capital cost.

The term $\left(\sum_{i\epsilon I} \sum_{g\epsilon G} \sigma_g\, \omega_{gi\tau}\, U_{gi\tau}\right)$ refers to the cost of the upgrading activity—that is, the cost of converting the ammonia unit based on coke-oven gas to one that uses natural gas as a feedstock. The estimated cost of this conversion is US$20 million, which is the value of $\omega_{gi\tau}$, while σ_g is the capital recovery factor and $U_{gi\tau}$ is the 0–1 variable.

DOMESTIC RECURRENT COST

$$\phi_{\psi t} = \sum_{c \in CR \cup CO} \sum_{i \in I} p^d_{cit} u_{cit} \tag{12.19}$$

With the exception of the addition of labor cost (labor requirements for new plants are included in the set CO), the treatment of domestic recurrent cost in the objective function of the dynamic model is similar to that in the static model. Prices similar to those in tables 17 and 18 have been used for miscellaneous inputs and raw materials; it is assumed that these prices will remain constant in real terms during the planning period. In the dynamic model, however, the number of raw materials is larger, and they are available at more sites. Table 26 gives the prices that have been assumed at the various relevant sites.

TRANSPORT COST

$$\begin{aligned} \phi_{\lambda t} = & \sum_{c \in CF} \Big(\sum_{i \in I} \sum_{j \in J} \mu_{cijt} x_{cijt} \\ & + \sum_{j \in J} \mu_{cjt} v_{cjt} + \sum_{i \in I} \sum_{l \in L} \mu_{cilt} e_{cilt} \Big) \\ & + \sum_{c \in CI} \Big(\sum_{i \in I} \sum_{\substack{i' \in I \\ i' \neq i}} \mu_{cii't} x_{cii't} \Big) \\ & + \sum_{c \in CR} \Big(\sum_{i \in I} \mu_{cit} v_{cit} \Big) \end{aligned} \tag{12.20}$$

Apart from the addition of the subscript t, the expression for transport cost in the dynamic model differs from that in the static model only in the sense that the dynamic model includes transport cost for exported fertilizers:

$$\sum_{i \in I} \sum_{l \in L} \mu_{cilt} e_{cilt}.$$

Moreover, as more plant sites and products are considered in the dynamic model, the amount of cost information is increased as well. It has been assumed, however, that transport cost rates remain constant in real terms. The complete information on road, rail, and

Table 26. *Prices of Raw Materials Used in the Dynamic Model by Plant Location*
(Egyptian pounds)

Plant location	*Electricity (per megawatt hour)*	*Coke-oven gas (per cubic meter)*	*Natural gas (per cubic foot)*	*Refinery gas (per cubic meter)*	*Phosphate rock (per ton)*	*Limestone (per ton)*
Talkha	—	—	0.56	—	—	1.2
Helwan	—	16.0	0.60	—	—	1.2
Suez	—	—	0.65	8.0	6.0	1.2
Aswan	1.0	—	—	—	—	1.2
Assiout	—	—	—	—	3.5	—
Kafr El Zayaat	—	—	—	—	5.0	—
Abu Zaabal	—	—	—	—	4.0	—
Abu Kir	—	—	0.56	—	—	—

— = not applicable.
Source: Institute of National Planning, Ministry of Planning.

Table 27. *Road Distances from Plants to Marketing Centers*
(kilometers)

Marketing center	*Abu Kir*	*Kafr El Zayaat*	*Talkha*	*Abu Zaabal*	*Hel-wan*	*Suez*	*Assi-out*	*Aswan*
Alexandria	16	119	187	210	244	362	607	1,135
Behera	76	42	120	50	184	288	547	1,065
Gharbia	150	20	55	65	122	226	485	1,003
Kafr El Sheikh	145	20	35	105	162	266	525	1,043
Dakahlia	208	58	3	138	152	219	515	1,033
Damietta	267	131	66	216	233	286	596	1,114
Sharkia	240	78	58	60	110	214	473	991
Ismailia	365	241	146	142	173	88	536	1,054
Suez	370	246	298	224	178	—	541	1,059
Menoufia	157	33	90	154	109	213	472	990
Kalubia	190	66	81	97	76	180	439	957
Giza	287	133	146	48	9	169	372	890
Beni Suef	359	248	261	163	105	270	257	775
Fayoum	341	230	243	145	88	252	308	826
Minia	384	372	386	288	230	394	132	650
Assiout	616	504	518	420	362	527	—	518
New Valley	815	703	717	619	561	726	199	519
Sohag	715	603	617	519	461	626	99	419
Quena	858	746	760	662	604	769	242	276
Aswan	1,134	1,022	1,036	938	880	1,045	518	—

— = not applicable.
Source: General Organization for Industrialization.

waterway distances used in the dynamic model is given in tables 27, 28, and 29.

WORKING CAPITAL

$$(12.21) \qquad \phi_{\mu t} = 0.025 \left(\phi_{\psi t} + \sum_{c \epsilon CR} \sum_{i \epsilon I} p^{v}_{cit} \, v_{cit}\right)$$

This amounts to the three months' value of recurrent cost and the cost of domestic and imported raw materials charged to the plant at an annual rate of 10 percent.

IMPORT COST

$$(12.22) \qquad \phi_{\pi t} = \sum_{c \epsilon CF} \sum_{j \epsilon J} p^{v}_{cjt} \, v_{cjt} + \sum_{c \epsilon CR} \sum_{i \epsilon I} p^{v}_{cit} \, v_{cit}$$

Table 28. *Rail Distances between Plants*
(kilometers)

Plant location	*Abu Kir*	*Kafr El Zayaat*	*Talkha*	*Abu Zaabal*	*Hel-wan*	*Suez*	*Assi-out*	*Aswan*
Abu Kir	—	113	191	218	252	365	599	1,103
Kafr El Zayaat	113	—	36	85	230	245	479	983
Talkha	191	36	—	139	168	298	517	1,021
Abu Zaabal	218	85	139	—	61	224	420	924
Helwan	252	230	168	61	—	166	400	904
Suez	365	245	298	224	166	—	516	1,020
Assiout	599	479	517	420	400	516	—	504
Aswan	1,103	983	1,021	924	904	1,020	504	—

— = not applicable.
Source: General Organization for Industrialization.

Table 29. *Import and Export Distances from Alexandria or Suez to Plant Locations*
(kilometers)

Plant location	*Distance by waterway*	*Distance by road*	*Total*
Abu Kir	16	6	22
Kafr El Zayaat	104	0.1	104.1
Talkha	199	—	199
Abu Zaabal	210	—	210
Helwan	183	—	183
Suez	—	10	10
Assiout	583	—	583
Aswan	1,087	10	1,097

— = not applicable.
Source: General Organization for Industrialization.

EXPORT REVENUE

(12.23) $$\phi_{\epsilon t} = \sum_{c \epsilon CF} \sum_{i \epsilon I} \sum_{l \epsilon L} p^{e}_{cilt}\, e_{cilt}$$

Since export of all final products is permitted in the dynamic model, the revenue that can thereby be generated should be taken into account in the objective function. To allow for transport and insurance cost, attainable export prices are assumed to be 70 percent of c.i.f. import cost, at Alexandria or Suez. The assumed export prices are given in table 30.

Table 30. *Attainable Export Prices for the Dynamic Model*
(1975 U.S. dollars)

Product	*Export price f.o.b. ex factory*
Urea	105
Calcium ammonium nitrate: 31 percent	77
Calcium ammonium nitrate: 33.5 percent	84
Ammonium sulfate	52.5
Monoammonium phosphate	154
Diammonium phosphate	147
Single superphosphate	56
Triple superphosphate: granular	105
Triple superphosphate: powdered	80.5
Nitrophosphates	105

Note: Attainable export prices f.o.b. (free on board) from the plant in Egypt are assumed to be equal to 70 percent of c.i.f. import prices for corresponding products.

The Mathematical Formulation of the Dynamic Model

A summary statement of the dynamic model used for the Egyptian fertilizer sector is given in this section. First, the symbols are categorized and defined.[2]

Symbol *Definition*

SETS AND INDEXES

$i \epsilon I$ Plant locations

Aswan
Helwan
Kafr El Zayaat
Assiout

Suez*
Talkha*
Abu Kir*
Abu Zaabal

2. An asterisk denotes items not included in the static model described in chapter 11.

Symbol *Definition*

SETS AND INDEXES (Continued)

$j \epsilon J$ Demand regions

Alexandria
Behera
Gharbia
Kafr El Sheikh
Dakahlia

Damietta
Sharkia
Ismailia
Suez
Menoufia

Kalubia
Giza
Beni Suef
Fayoum
Minia

Assiout
New Valley
Sohag
Quena
Aswan

$l \epsilon L$ Export ports of exit*

Alexandria*
Suez*

$m \epsilon M$ Productive units

Sulfuric acid: sulfur
Sulfuric acid: pyrites
Nitric acid
Ammonia: water electrolysis
Ammonia: coke-oven gas

Ammonia: natural gas*
Ammonia: refinery gas*
Phosphoric acid*
Calcium ammonium nitrate
Ammonium sulfate

Urea*
Ammonium phosphate*
Single superphosphate
Triple superphosphate*
Nitrophosphate*

Symbol	*Definition*
SETS AND INDEXES (Continued)	
$p \epsilon P$	Processes
	Sulfuric acid: sulfur
	Sulfuric acid: pyrites
	Nitric acid
	Ammonia: water electrolysis
	Ammonia: coke-oven gas
	Ammonia: natural gas*
	Ammonia: refinery gas*
	Phosphoric acid*
	Calcium ammonium nitrate: 31 percent
	Calcium ammonium nitrate: 33.5 percent
	Ammonium sulfate
	Urea*
	Diammonium phosphate*
	Monoammonium phosphate*
	Single superphosphate
	Powdered triple superphosphate*
	Granular triple superphosphate*
	Nitrophosphate*
$g \epsilon G$	Upgrading (conversion) activity
	Ammonia: coke-oven gas*
$c' \epsilon CQ$	Nutrients
	Nitrogen
	Phosphorus
$c \epsilon CF$	Final products (fertilizers)
	Urea
	Calcium nitrate*
	Calcium ammonium nitrate: 31 percent
	Calcium ammonium nitrate: 33.5 percent
	Ammonium sulfate
	Monoammonium phosphate*
	Diammonium phosphate
	Single superphosphate
	Powdered triple superphosphate*
	Granular triple superphosphate*
	Nitrophosphate*
$c \epsilon CI$	Intermediate products
	Ammonia
	Nitric acid
	Sulfuric acid
	Phosphoric acid*

Symbol	*Definition*
SETS AND INDEXES (Continued)	
$c \epsilon CR$	Domestic raw materials and miscellaneous inputs
	Electricity
	Coke-oven gas
	Natural gas*
	Refinery gas*
	Phosphate rock
	Limestone
	Elemental sulfur
	Pyrites
	Blast-furnace gas
	Cooling water
	Steam
	Bags
$c \epsilon CO$	Labor skill class
	Total labor
$t \epsilon T$	Time periods
	1 = 1979–81
	2 = 1982–84
	3 = 1985–87
THE VARIABLES	
z	Process level (production level)
x	Domestic shipment activity
v	Imports
e	Exports*
u	Domestic raw material purchases
h	Capacity expansion*
U, y	Binary variable (0–1)*
ξ	Total cost (discounted)
ϕ_k	Capital cost*
ϕ_ψ	Domestic recurrent cost
ϕ_λ	Transport cost
ϕ_μ	Working capital cost*
ϕ_π	Import cost
ϕ_ϵ	Export revenue*
THE PARAMETERS	
a	Input (−) or output (+) coefficient
b	Capacity utilization coefficient
$e, \hat{e}, \bar{e}$	Maximum exports*
f	Capacity conversion (retirement/addition)*
$\bar{h}$	Maximum capacity expansion*

Symbol	*Definition*
THE PARAMETERS (Continued)	
k	Initial capacity
λ	Export market growth rate*
p^d	Domestic price
p^v	Import price (c.i.f.)
p^e	Export price (f.o.b.)*
d	Demand or market requirement
ζ_m	Life of productive unit*
δ	Discount factor*
μ	Transport cost
ρ	Opportunity cost of capital*
σ	Capital recovery factor*
θ	Gestation lag*
α	Nutrient content
η	Urea consumption restriction*
ν	Variable portion of investment or labor cost*
ω	Fixed-charge portion of investment or labor cost*

Second, the constraints of the dynamic model are specified.

MATERIAL BALANCE CONSTRAINTS ON DEMAND

$$\sum_{c \in CF} \sum_{i \in I} \alpha_{cc'} x_{cijt} + \sum_{c \in CF} \alpha_{cc'} v_{cjt} \geq d_{c'jt} \qquad c' \in CQ,\ j \in J,\ t \in T \tag{12.24}$$

MATERIAL BALANCE CONSTRAINTS ON UREA CONSUMPTION[3]

$$\sum_{i \in I} \alpha_{cc'} x_{cijt} + \alpha_{cc'} v_{cjt} \leq \eta_t d_{c'jt} \qquad c = \text{urea},\ c' = \text{nitrogen},\ j \in J,\ t \in T \tag{12.25}$$

MATERIAL BALANCE CONSTRAINTS ON FINAL PRODUCTS

$$\sum_{p \in \Gamma} a_{cpit} z_{pit} \geq \sum_{j \in J} x_{cijt} + \sum_{l \in L} e_{cilt} \qquad c \in CF,\ i \in I,\ t \in T \tag{12.26}$$

3. In chapter 13, seven scenarios or different project planning strategies are analyzed. This constraint is not included in scenario VII.

MATERIAL BALANCE CONSTRAINTS ON INTERMEDIATE PRODUCTS

(12.27)

$$\sum_{p\epsilon P} a_{cpit}\, z_{pit} + \sum_{\substack{i'\epsilon I \\ i'\neq i}} x_{ci'it} + v_{cit} \geq \sum_{\substack{i'\epsilon I \\ i'\neq i}} x_{cii't} + \sum_{l\epsilon L} e_{cilt} \qquad \begin{matrix} c \,\epsilon\, CI \\ i \,\epsilon\, I \\ t \,\epsilon\, T \end{matrix}$$

MATERIAL BALANCE CONSTRAINTS ON RAW MATERIALS AND MISCELLANEOUS INPUTS

(12.28)

$$\sum_{p\epsilon P} a_{cpit}\, z_{pit} + u_{cit} + v_{cit} \geq 0 \qquad \begin{matrix} c \,\epsilon\, CR \\ i \,\epsilon\, I \\ t \,\epsilon\, T \end{matrix}$$

MATERIAL BALANCE CONSTRAINTS ON LABOR

(12.29)

$$u_{cit} - \sum_{\substack{\tau\epsilon T \\ \tau\leq t}} \sum_{m\epsilon M} (\omega_{ci\tau}\, y_{mi\tau} + \nu_{ci\tau}\, h_{mi\tau}) \geq 0 \qquad \begin{matrix} c \,\epsilon\, CO \\ i \,\epsilon\, I \\ t \,\epsilon\, T \end{matrix}$$

CAPACITY CONSTRAINTS

(12.30)

$$\sum_{p\epsilon P} b_{mpit}\, z_{pit} \leq k_{mi} + \sum_{\substack{\tau\epsilon T \\ \tau\leq t}} \left[h_{mi\tau} + \sum_{g\epsilon G} (f_{mgi} U_{gi\tau}) \right] \qquad \begin{matrix} i \,\epsilon\, I \\ m \,\epsilon\, M \\ t \,\epsilon\, T \end{matrix}$$

MAXIMUM CAPACITY EXPANSION CONSTRAINTS

(12.31)

$$h_{mit} \leq \bar{h}_{mit}\, y_{mit} \qquad \begin{matrix} i \,\epsilon\, I \\ m \,\epsilon\, M \\ t \,\epsilon\, T \end{matrix}$$

MUTUAL EXCLUSIVITY CONSTRAINTS

(12.32)

$$\sum_{t\epsilon T} U_{git} \leq 1 \qquad \begin{matrix} g \,\epsilon\, G \\ i \,\epsilon\, I \end{matrix}$$

INTEGRALITY CONSTRAINTS

(12.33)

$$y_{mit} = 0 \quad \text{or} \quad 1 \qquad \begin{matrix} i \,\epsilon\, I \\ m \,\epsilon\, M \\ t \,\epsilon\, T \end{matrix}$$

(12.34)

$$U_{git} = 0 \quad \text{or} \quad 1 \qquad \begin{matrix} g \,\epsilon\, G \\ i \,\epsilon\, I \\ t \,\epsilon\, T \end{matrix}$$

EXPORT CONSTRAINTS BY COMMODITY AND PLANT SITE[4]

$$\sum_{l \epsilon L} e_{cilt} \leq \sum_{l \epsilon L} \bar{e}_{cilt} \qquad c \epsilon CF,\ i \epsilon I,\ t \epsilon T \tag{12.35}$$

AGGREGATE EXPORT CONSTRAINT[5]

$$\sum_{c \epsilon CF} \sum_{i \epsilon I} \sum_{l \epsilon L} \bar{e}_{cilt} \leq \hat{e}_t \qquad t \epsilon T \tag{12.36}$$

$$\sum_{c \epsilon CF} \sum_{i \epsilon I} \sum_{l \epsilon L} \bar{e}_{cilt} \leq \hat{e}_t \qquad t = 1 \tag{12.37}$$

EXPORT CONSTRAINT BY MARKET SHARE[6]

$$\sum_{c \epsilon CF} \sum_{i \epsilon I} \sum_{l \epsilon L} \bar{e}_{cilt+1} \leq \lambda_t \sum_{c \epsilon CF} \sum_{i \epsilon I} \sum_{l \epsilon L} e_{cilt} \qquad t \epsilon \{T - 1\} \tag{12.38}$$

$$\sum_{c \epsilon CF} \sum_{i \epsilon I} \sum_{l \epsilon L} \bar{e}_{cilt+1} \geq \sum_{c \epsilon CF} \sum_{i \epsilon I} \sum_{l \epsilon L} e_{cilt} \tag{12.39}$$

NONNEGATIVITY CONSTRAINTS

$$z_{pit},\ x_{cijt},\ x_{cii't},\ v_{cit},\ v_{cjt},\ e_{cilt},\ u_{cit},\ h_{mi\tau},\ y_{mi\tau},\ U_{gi\tau} \geq 0 \qquad c \epsilon C,\ g \epsilon G,\ i, i' \epsilon I,\ j \epsilon J,\ l \epsilon L,\ m \epsilon M,\ p \epsilon P \tag{12.40}$$

OBJECTIVE FUNCTION

$$\min \xi = \sum_{t \epsilon T} \delta_t (\phi_{\kappa t} + \phi_{\psi t} + \phi_{\lambda t} + \phi_{\mu t} + \phi_{\pi t} - \phi_{\epsilon t}) \tag{12.41}$$

where

$$\delta_t = \sum_{\tau=1}^{\theta} (1 + \rho)^{-\theta(t-1)-\tau} \tag{12.42}$$

4. Not utilized in scenarios III, IV, and V.
5. Constraint (12.36) not utilized in scenarios III, IV, and V; constraint (12.37) utilized in scenarios IV and V only.
6. Utilized in scenarios IV and V only.

CAPITAL COST CHARGES

$$(12.43) \qquad \phi_{\kappa t} = \sum_{\substack{\tau \epsilon T \\ \tau \leq t}} \Bigg[\sum_{i \epsilon I} \sum_{m \epsilon M} \sigma_m (\omega_{mi\tau}\, y_{mi\tau} + \nu_{mi\tau}\, h_{mi\tau}) + \sum_{i \epsilon I} \sum_{g \epsilon G} \sigma_g\, \omega_{gi\tau}\, U_{gi\tau} \Bigg]$$

where

$$(12.44) \qquad \sigma_m = \frac{\rho(1+\rho)^{\zeta_m}}{(1+\rho)^{\zeta_m} - 1}$$

DOMESTIC RECURRENT COST

$$(12.45) \qquad \phi_{\psi t} = \sum_{c \epsilon CR \cup CO} \sum_{i \epsilon I} p^d_{cit}\, u_{cit}$$

TRANSPORT COST

$$(12.46) \qquad \phi_{\lambda t} = \sum_{c \epsilon CF} \Bigg(\sum_{i \epsilon I} \sum_{j \epsilon J} \mu_{cijt}\, x_{cijt} + \sum_{j \epsilon J} \mu_{cjt}\, v_{cjt} + \sum_{i \epsilon I} \sum_{l \epsilon L} \mu_{cilt}\, e_{cilt} \Bigg) + \sum_{c \epsilon CI} \sum_{i \epsilon I} \sum_{\substack{i' \epsilon I \\ i' \neq i}} \mu_{cii't}\, x_{cii't} + \sum_{c \epsilon CR} \sum_{i \epsilon I} \mu_{cit}\, v_{cit}$$

WORKING CAPITAL

$$(12.47) \qquad \phi_{\mu t} = 0.025 \Bigg(\phi_{\psi t} + \sum_{c \epsilon CR} \sum_{i \epsilon I} p^v_{cit}\, v_{cit} \Bigg)$$

IMPORT COST

$$(12.48) \qquad \phi_{\pi t} = \sum_{c \epsilon CF} \sum_{j \epsilon J} p^v_{cjt}\, v_{cjt} + \sum_{c \epsilon CR} \sum_{i \epsilon I} p^v_{cit}\, v_{cit}$$

EXPORT REVENUE

$$(12.49) \qquad \phi_{\epsilon t} = \sum_{c \epsilon CF} \sum_{i \epsilon I} \sum_{l \epsilon L} p^e_{cilt}\, e_{cilt}$$

13

Results of the Dynamic Analysis

THE KIND OF RESULTS obtained with the model outlined in the previous chapter are described in this chapter. This description is intended primarily to convey a flavor of the nature of these results, not to report on them in exhaustive detail.[1]

The model has been used to address several of the basic questions facing the planners of the Egyptian fertilizer sector, but two general concerns dominate. First, with regard to domestic demand, what is the optimal, or least-cost, pattern of supply to meet specified regional requirements for fertilizer material over the planning period? This question involves investigating the relative cost of domestic supply patterns of raw materials, intermediates, and fertilizer products. In this context, specific questions may have to be addressed: for example, what is the likely rate of adoption by Egyptian farmers of relatively new fertilizers such as urea, and what should be done with

1. For a more detailed examination of these results, see Armeane Choksi, Alexander Meeraus, and Ardy Stoutjesdijk, "A Planning Study of the Egyptian Fertilizer Sector," Staff Working Paper, no. 269 (Washington, D.C.: World Bank, July 1977).

individual existing plants, particularly those that turn out to be relatively inefficient?

The second main area of concern relates to the role of exports. In terms of raw materials, Egypt could well be in a favorable position to build up a substantial export-oriented fertilizer industry. Even though the model is not particularly well-suited to determine the most efficient export strategy, it can be used to assess the implications of the different forms an export strategy may take.

This chapter is structured as follows. To begin with, the set of "basic" results—referred to as the reference solution—of the dynamic analysis are presented in summary form; these results are obtained on the basis of what are considered the most likely assumptions, including highly restricted exports of fertilizers and a relatively slow adoption rate for urea.

Then, a number of specific alternatives to the basic assumptions are investigated. First, various postulated production strategies at Suez are investigated. Second, several more optimistic export strategies—varying mainly in terms of the total volume of exports thought to be feasible—are analyzed. Finally, a complete import substitution policy and the complete elimination of the urea consumption restrictions are examined.

Next, a brief discussion focuses on the use of the model's results to obtain measures of domestic resource costs. The chapter concludes with a sensitivity analysis of the results. It focuses on the most important price and cost parameters in the model, as well as the demand projections that underlie the results. An appendix to this chapter presents the main numerical results in a series of summary tables.

Basic Results: The Reference Solution

Depending upon one's confidence in the robustness of the numerous assumptions underlying the estimates of the parameters of the dynamic model, one can consider the numerical results obtained with this model as more or less basic. Sectoral analysis carried out without a formal planning model can frequently offer the policymaker only basic results. The present approach, however, has two major advantages. First and foremost, the full set of assumptions made in the analysis must be explicitly stated; this was done in the previous chapter. Second, once a basic set of solutions to the model has been obtained, alternative scenarios can be generated on the basis of different assumptions, and thorough sensitivity analysis of crucial parameter estimates can be easily carried out.

With a model of this type, it is standard procedure to solve the model using estimates of the parameters that the analyst considers most likely to materialize. Since many of these estimates involve projections into the future, the values eventually chosen may reflect a certain degree of compromise among the diverging opinions of planners involved in the study. These, in turn, provide a useful demarcation of the range of values to be investigated in the subsequent sensitivity analysis.

An overview

An overview of the main results of the basic solution to the dynamic model is given in table 31. There, the results are divided into nine broad categories: cost, demand, production, capacity expansion, imports, exports, shipments of final products, interplant shipments, and transportation requirements. The years specified in the table—1980, 1983, and 1986—refer to the mid-point of each time period, and they are considered as representative for each time period.

Several broad conclusions can be drawn from the information in this table. First, domestic products are fairly competitive with imports in the Egyptian fertilizer sector, with only relatively small quantities of final product (triple superphosphate) being required from outside sources in the second and third periods. Since Egypt is not self-sufficient in raw materials, several of these need to be imported. Second, exports of fertilizers are sufficiently attractive to take place up to the specified maximum level of 100,000 a year. Third, the only capacity expansion that should occur is at Abu Zaabal, where a phosphoric acid plant is expanded by 134,000 tons to permit the production of powdered triple superphosphate at that location. Finally, interplant shipments of surplus intermediate product are efficient in some cases—in particular, for ammonia from Suez to Helwan.

The production of final and intermediate products

The production of final and intermediate products is detailed in table 32. The figures presented are the current costs for the relevant time period.

Table 31. *Summary of the Results of the Reference Solution*
(objective function value = 177.28 million Egyptian pounds)[a]

Category	*1980*	*1983*	*1986*
Cost (millions of Egyptian pounds)			
Transport cost	6.08	6.24	6.83
Domestic raw materials cost	13.15	14.92	16.12
Operating cost	17.01	18.57	19.56
Working capital cost	0.81	0.90	0.95
Capital cost	1.21	1.21	1.21
Import cost			
Raw materials	2.24	2.52	2.52
Final products	0.01	1.07	4.07
Export revenue	−3.50	−3.78	−3.78
Total cost	37.01	41.64	47.48
Total demand (thousands of tons)			
Nutrient demand			
Nitrogen	496	552	607
Phosphorus	112	135	158
Fertilizer demand	1,691	1,881	1,997
Production (thousands of tons)			
Final products	1,783	1,973	2,089
Intermediate products	1,664	1,737	1,788
Capacity expansion (thousands of tons)			
Phosphoric acid (at Abu Zaabal)	134	0	0
Imports (thousands of tons)			
Final products (TSP)	0	18	68
Raw materials	141	158	158
Exports (thousands of tons)			
Final products	100	100	100
Shipments of final products to governorates from following plants (thousands of tons)			
Aswan (CAN 33.5 percent)	317	311	344
Helwan (CAN 33.5 percent + AS)	67	67	67
Kafr El Zayaat (SSP)	69	168	167
Assiout (SSP)	178	178	178
Suez (CN)	23	1	3
Abu Kir (urea)	133	281	421
Talkha (CAN 33.5 percent + urea)	740	712	653
Abu Zaabal (TSP)	163	163	163
Total shipments	1,691	1,881	1,997

Table 31 (*continued*)

Category	*1980*	*1983*	*1986*
Interplant shipments of intermediate products from following plants (thousands of tons)			
Aswan	—	—	—
Helwan	—	—	—
Kafr El Zayaat (sulfuric acid to Abu Zaabal)	1	1	1
Assiout	—	—	—
Suez (ammonia to Helwan)	36	36	36
Abu Kir	—	—	—
Talkha	—	—	—
Abu Zaabal	—	—	—
Total shipments	37	37	37

Note: Details may not sum to totals because of rounding.
a. Discounted total cost in 1975 Egyptian pounds for the period 1979–87.

At Aswan, the calcium ammonium nitrate produced is entirely in the form of CAN 33.5 percent rather than the 31 percent variety produced until now. This is because of the lower transport cost per ton of nutrient of the higher-nutrient fertilizer. In addition, excess capacity is available for all products in all time periods, except for ammonia in the third time period. The unutilized capacity ranges from 2,000 tons a year for nitric acid in 1986 to 52,000 tons a year for CAN 33.5 percent in 1983. The reason for this is that the demand for CAN in the regions of Upper Egypt, where the Aswan plant competes with other sources of supply, is not sufficient to permit full-capacity utilization. The ammonia capacity is fully utilized only in the third time period. This constrains the production of CAN 33.5 percent to 344,000 tons a year; this level of production just satisfies the demands of the surrounding governorates in this time period. The marginal costs of all products remain the same in the first two time periods, but the rental of 2.5 Egyptian pounds a ton incurred on ammonia capacity in the third time period causes proportional increases in the marginal cost of nitric acid and CAN 33.5 percent.

During periods of excess capacity, the production of any product to the full-capacity level will necessitate sales to sectors other than the fertilizer sector at a price equal to at least the relevant marginal

Table 32. *The Production of Final and Intermediate Products under the Reference Solution*

Plant location and product	*Time period*	*Production (thousands of tons)*	*Unutilized capacity (thousands of tons)*	*Maximum possible production (thousands of tons)*	*Marginal cost (Egyptian pounds per ton)*[a]
Aswan					
Ammonia:	1980	137	11	148	12.3
water electrolysis	1983	134	14	148	12.3
	1986	148	0	148	14.8
Nitric acid	1980	241	23	264	5.3
	1983	237	27	264	5.3
	1986	262	2	264	6.0
CAN 33.5 percent[b]	1980	317	46	363	15.3
	1983	311	52	363	15.3
	1986	344	19	363	16.4
Helwan					
Ammonia: coke-oven gas	1980	0	39	39	17.32
	1983	0	39	39	17.32
	1986	0	39	39	17.32
Nitric acid	1980	64	1	65	6.73
	1983	64	1	65	6.73
	1986	64	1	65	6.73
CAN 33.5 percent	1980	84	0	84	25.73
	1983	84	0	84	20.64
	1986	84	0	84	19.84
Ammonium sulfate	1980	8	0	8	15.58
	1983	8	0	8	12.29
	1986	8	0	8	11.96
Kafr El Zayaat					
Sulfuric acid:	1980	0	14	14	9.96
pyrites	1983	14	0	14	19.50
	1986	14	0	14	18.46
Sulfuric acid:	1980	40	16	56[c]	9.18
sulfur	1983	56	0	56[c]	19.50
	1986	56	0	56[c]	18.46

Table 32 (*continued*)

Plant location and product	*Time period*	*Production (thousands of tons)*	*Unutilized capacity (thousands of tons)*	*Maximum possible production (thousands of tons)*	*Marginal cost (Egyptian pounds per ton)*[a]
SSP 15.5 percent	1980	94	74	168	13.53
	1983	168	0	168	19.36
	1986	168	0	168	19.51
Powdered TSP	1980	0	0	0	44.61
	1983	0	0	0	66.79
	1986	0	0	0	65.60
Assiout					
Sulfuric acid:					
sulfur	1980	73	1	74	9.45
	1983	73	1	74	9.36
	1986	73	1	74	9.42
SSP 15.5 percent	1980	178	0	178	12.78
	1983	178	0	178	18.79
	1986	178	0	178	18.93
Powdered TSP	1980	0	0	0	53.76
	1983	0	0	0	78.40
	1986	0	0	0	78.70
Suez					
Ammonia:					
refinery gas	1980	41	12	53[d]	8.86
	1983	36	17	53[d]	8.86
	1986	37	16	53[d]	8.86
Nitric acid	1980	15	117	132	4.24
	1983	1	131	132	4.28
	1986	2	130	132	4.28
Calcium nitrate	1980	23	152	175	9.61
	1983	1	174	175	9.57
	1986	3	172	175	9.51
Ammonium sulfate	1980	0	46	46	23.40
	1983	0	46	46	20.93
	1986	0	46	46	20.08

(*Table continues on the following pages*)

Table 32. (*continued*)

Plant location and product	*Time period*	*Production (thousands of tons)*	*Unutilized capacity (thousands of tons)*	*Maximum possible production (thousands of tons)*	*Marginal cost (Egyptian pounds per ton)*[a]
Abu Kir					
Ammonia:					
natural gas	1980	92	205	297	19.48
	1983	177	120	297	10.29
	1986	258	39	297	10.28
Urea	1980	158	287	445	20.08
	1983	305	140	445	20.07
	1986	445	0	445	23.88
Talkha					
Ammonia:					
natural gas	1980	400	49	449	19.48
	1983	402	47	449	19.50
	1986	376	73	449	19.51
Nitric acid	1980	226	86	312	7.35
	1983	207	105	312	7.35
	1986	162	150	312	7.33
CAN 31 percent[e]	1980	0	0	0	15.17
	1983	0	0	0	17.93
	1986	0	0	0	17.89
CAN 33.5 percent	1980	297	0	297	25.66
	1983	272	25	297	18.43
	1986	213	84	297	18.46
Urea	1980	468	22	490	20.08
	1983	490	0	490	21.43
	1986	490	0	490	25.50
Abu Zaabal					
Sulfuric acid: pyrites	1980	64	0	64	15.15
	1983	64	0	64	25.50
	1986	64	0	64	24.50
Sulfuric acid: sulfur	1980	152	0	152	15.19
	1983	152	0	152	25.50
	1986	152	0	152	25.50

Table 32 (*continued*)

Plant location and product	*Time period*	*Production (thousands of tons)*	*Unutilized capacity (thousands of tons)*	*Maximum possible production (thousands of tons)*	*Marginal cost (Egyptian pounds per ton)*[a]
Phosphoric acid[e]	1980	120	0	120	45.14
	1983	120	0	120	70.07
	1986	120	0	120	70.60
SSP 15.5 percent	1980	0	0	0	15.35
	1983	0	0	0	19.57
	1986	0	0	0	19.03
Powdered TSP	1980	163	6	169	41.92
	1983	163	6	169	60.36
	1986	163	6	169	60.80

a. These are the current (undiscounted) marginal costs of obtaining the product.
b. All CAN production has shifted from the 31 percent variety to the 33.5 percent form.
c. Includes interplant shipment to Abu Zaabal.
d. Includes interplant shipment of 36,000 tons to Helwan in each time period.
e. Capacity expansion of 134,000 tons at a cost of US$22.95 million.

cost. For example, the sale of nitric acid from Aswan may be undertaken at a price of at least 5.3 Egyptian pounds a ton in 1980 and 1983 and 6.0 Egyptian pounds a ton in 1986. Sales at any price lower than this marginal cost would make this incremental production unattractive.

Though this model does not explicitly consider exports of CAN 33.5 percent from Aswan to the Sudan, it is possible to assess the possibility of an export-oriented strategy to that country by inspecting the marginal production costs. If the fertilizer can be exported to the Sudan at an f.o.b. price that is at least equal to the marginal production costs plus transport cost to the border, such a strategy would be beneficial to Egypt.

At Helwan, CAN production is restricted entirely to the 33.5 percent variety, for the same reason it is at Aswan. Ammonium sulfate is produced at its full-capacity level. No ammonia is produced by either the coke-oven gas process, which is already in existence, or by the natural gas technology, which could be used by converting the existing equipment, because the marginal cost of obtaining ammonia from Suez is lower. Thus, production of ammonia at Helwan would cause the fertilizer sector as a whole to incur a higher total cost than necessary. The production of CAN 33.5 percent at full capacity of 84,000 tons a year in each time period is distributed between shipments to the surrounding governorates (59,000 tons a year) and exports.

At Kafr El Zayaat and Assiout, the production pattern is self-explanatory. In both cases, no powdered triple superphosphate is produced because its marginal cost is too high, and all single superphosphate units operate at full capacity except at Kafr El Zayaat in the first time period. This plant produces 94,000 tons a year of SSP in the first time period, of which 69,000 tons are shipped to the governorates of Kafr El Sheikh and Menoufia and the remainder is exported. All of Assiout's production of 178,000 tons a year of SSP is shipped to surrounding governorates. All the sulfuric acid produced in the first time period is made from sulfur because the marginal production cost for this acid (9.18 Egyptian pounds a ton) is lower than for that made from pyrites (9.96 Egyptian pounds a ton). At Kafr El Zayaat, the excess capacity of 14,000 tons of sulfuric acid from pyrites may be utilized if the plant can sell this acid to the pulp and paper sector or to some other sector at a price of at least 9.96 Egyptian pounds a ton. In the second and third time periods, however, the increased demand for the final product forces all units to operate at full capacity.[2] This accounts for the quantum jump in marginal costs of single superphosphate in the second period from 13.53 Egyptian pounds a ton to 19.36 Egyptian pounds a ton, since the plant now incurs a rental on its capacity of 5.83 Egyptian pounds a ton.

The production pattern at Suez is determined by the urea "learning curve" incorporated into the model. In the first time period, when consumption of urea is most restricted, calcium nitrate is produced at the rate of 23,000 tons a year to supply the governorates of Ismailia, Suez, and Kalubia. No ammonium sulfate is produced because of its relatively high marginal cost. As the urea restrictions are relaxed in the subsequent time periods, calcium nitrate production declines drastically (to 1,000 tons a year and 3,000 tons a year, respectively) to supply only the governorate of Suez. The production of ammonia and nitric acid declines, but the decline in production

2. Minor quantities of acid are shipped to Abu Zaabal from Kafr El Zayaat in all three time periods.

of ammonia is less than that of nitric acid because the Suez plant ships 36,000 tons of ammonia to Helwan in each time period. This implies that there is unbalanced excess capacity of ammonia (at Helwan) and calcium nitrate (at Suez). This provides a fallback position for the nitrogen fertilizer sector. In times of emergency or unanticipated demand, imports could only be justified, assuming the availability of foreign exchange, if the delivered price were less than the marginal cost of calcium nitrate plus the relevant transport cost. What is most noticeable is that, even in the first time period of maximum production, there is substantial excess capacity of the final product—152,000 tons a year. The low nutrient content of this product (15.5 percent nitrogen) makes its production and transport an uneconomical proposition under most conditions.[3]

The production of urea at Abu Kir is obviously determined by the restrictions on urea consumption. As these restrictions are relaxed, more urea production comes on stream. The favorable location of the plant, and the superior economics of production, make this an ideal export-based production unit.[4] In each time period, the plant exports to the maximum limit of 25,000 tons a year. In all three periods, the bulk of the urea is transported to the neighboring governorate of Behera.[5] The second largest shipment goes as far south as Minia. Thus, Minia's nitrogen requirements are supplied entirely by Abu Kir rather than by the relatively closer Helwan or Aswan. The high nutrient content of urea makes this supply pattern efficient, while Helwan and Aswan are restricted to supplying the surrounding governorates closest to them, thus minimizing the total cost to the sector.

The production pattern of Talkha is characterized by a switch from producing CAN 31 percent to CAN 33.5 percent and urea. Again, the urea consumption restrictions determine the production pattern. In the first time period, CAN production is at its full capacity of 297,000 tons a year and urea production has some excess capacity

3. In general, if the transport cost per ton of final product is the same, transporting calcium nitrate is three times more expensive than transporting urea on a nutrient basis. In addition, calcium nitrate production involves a relatively high-cost technology.

4. The plant has been financed, however, under the condition that it does not export its product.

5. The amount of urea transported is 70,000 tons a year, 97,000 tons a year, and 121,000 tons a year in the three time periods, respectively.

of 22,000 tons a year. In the second time period, as the urea restrictions are relaxed, urea is produced at its full capacity of 490,000 tons a year, with CAN production declining to 272,000 tons a year.[6] This decline continues through the last time period. The increasing nitrogen requirements are now met through urea production at Abu Kir, because the Talkha production of urea cannot increase any further. The ammonia and nitric acid production adjust accordingly. What is obvious is the excess capacity available for these intermediate products in all three time periods. Further, in the first time period, Talkha exports only urea and all CAN production is utilized for domestic consumption. As the increasing nitrogen requirements are met by urea in the next two time periods, however, CAN production is released for exports. Thus, in the last two time periods, exports of both CAN and urea take place. Urea production at Talkha attains full-capacity utilization before that at Abu Kir because Talkha has a more favorable location from the point of view of domestic supply. Total costs are minimized by shipping urea from Talkha rather than from Abu Kir, despite the slightly higher marginal costs in the latter two periods at Talkha. The higher marginal costs at Talkha in the second time period are explained by the rental on capacity incurred and the higher rental incurred in the third time period at Talkha compared with Abu Kir.

Abu Zaabal is the only location where capacity expansion takes place. This is in the form of a phosphoric acid plant of 134,000 tons a year of product in the first time period. The total cost of this expansion is US$22.95 million, of which US$17.65 million is for the plant and US$5.30 million for the off-site facilities. Assuming 90 percent capacity utilization, this new plant operates at full capacity of 120,000 tons a year from the start. In addition, Abu Zaabal no longer produces SSP 15.5 percent, but uses the phosphoric acid to produce powdered TSP using the existing capital equipment with minor alterations to the den. Sulfuric acid from both sulfur and pyrites is utilized to capacity limitations in the production of phosphoric acid. Despite the higher marginal costs of powdered TSP relative to SSP, the production of high-analysis TSP is justified on the basis of its lower delivered price because of the lower transport cost per ton of nutrient.

6. Helwan produces at full capacity, but this is only possible because of the availability of cheap ammonia from Suez.

Table 33. *Exports of Final Products under the Reference Solution*
(thousands of tons)

	1980			1983			1986		
Plant location	SSP	CAN[a]	*Urea*	SSP	CAN[a]	*Urea*	SSP	CAN[a]	*Urea*
Aswan	0	0	0	0	0	0	0	0	0
Helwan	0	25	0	0	25	0	0	25	0
Kafr El Zayaat	0	0	0	0	0	0	0	0	0
Assiout	25	0	0	0	0	0	0	0	0
Suez	0	0	0	0	0	0	0	0	0
Abu Kir	0	0	25	0	0	25	0	0	25
Talkha	0	0	25	0	25	25	0	25	25
Abu Zaabal	0	0	0	0	0	0	0	0	0
Total	25	25	50	0	50	50	0	50	50

a. 33.5 percent nitrogen.

Exports

The exports of fertilizer products in the three time periods are shown in table 33.[7] In 1980, SSP, CAN 33.5, and urea are exported. In that period, P_2O_5 production is sufficient to meet all domestic demand and to earn some foreign exchange. In the second and third time periods, however, P_2O_5 domestic production falls short of demand, necessitating imports and a cessation of SSP exports. During these same two periods, urea consumption restrictions are relaxed, which permits more urea production at Talkha and Abu Kir and a reduction of CAN 33.5 percent production at Talkha. This reduction is mitigated, however, by exports of CAN 33.5 percent from Talkha, which were not possible in the first time period because of the urea restrictions. These changing restrictions, combined with increased demand for phosphorus, cause a shift in the export pattern from the first time period to the second; this pattern is then maintained in the third period. Alternative export strategies and potentials are investigated in greater detail later in this chapter.

7. The export constraints in the model permit exports from an individual plant of a maximum of 25,000 tons a year of a product and total exports from the country of 100,000 tons a year. All products shown in table 31 attain the upper bound stated in the model.

Table 34. *Transport Requirements by Mode under the Reference Solution*
(millions of ton-kilometers)

Mode	*1975*	*1980*	*1983*	*1986*
Barge	19.2	37.3	39.1	39.1
Rail	27.6	18.2	20.6	20.6
Road	332.0	294.9	291.9	328.4
Total	378.8	350.4	351.6	388.1

Transport requirements

The amount of transport capacity utilized by the fertilizer sector over the planning period is given in table 34. The change in the barge capacity between the first and the second time periods is explained by the increase in the import of raw materials from 141,000 tons a year in 1980 to 158,000 tons a year in the subsequent periods (see table 31). The change in the rail requirements is explained by the shift from exports of SSP produced at Kafr El Zayaat in the first time period to exports of CAN 33.5 percent produced at Talkha in the next two time periods. The latter plant is farther from the port of exit (Alexandria) than the former. The changes in road requirements are a function of two variables: first, the nutrient content of the fertilizer; and, second, the nutrient demand. As the nutrient content rises, the transport requirement tends to decline; as the demand grows, however, this requirement increases.

The transport sector is considered to be a major bottleneck in the distribution of fertilizers: there is a shortage of rail wagons, and not enough use is made of river transport. This study has not sought to determine the optimum mode of transport; rather, it has taken the existing modes as given. In this context, an interesting conclusion emerges from the requirements listed in table 34: The existing total transport capacity available to the fertilizer sector will be sufficient to distribute the products of the sector to the plants and governorates until 1984. After that a slight increase in transport capacity will be required. In 1975, the requirement was 378.8 million ton-kilometers. This is not exceeded until the start of the third time period. The net decline in the first two time periods, as compared with 1975, is caused by three factors. First, the change to higher-analysis fertilizers such as CAN 33.5 percent, urea, and TSP lowers the road transport requirements. Second, the decline in interplant shipments lowers the rail transport requirements. Finally, increasing imports of raw materials (because of increased demand for phosphatic fertilizers) increases the demand for barge capacity.

Alternative Scenarios at Suez: Scenarios I and II

Since the 1967 war between Egypt and Israel, no fertilizers have been produced at Suez. The calcium nitrate plant has, however, been repaired and is now operational. The question faced by planners in Egypt is what should be done with this plant? It is clear from the preceding section that the optimal strategy at Suez would be to operate all the units in the first time period to produce 23,000 tons a year of calcium nitrate, but to reduce significantly the amount of this fertilizer produced in the subsequent periods while continuing to produce and ship ammonia to Helwan (see table 32). In view of the existing capacity and the various ramifications of bringing the Suez plant into operation, this section investigates the cost and impact of two alternative strategies. The first considers constructing a nitrophosphate unit that would produce nitrophosphate (20–20–0) and calcium nitrate in a fixed nitrogen ratio of 1:1. The second strategy involves operating the existing calcium nitrate plant at a minimum production rate of 150,000 tons a year of product. These two scenarios are compared with one another and with the basic reference solution presented in the previous section.

The production of nitrophosphate and calcium nitrate at Suez: Scenario I

A general overview of the results of the strategy of producing nitrophosphate and calcium nitrate at the Suez plant is presented in table 53 in the appendix to this chapter. Clearly, since the erection of this plant was forced into the solution, it represents a nonoptimal policy and has an associated cost. This cost is given by the difference between the value of the objective function in this scenario and that in the reference solution. This amounts to 2.53 million Egyptian pounds (1975 constant pounds), or 1.5 percent more than the reference solution. This is not the cost of the plant alone, but the total cost associated with such a policy to the entire sector, including the costs of transportation, operation, raw materials, and so forth.

In this scenario, the entire production of Aswan, Assiout, and Abu Zaabal is shipped to the governorates for domestic consumption, whereas production of the other plants—including the nitrophosphate production at Suez—is for exports as well as for domestic consumption. The Suez plant exports 25,000 tons a year in the first period; after that, its annual production of 34,000 tons is used entirely for domestic consumption. As in the reference solution, Suez produces ammonia for use at Helwan.

A comparison of the production pattern of final and intermediate products under Scenario I with the pattern under the reference solution is presented in table 35. The changes are at Aswan and Kafr El Zayaat in the first time period, at Abu Kir and Talkha in the second and third time periods, and at Suez in all three time periods. The capacity expansion in this scenario includes a phosphoric acid plant with a capacity of 134,000 tons a year at Abu Zaabal (as in the reference solution) and a nitrophosphate plant with a capacity of 88,000 tons a year at Suez. Both plants are erected in the first time period; the investment cost for the acid plant is US$22.95 million, and for the nitrophosphate plant it is US$18.41 million. These costs include the site costs.

Given that the nutrient demand in each time period is the same in both cases, the new production of nitrophosphate and calcium nitrate at Suez alters the shipment patterns and therefore the production patterns of other plants. Thus, in the first time period, Suez satisfies part of the nitrogen and phosphorus requirements at Kalubia by supplying 31,000 tons a year of calcium nitrate and 9,000 tons a year of nitrophosphate. The rest of the nitrophosphate produced, 25,000 tons, is exported. This causes the Abu Zaabal plant to reduce its shipments of TSP to Kalubia by an equal amount and ship that TSP instead to Kafr El Sheikh. Thus, the production level at Abu Zaabal does not change; only the direction of its TSP shipment alters. This causes the shipment of SSP from Kafr El Zayaat to Kafr El Sheikh to be reduced by 12,000 tons a year, and the exports of SSP from Kafr El Zayaat to be reduced. The change in the production pattern at Aswan can be explained as follows: Under Scenario I, 31,000 tons a year of calcium nitrate from Suez are shipped to Kalubia, which causes the shipment of CAN from Helwan to Kalubia to be reduced. The Helwan CAN is now shipped to Beni Suef instead. Aswan, which supplied Beni Suef in the reference solution, must thus reduce its production of CAN from 317,000 tons a year to 295,000 tons. In all cases, the production of the intermediate products adjusts proportionately.

Table 35. *The Production of Final and Intermediate Products under Scenario I*
(thousands of tons)

Plant location and product	*1980* Reference solution	*1980* Scenario I	*1983* Reference solution	*1983* Scenario I	*1986* Reference solution	*1986* Scenario I
Aswan						
Ammonia	137	127	134	134	148	149
Nitric acid	241	224	237	237	262	262
CAN 33.5 percent	317	295	311	311	344	344
Helwan						
Ammonia	0	0	0	0	0	0
Nitric acid	64	64	64	64	64	64
CAN 33.5 percent	84	84	84	84	84	84
Ammonium sulfate	8	8	8	8	8	8
Kafr El Zayaat						
Sulfuric acid: pyrites	0	0	14	14	14	14
Sulfuric acid: sulfur	40	28	56	56	56	56
SSP	94	65	168	168	168	168
Powdered TSP	0	0	0	0	0	0
Assiout						
Sulfuric acid: sulfur	73	73	73	73	73	73
SSP	178	178	178	178	178	178
Powdered TSP	0	0	0	0	0	0
Suez						
Ammonia	41	53	36	53	37	53
Nitric acid	15	40	1	40	2	40
Calcium nitrate	23	45	1	45	3	45
Ammonium sulfate	0	0	0	0	0	0
Nitrophosphate	0	34	0	34	0	34
Abu Kir						
Ammonia	92	92	177	173	258	238
Urea	158	158	305	298	445	445
Talkha						
Ammonia	400	400	402	388	376	359
Nitric acid	226	226	207	183	162	132
CAN 31 percent	0	0	0	0	0	0
CAN 33.5 percent	297	297	272	241	213	173
Urea	468	268	490	490	490	490
Abu Zaabal						
Sulfuric acid: pyrites	64	64	64	64	64	64
Sulfuric acid: sulfur	152	152	152	152	152	152
Phosphoric acid	120	120	120	120	120	120
SSP 15.5 percent	0	0	0	0	0	0
Powdered TSP	163	163	163	163	163	163

In the second and third time periods, as the demand for nitrogen and phosphorus grows, the 25,000 tons a year of nitrophosphate that were exported in the first time period are diverted for domestic use. The bulk of this nitrophosphate is shipped to the governorates of Ismailia, Suez, Kalubia, and Minia. The nitrogen requirements of these governorates were previously supplied by CAN from Talkha and urea from Abu Kir. Thus, under Scenario I, CAN production at Talkha and urea production at Abu Kir are reduced in the second period.

The domestic availability of nitrophosphates also causes a reduction in the imports of TSP. This results in savings in import costs (for final products only) of 880,000 Egyptian pounds a year. These savings are, however, more than offset by an increase in the other cost categories, primarily capital and operating costs. Therefore, even though this strategy may make Egypt more independent of foreign supply sources, and may permit fertilizer production for Suez, the price of this incremental independence will amount to more than 2.5 million Egyptian pounds.

The production of calcium nitrate at Suez: Scenario II

In Scenario II, the calcium nitrate plant at Suez operates at a minimum of 150,000 tons a year in each time period. This is 60 percent of the rated design capacity of the plant. Since the reference solution indicated a low level of production in the first time period (23,000 tons a year), which subsequently declined to 1,000 tons a year in the second time period and to 3,000 tons a year in the third time period, forcing a production level of 150,000 tons in each year will distort the optimal patterns of production and consumption, thus involving a cost to the fertilizer sector. This cost, which is the difference between the objective function values of the two solutions, amounts to 1.86 million Egyptian pounds, or 1 percent of the reference solution, over the planning period. This is, however, less than the cost incurred under Scenario I.

In this scenario, all costs increase except capital cost and import cost (see table 54 in the appendix to this chapter). These cost increases can be explained by the change in the production pattern from using relatively efficient technology that produces high-analysis fertilizers to a relatively inefficient technology that produces a much lower analysis fertilizer, calcium nitrate. This low-analysis calcium nitrate necessitates higher levels of production to meet nutrient demand, which leads to higher transport cost on a nutrient basis.

Table 36. *The Production of Final and Intermediate Products under Scenario II*
(thousands of tons)

Plant location and product	*1980*		*1983*		*1986*	
	Reference solution	*Scenario II*	*Reference solution*	*Scenario II*	*Reference solution*	*Scenario II*
Aswan						
Ammonia	137	127	134	135	148	149
Nitric acid	241	224	237	237	262	261
CAN 33.5 percent	317	295	311	311	344	344
Helwan						
Ammonia	0	0	0	0	0	0
Nitric acid	64	56	64	42	64	43
CAN 33.5 percent	84	74	84	56	84	56
Ammonium sulfate	8	8	8	8	8	8
Kafr El Zayaat						
Sulfuric acid: pyrites	0	0	14	14	14	14
Sulfuric acid: sulfur	40	30	56	56	56	56
SSP	94	69	168	168	168	168
Powdered TSP	0	0	0	0	0	0
Assiout						
Sulfuric acid: sulfur	73	73	73	73	73	73
SSP	178	178	178	178	178	178
Powdered TSP	0	0	0	0	0	0
Suez						
Ammonia	41	53	36	53	37	53
Nitric acid	15	99	1	99	2	99
Calcium nitrate	23	150	1	150	3	150
Ammonium sulfate	0	0	0	0	0	0
Nitrophosphate	0	0	0	0	0	0
Abu Kir						
Ammonia	92	92	177	172	258	258
Urea	158	158	305	297	445	445
Talkha						
Ammonia	400	407	402	389	376	359
Nitric acid	226	226	207	185	162	131
CAN 31 percent	0	0	0	0	0	0
CAN 33.5 percent	297	297	272	243	213	173
Urea	468	468	490	490	490	490
Abu Zaabal						
Sulfuric acid: pyrites	64	64	64	64	64	64
Sulfuric acid: sulfur	152	152	152	152	152	152
Phosphoric acid	120	120	120	120	120	120
SSP 15.5 percent	0	0	0	0	0	0
Powdered TSP	163	163	163	163	163	163

In addition, the use at Suez of the relatively inefficient technology that produces the required ammonia from refinery gas, and subsequently nitric acid and calcium nitrate, leads to higher raw materials, operating, and working capital costs.

In this scenario, only Helwan, Abu Kir, and Talkha produce for both foreign and domestic markets. The other plants ship all their production to the governorates. Table 36 shows the production levels at all plants.

Alternative Export Strategies: Scenarios III, IV, and V

In this section, three alternative export-oriented scenarios for Egypt are investigated. These scenarios are based on varying assumptions regarding Egypt's ability to export fertilizers. In the first case, it is assumed that no capacity expansion will be undertaken over the planning period and that the sector may export as much final product as is possible with the given capacity. In the second case, capacity expansion is permitted, but the total exports in the first time period are restricted to an upper limit (that is, a maximum) of 500,000 tons a year. In this scenario, an export market share is secured by Egypt in the first time period and is then maintained in the following periods or is increased by, at most, 10 percent year. The third strategy lowers the maximum of the first time period from 500,000 tons a year to 250,000 tons a year but permits capacity expansion and retention and growth of the export market share as in the previous case. Since this section is intended to investigate the export side of the market, the details of product shipments to the various governorates is not discussed.

No capacity expansion with unbounded exports: Scenario III

Scenario III investigates the potential for exports of fertilizer products from Egypt with no change in the capacities of the existing plants; that is, no capacity expansion is permitted.[8] Thus, this sce-

8. It is essential to constrain the model to no capacity expansion. Permitting expansion plus unlimited exports would yield new capacity in all time periods up to the maximum limit on capacity expansion. This would be a meaningless result.

nario assumes that fertilizer products will be exported by Egypt up to the existing capacity limit as long as the country has a comparative advantage in exports—that is, as long as the marginal cost of production plus transport cost from the plant to the port of exit is less than the f.o.b. price. Given the cost-minimization objective function of the model, the products yielding the largest amount of export revenue will be selected. It may be argued that, given the assumption of a perfectly elastic demand for exports (that is, the small country assumption, since Egypt will not be able to influence world prices), there may be nonprice variables that will limit the total amount of exports from Egypt. Since this scenario is incorporated into the analysis to study the production, import, and export behavior under the most optimistic conditions, there is no upper bound on the exports.

Table 55 in the appendix to this chapter presents a summary of the results. The objective function value of 163.19 million Egyptian pounds indicates that this scenario is clearly superior to the reference solution, which permits capacity expansion. The objective function in the reference solution is 177.28 million Egyptian pounds. Thus, a strategy of no capacity expansion, with Egypt exporting as much as possible, would yield a saving of 14.09 million Egyptian pounds, or 8 percent of the total discounted cost under the basic assumptions, over the period under consideration. This is evident from the fact that the increases in the first two time periods in the transport, domestic raw materials, operating, import, and working capital costs are more than offset by the decrease in the capital charges (because capacity is not expanded) and by the increase in the export revenues.

With the exception of the plant at Abu Kir, all plants produce for domestic consumption only. Table 37 indicates that all plants, except that at Suez, will operate at full capacity in all time periods. The Suez plant, which produces the lowest-analysis fertilizer (calcium nitrate), is the last to reach full-capacity utilization.

Because capacity expansion is not permitted, the phosphoric acid plant is not built at Abu Zaabal. Thus, as table 37 indicates, all phosphate plants operate at full capacity, producing the low-analysis fertilizer SSP. This is not sufficient to meet domestic nutrient requirements, and larger imports of TSP are needed than in the reference solution.

The only product exported is urea from Abu Kir. The plant's coastal location provides it with a competitive edge over Talkha. The marginal export revenue (f.o.b. price) equals the marginal cost

Table 37. *The Production of Final and Intermediate Products under Scenario III*
(thousands of tons)

Plant location and product	*1980*		*1983*		*1986*	
	Reference solution	*Scenario III*	*Reference solution*	*Scenario III*	*Reference solution*	*Scenario III*
Aswan						
Ammonia	137	149	134	148	148	148
Nitric acid	241	261	237	262	262	262
CAN 33.5 percent	317	344	311	344	344	344
Helwan						
Ammonia	0	0	0	0	0	0
Nitric acid	64	56	64	42	64	43
CAN 33.5 percent	84	84	84	84	84	84
Ammonium sulfate	8	8	8	8	8	8
Kafr El Zayaat						
Sulfuric acid: pyrites	0	14	14	14	14	14
Sulfuric acid: sulfur	40	56	56	56	56	56
SSP	94	168	168	168	168	168
Powdered TSP	0	0	0	0	0	0
Assiout						
Sulfuric acid: sulfur	73	73	73	73	73	73
SSP	178	178	178	178	178	178
Powdered TSP	0	0	0	0	0	0
Suez						
Ammonia	41	53	36	53	37	53
Nitric acid	15	101	1	108	2	116
Calcium nitrate	23	150	1	163	3	175
Ammonium sulfate	0	0	0	0	0	0
Nitrophosphate	0	0	0	0	0	0
Abu Kir						
Ammonia	92	258	177	258	258	258
Urea	158	445	305	445	445	445
Talkha						
Ammonia	400	425	402	427	376	429
Nitric acid	226	226	207	226	162	226
CAN 31 percent	0	0	0	0	0	0
CAN 33.5 percent	297	297	272	297	213	297
Urea	468	490	490	490	490	490
Abu Zaabal						
Sulfuric acid: pyrites	64	0	64	0	64	0
Sulfuric acid: sulfur	152	69	152	69	152	69
Phosphoric acid	120	0	120	0	120	0
SSP 15.5 percent	0	168	0	168	0	168
Powdered TSP	163	0	163	0	163	0

Table 38. *Exports of Final Products under Scenario III*
(thousands of tons)

Plant location and product	*1980*	*1983*	*1986*
Abu Kir: urea	440	323	206

of 42 Egyptian pounds a ton.[9] As the urea consumption restrictions relax over time, however, and as the nitrogen demand increases simultaneously, the exports of urea decline in order to meet the increasing domestic demand (see table 38). Since the marginal import cost is greater than the f.o.b. export price, the increase in domestic demand will always be met by reducing exports.

The costs of establishing export markets are not captured in this model. In reality, these costs—which may include establishing foreign trade agencies abroad, advertising, and so forth—will be quite substantial. Therefore, it may be argued that, once Egypt has established itself in the world market for urea (or any fertilizer), it is unlikely that the country would reduce its exports and thus its foreign exchange earnings to supply the increasing domestic demand from existing capacity. This argument carries added strength given the desire of the government to develop and promote an export-oriented industry. The relevant question then becomes: if Egypt is at least to maintain its world market share, established in the first time period, is it optimal for the country to expand domestic capacity in order to meet increasing domestic demand? This question is addressed in the next two scenarios.

Bounded export growth with maximum first-period exports of 500,000 tons a year: Scenario IV

The second export strategy analyzes the expansion of domestic capacity in the fertilizer sector in Egypt that would permit growing exports of fertilizer products. In Scenario III, the first-period exports of fertilizer (urea) amounted to 440,000 tons a year, without capacity expansion. In Scenario IV, an upper bound of 500,000 tons a year is placed on first-period exports. In addition, it is assumed that, once a market share in the exports of fertilizers is established in the

9. This includes the transport cost from Abu Kir to Alexandria.

first time period, at least the same amount of fertilizers can be exported in the subsequent time periods, and that exports can grow by, at most, 10 percent a year. Thus, the first time period has only an upper bound on total exports, whereas the second and third time periods have both an upper and a lower bound.

Table 56 in the appendix to this chapter indicates that this scenario is superior to the reference solution. The objective function value of Scenario IV (158.09 million Egyptian pounds) is 19.19 million Egyptian pounds, or almost 11 percent, less than that of the reference solution. The increase in export revenues easily offsets the increase in the other cost components, despite the increased cost of capacity expansion.

Exports in the first time period attain the upper bound of 500,000 tons, and they then grow at the rate of 10 percent a year. As in all other solutions involving capacity expansion, a phosphoric acid plant with a capacity of 134,000 tons a year is built at Abu Zaabal in 1980, which leads to a conversion of the superphosphate production from SSP to TSP. In addition, to accommodate the increase in domestic demand as well as the exports, an ammonia/urea complex is constructed at Suez in the second time period.[10] Interestingly, urea capacity is installed in both the second and the third time periods, whereas ammonia capacity is constructed only in the second period. The total cost, including site cost, of the new complex at Suez is US$214.27 million. Table 39 gives the detailed breakdown.

Table 40 shows the production levels of final and intermediate products for Scenario IV and compares them to the levels for the reference solution. Most of the changes take place in the nitrogen fertilizer industry. The major exception is the increase in the production of SSP at Kafr El Zayaat in the first time period from 94,000 tons a year to 151,000 tons a year; this change is explained by the increase in the amount of exports of SSP from 25,000 tons a year to 82,000 tons a year (see table 41). The increased production of SSP necessitates an increase in the production of sulfuric acid. The acid production process using sulfur reaches its capacity limit at 56,000 tons a year, thus forcing the production of the higher-cost acid using pyrites. The production of sulfuric acid using the pyrites process

10. Abu Kir is the preferred location for this plant, but there is insufficient space to accommodate another complex. Area is not a binding constraint at Suez, which is the next most preferred location.

Table 39. *Plant Investment under Scenario IV*

Plant location and product	*Time period*	*Capacity (thousands of tons a year)*	*Investment (millions of U.S. dollars)*	*Site cost (millions of U.S. dollars)*	*Total cost (millions of U.S. dollars)*
Abu Zaabal					
Phosphoric acid	1980	134	17.65	5.30	22.95
Suez					
Ammonia:					
natural gas	1983	431	92.64	27.79	120.43
Urea	1983	424	38.83	11.65	50.48
Urea	1986	319	33.35	10.01	43.36
Total			182.47	54.75	237.22

reaches its capacity limit in the second time period, thus necessitating an increase in the imports of pyrites, which is reflected in the imports and import cost categories in table 56 in the appendix.

Table 41 shows the amount of exports undertaken by the plants. All plants not listed in that table produce for domestic consumption and ship their products to governorates (see table 56). The urea production at Abu Kir is directed toward both the export and the domestic markets. Interestingly, the first-period exports of urea from Abu Kir are 419,000 tons, as compared with 440,000 tons under Scenario III. Therefore, it is more profitable for the entire sector to reduce urea exports from that location and increase SSP exports.

In the second and third time periods, the export market is supplied by the new urea capacity at Suez, causing a decline in the exports from Abu Kir and an increase in the domestic supply of urea from this location. As a result, calcium nitrate production declines to 1,000 tons a year in the second time period, since this fertilizer cannot compete domestically with urea. As domestic demand increases in the third time period, however, calcium nitrate production increases back to 87,500 tons a year. As table 41 indicates, Suez becomes basically an "export plant" and Abu Kir's production shifts toward domestic consumption. In the last time period, approximately 50 percent of the urea produced at Abu Kir is exported, as compared with 94 percent in the first time period. In the third time period, 94 percent of total output at Suez is exported, and this accounts for around 75 percent of Egypt's total exports.

Table 40. *The Production of Final and Intermediate Products under Scenario IV*
(thousands of tons)

Plant location and product	1980 Reference solution	1980 Scenario IV	1983 Reference solution	1983 Scenario IV	1986 Reference solution	1986 Scenario IV
Aswan						
Ammonia	137	149	134	148	148	148
Nitric acid	241	261	237	262	262	262
CAN 33.5 percent	317	344	311	344	344	344
Helwan						
Ammonia	0	0	0	0	0	0
Nitric acid	64	64	64	64	64	64
CAN 33.5 percent	84	84	84	84	84	84
Ammonium sulfate	8	8	8	8	8	8
Kafr El Zayaat						
Sulfuric acid: pyrites	0	7	14	14	14	14
Sulfuric acid: sulfur	40	56	56	56	56	56
SSP	94	151	168	168	168	168
Powdered TSP	0	0	0	0	0	0
Assiout						
Sulfuric acid: sulfur	73	73	73	73	73	73
SSP	178	178	178	178	178	178
Powdered TSP	0	0	0	0	0	0
Suez						
Ammonia: refinery gas	41	53	36	36	37	53
Ammonia: natural gas	0	0	0	222	0	388
Nitric acid	15	58	1	1	2	58
Calcium nitrate	23	88	1	1	3	88
Ammonium sulfate	0	0	0	0	0	0
Nitrophosphate	0	0	0	0	0	0
Urea	0	0	0	382	0	669
Abu Kir						
Ammonia	92	258	177	258	258	258
Urea	158	445	305	445	445	445
Talkha						
Ammonia	400	413	402	413	376	413
Nitric acid	226	226	207	226	162	226
CAN 31 percent	0	0	0	0	0	0
CAN 33.5 percent	297	297	272	297	213	297
Urea	468	490	490	490	490	490

Table 40 (*continued*)

Plant location and product	*1980*		*1983*		*1986*	
	Reference solution	*Scenario IV*	*Reference solution*	*Scenario IV*	*Reference solution*	*Scenario IV*
Abu Zaabal						
Sulfuric acid: pyrites	64	64	64	64	64	64
Sulfuric acid: sulfur	152	152	152	152	152	152
Phosphoric acid	120	120	120	120	120	120
SSP 15.5 percent	0	0	0	0	0	0
Powdered TSP	163	163	163	163	163	163

Table 41. *Exports of Final Products under Scenario IV*
(thousands of tons)

Plant location and product	*1980*	*1983*	*1986*
Kafr El Zayaat:			
SSP 15.5 percent	81	0	0
Suez: Urea	0	373	631
Abu Kir: Urea	419	277	214
Total	500	650	845

Bounded export growth with maximum first-period exports of 250,000 tons a year: Scenario V

The third export strategy, Scenario V, is identical to the previous one, except that the upper bound in the first period on exports is 250,000 tons a year rather than 500,000 tons. The maximum permissible annual growth rate is still 10 percent.

On the basis of the value of the objective function, Scenario V is worse than Scenario IV, but is superior to the reference solution and Scenario III (unbounded exports, no capacity expansion). Table 57 in the appendix shows that the cost of exporting 250,000 tons a year is 3.87 million Egyptian pounds greater than the cost of exporting 500,000 tons over the planning period. Scenario V and the reference solution both involve the same phosphoric acid capacity

Table 42. *The Production of Final and Intermediate Products under Scenario V*
(thousands of tons)

Plant location and product	1980 Reference solution	1980 Scenario V	1983 Reference solution	1983 Scenario V	1986 Reference solution	1986 Scenario V
Aswan						
Ammonia	137	128	134	148	148	148
Nitric acid	241	226	237	262	262	262
CAN 33.5 percent	317	297	311	344	344	344
Helwan						
Ammonia	0	0	0	0	0	0
Nitric acid	64	64	64	64	64	64
CAN 33.5 percent	84	84	84	84	84	84
Ammonium sulfate	8	8	8	8	8	8
Kafr El Zayaat						
Sulfuric acid: pyrites	0	0	14	14	14	14
Sulfuric acid: sulfur	40	30	56	56	56	56
SSP	94	69	168	168	168	168
Powdered TSP	0	0	0	0	0	0
Assiout						
Sulfuric acid: sulfur	73	73	73	73	73	73
SSP	178	178	178	178	178	178
Powdered TSP	0	0	0	0	0	0
Suez						
Ammonia	41	39	36	53	37	53
Nitric acid	15	8	1	58	2	116
Calcium nitrate	23	12	1	87	3	175
Ammonium sulfate	0	0	0	0	0	0
Nitrophosphate	0	0	0	0	0	0
Abu Kir						
Ammonia	92	222	177	258	258	258
Urea	158	383	305	445	445	445
Talkha						
Ammonia	400	385	402	413	376	429
Nitric acid	226	226	207	226	162	226
CAN 31 percent	0	0	0	0	0	0
CAN 33.5 percent	297	297	272	297	213	297
Urea	468	443	490	490	490	490

Table 42 (*continued*)

Plant location and product	*1980*		*1983*		*1986*	
	Reference solution	*Scenario V*	*Reference solution*	*Scenario V*	*Reference solution*	*Scenario V*
Abu Zaabal						
Sulfuric acid: pyrites	64	64	64	64	64	64
Sulfuric acid: sulfur	152	152	152	152	152	152
Phosphoric acid	120	120	120	120	120	120
SSP 15.5 percent	0	0	0	0	0	0
Powdered TSP	163	163	163	163	163	163

Table 43. *Exports of Final Products under Scenario V*
(thousands of tons)

Plant location and product	*1980*	*1983*	*1986*
Abu Kir: Urea	250	297	205
Kafr El Zayaat: SSP	0	0	92
Total	250	297	297

expansion, but the reference solution involves an export upper bound (100,000 tons a year) that is smaller than that of Scenario V.

The production pattern under Scenario V is presented in table 42; the exports are shown in table 43, which indicates that the only products exported are urea from Abu Kir and SSP from Kafr El Zayaat. All other production is channeled toward domestic consumption (see table 57). Unlike in Scenario IV, the total exports in Scenario V remain the same in the last two time periods; that is, exports grow by 10 percent a year during the first two time periods, but there is no subsequent increase. This 10 percent annual growth of exports is not large enough to justify new nitrogen capacity expansion (as was the case in the previous scenario). Therefore, the increasing domestic demand and the relaxation of the urea consumption restrictions causes an increase in the production of calcium nitrate at Suez from 12,000 tons a year to 175,000 tons a year and a decline in urea exports from Abu Kir from 297,000 tons a year to 205,000 tons a year in the third period. Since total exports have a lower bound of 297,000 tons a year in the third time period, the difference of 92,000 tons is made up by exporting SSP from Kafr El Zayaat. This, however, causes a positive excess demand domestically for the phosphorus nutrient, which is satisfied by annual imports of 98,000 tons of TSP. Clearly, this is a somewhat unlikely pattern of trade, caused solely by the specification of a lower bound on exports.

A Complete Import Substitution Policy: Scenario VI

Scenario VI evaluates the costs of a policy that bans the imports of all final products: that is, a policy of substituting all final product imports with domestic production.[11]

As table 58 in the appendix indicates, the objective function value under the import substitution policy is marginally higher than that under the reference solution, amounting to 178.66 million Egyptian pounds; the difference, or the discounted cost of the policy, is therefore 1.38 million Egyptian pounds over the planning period. It is not surprising that this difference—less than 0.8 percent of the cost of the reference solution—is so small since the imports substituted

Table 44. *Plant Investment under Scenario VI*

Plant location and product	*Time period*	*Capacity (thousands of tons a year)*	*Investment (millions of U.S. dollars)*	*Site cost (millions of U.S. dollars)*	*Total cost (millions of U.S. dollars)*
Abu Zaabal					
Phosphoric acid	1980	214	22.20	6.66	28.86
Sulfuric acid	1983	146	13.32	4.00	17.32
Total		360	35.52	10.66	46.18

11. The imports of raw materials—namely, pyrites and sulfur—are still permitted because these products are not available domestically.

Table 45. *The Production of Final and Intermediate Products under Scenario VI*
(thousands of tons)

Plant location and product	*1980* Reference solution	*1980* Scenario VI	*1983* Reference solution	*1983* Scenario VI	*1986* Reference solution	*1986* Scenario VI
Aswan						
Ammonia	137	137	134	134	148	149
Nitric acid	241	241	237	237	262	262
CAN 33.5 percent	317	317	311	311	344	344
Helwan						
Ammonia	0	0	0	0	0	0
Nitric acid	64	64	64	64	64	64
CAN 33.5 percent	84	84	84	84	84	84
Ammonium sulfate	8	8	8	8	8	8
Kafr El Zayaat						
Sulfuric acid: pyrites	0	0	14	0	14	0
Sulfuric acid: sulfur	40	40	56	43	56	31
SSP	94	77	168	0	168	76
Powdered TSP	0	0	0	91	0	93
Assiout						
Sulfuric acid: sulfur	73	73	73	43	73	73
SSP	178	178	178	105	178	178
Powdered TSP	0	0	0	0	0	0
Suez						
Ammonia	41	41	36	36	37	37
Nitric acid	15	15	1	1	2	2
Calcium nitrate	23	23	1	1	3	3
Ammonium sulfate	0	0	0	0	0	0
Nitrophosphate	0	0	0	0	0	0
Abu Kir						
Ammonia	92	92	177	172	258	258
Urea	158	158	305	305	445	445
Talkha						
Ammonia	400	400	402	402	376	376
Nitric acid	226	226	207	207	162	162
CAN 31 percent	0	0	0	0	0	0
CAN 33.5 percent	297	297	272	272	213	213
Urea	468	468	490	490	490	490
Abu Zaabal						
Sulfuric acid: pyrites	64	64	64	62	64	64
Sulfuric acid: sulfur	152	152	152	284	152	284
Phosphoric acid	120	125	120	192	120	193
SSP 15.5 percent	0	0	0	0	0	0
Powdered TSP	163	168	163	168	163	168

through domestic production in the reference solution amount to only 258,000 tons over the planning horizon. In the reference solution, the only imports of final product required were those of TSP in the second and third time periods (see table 31). The imports in the second time period amounted to 18,000 tons a year and those in the third time period to 68,000 tons a year.

Comparing the results for the reference solution (table 31) and those for Scenario VI (table 58) shows that major changes occur only in capacity expansion and interplant shipments. In the reference solution, the capacity expansion involved a phosphoric acid plant with a capacity of 134,000 tons a year at Abu Zaabal, and the interplant shipments involved transporting sulfuric acid from Kafr El Zaayat to Assiout and ammonia from Suez to Helwan; Scenario VI necessitates a phosphoric acid plant with a capacity of 214,000 tons a year capacity (at a cost of US$29 million) and a sulfuric acid plant with a capacity of 146,000 tons a year in the second time period (at a cost of US$17 million). The detailed breakdown is presented in table 44. The interplant shipments now involve an additional shipment of phosphoric acid from Abu Zaabal to Kafr El Zayaat.

The production pattern under Scenario VI is shown in table 45.

The Elimination of the Urea Consumption Restrictions: Scenario VII

The preceding scenarios have all assumed that the Egyptian farmer would require time to adjust to the consumption of the higher-analysis fertilizer urea. Thus, consumption restrictions were imposed so that no more than 60 percent of all nitrogen could be consumed in the form of urea in the first time period; this figure was increased to 75 percent and 85 percent in the second and third time periods, respectively. Since this consumption pattern is less than optimal, an opportunity cost is associated with this constraint. To determine this cost, the production-consumption pattern was determined without these restrictions on urea.

Table 59 in the appendix shows that the discounted objective function value of Scenario VII is 172.31 million Egyptian pounds, which is 4.97 million Egyptian pounds less than the value of the reference solution. Comparing the individual cost categories of Scenario VII with those of the reference solution (see table 31)

Table 46. *The Production of Final and Intermediate Products under Scenario VII*
(thousands of tons)

Plant location and product	*1980* Reference solution	*1980* Scenario VII	*1983* Reference solution	*1983* Scenario VII	*1986* Reference solution	*1986* Scenario VII
Aswan						
Ammonia	137	149	134	148	148	148
Nitric acid	241	193	237	262	262	262
CAN 33.5 percent	317	253	311	344	344	344
Helwan						
Ammonia	0	0	0	0	0	0
Nitric acid	64	24	64	64	64	64
CAN 33.5 percent	84	31	84	84	84	84
Ammonium sulfate	8	8	8	8	8	8
Kafr El Zayaat						
Sulfuric acid: pyrites	0	0	14	14	14	14
Sulfuric acid: sulfur	40	29	56	56	56	56
SSP	94	69	168	168	168	168
Powdered TSP	0	0	0	0	0	0
Assiout						
Sulfuric acid: sulfur	73	73	73	73	73	73
SSP	178	178	178	178	178	178
Powdered TSP	0	0	0	0	0	0
Suez						
Ammonia	41	14	36	37	37	37
Nitric acid	15	0	1	2	2	2
Calcium nitrate	23	0	1	3	3	3
Ammonium sulfate	0	0	0	0	0	0
Nitrophosphate	0	0	0	0	0	0
Abu Kir						
Ammonia	92	258	177	258	258	258
Urea	158	445	305	445	445	445
Talkha						
Ammonia	400	295	402	258	376	258
Nitric acid	226	19	207	35	162	162
CAN 31 percent	0	0	0	0	0	0
CAN 33.5 percent	297	25	272	47	213	213
Urea	468	490	490	490	490	490
Abu Zaabal						
Sulfuric acid: pyrites	64	64	64	64	64	64
Sulfuric acid: sulfur	152	152	152	152	152	152
Phosphoric acid	120	120	120	120	120	120
SSP 15.5 percent	0	0	0	0	0	0
Powdered TSP	163	163	163	163	163	163

Table 47. *Exports of Final Products under Scenario VII*
(thousands of tons)

Plant location and product	*1980*	*1983*	*1986*
Helwan			
CAN 33.5 percent	25	25	25
Abu Kir			
Urea	25	25	25
Talkha			
CAN 33.5 percent	25	25	25
Urea	25	25	25
Total	100	100	100

shows that the decline in the objective function is caused chiefly by the saving in transport cost (1.31 million Egyptian pounds) and in operating cost (3.64 million Egyptian pounds).

These changes can be explained by the production pattern shown in table 46. Since the urea restrictions primarily affect the nitrogen fertilizer industry, all changes in production levels are restricted to that industry except for the production of SSP at Kafr El Zayaat, which drops from 94,000 tons a year to 69,000 tons a year in the first time period. This decline of 25,000 tons a year does not represent a change in domestic consumption, but rather a change in the export pattern. The exports of SSP are substituted for by the exports of the more profitable CAN 33.5 percent from Talkha (see table 47). This switch is possible because eliminating the urea restriction permits Talkha CAN production to be diverted away from the domestic market to the export market.

The most important impact of the elimination of this restriction is the production at full capacity of urea plants at both Talkha and Abu Kir in all time periods. All urea—490,000 tons a year at Talkha and 446,000 tons a year at Abu Kir—is shipped domestically (see table 59) except for exports of 25,000 tons a year from each location (see table 47). This level of urea production necessitates a reduction in the first time period in the production of the relatively more expensive nitrogen products at Helwan, Aswan, Suez, and Talkha. As nitrogen demand increases in subsequent time periods, however, Helwan and Aswan produce CAN at full capacity in the second and third periods, Suez produces small amounts of calcium nitrate in the second and third periods to satisfy local demand, and Talkha increases its production of CAN to 47,000 tons a year in the second period and to full capacity in the last period.

Thus, nitrogen capacity in Egypt is sufficient to satisfy domestic demand up to 1987, even in the absence of restrictions on urea consumption. The production and consumption patterns so obtained result in a savings of about 5 million Egyptian pounds over the planning period. This implies that, if the cost of educating farmers to use urea is less than or equal to 5 million Egyptian pounds, such extension would be worth considering.

Measures of the Domestic Resource Cost

On the basis of the available cost data, the domestic resource cost (DRC) associated with the various scenarios can be evaluated. These measures provide estimates of the unit opportunity cost of the domestically owned factors of production employed directly (in the fertilizer sector) and indirectly (in the associated home goods industries) as a function of the net change in Egypt's trade balance that would occur if the level of output were expanded or contracted by one unit. The DRC criterion is analogous to the "rate of return" criterion using the foreign exchange factor as the numeraire rather than the capital factor.

Within the context of this study, the DRC is computed for the entire investment program over the planning horizon. Therefore, the numerator and the denominator are expressed in present value terms with the costs (both foreign exchange and domestic) discounted back to the beginning of the planning period. In addition, since this calculation is undertaken within the framework of a process analysis, economic cost can be defined as the value of the final and intermediate goods that could be produced in the sector through resource allocation and trade, which takes into account the possibility of substitution in production and consumption. Thus, such a measure of cost does not undertake the welfare loss attributable to a system that assumes an unaltered pattern of final consumption.

Throughout this section, it is assumed that the foreign exchange component of the various cost categories are as follows: transport cost, 40 percent; domestic raw materials cost, 30 percent; operating cost, 30 percent; working capital charge, 50 percent; and capital charge, 70 percent.

Three approaches are followed in calculating the domestic resource cost, thus yielding three different measures.[12] The first approach (DRC_o) ignores substitution in consumption, whereas the other two (DRC_s and IDRC) do not. In addition, the last approach (IDRC) is, strictly speaking, an incremental (or marginal) DRC that evaluates the opportunity cost of domestic resources per unit of foreign exchange on the incremental capacity expansion only; it thus takes the existing domestic capacity as given.

The first approach (DRC_o) calculates the foreign exchange cost on the assumption that all fertilizers consumed domestically are imported—that is, these fertilizers are valued at their c.i.f. import prices. The fertilizer consumption pattern is taken to be identical to the pattern implicit in the relevant capacity-expansion scenario. Then, the direct and indirect foreign exchange cost and the domestic cost associated with such a capacity-expansion scenario are obtained (see table 48). The foreign exchange savings or earnings so generated and the associated domestic cost are calculated, yielding a measure of the domestic resource cost (denoted DRC_o). The resource cost coefficient, expressed as a ratio of the domestic resource cost to the exchange rate, is subsequently obtained for both the shadow and the official exchange rate.[13] These ratios are expressed in percentage terms. This approach, however, ignores all substitution in the final consumption of fertilizers.

The second approach (DRC_s) calculates the significance of consumption substitution; it takes into account the change in the final product mix and thus the consumption brought about by new capacity expansion. Table 49 compares the production and import patterns when no new capacity expansion is permitted with those when there is new capacity. The no-capacity-expansion situation permits domestic production from existing plants only, with the

12. All three measures of DRC are based on marginal costs for the existing plants. All the associated committed costs are treated as sunk costs since they involve decisions that have already been made and that are irreversible.

13. Excluding the multiple exchange rates generated by the "own imports" scheme in Egypt, three exchange rates can be observed: the official rate (US$1 = 0.4 Egyptian pounds), the parallel market rate (US$1 = 0.59 Egyptian pounds), and the black market rate (US$1 = 0.70 Egyptian pounds). The shadow exchange rate used here (US$1 = 0.65 Egyptian pounds) therefore appears to be reasonable.

Table 48. *The Domestic and Foreign Exchange Cost Components of the Various Scenarios*
(millions of currency units)

Cost category	*Reference solution*		*Scenario I*		*Scenario II*		*Scenario III*	
	Foreign exchange cost (U.S. dollars)	*Domestic cost (Egyptian pounds)*	*Foreign exchange cost (U.S. dollars)*	*Domestic cost (Egyptian pounds)*	*Foreign exchange cost (U.S. dollars)*	*Domestic cost (Egyptian pounds)*	*Foreign exchange cost (U.S. dollars)*	*Domestic cost (Egyptian pounds)*
Transport cost	16.76	16.34	16.57	16.15	17.24	16.81	16.94	16.52
Domestic raw materials cost	28.78	43.65	28.71	43.54	28.70	43.53	32.48	49.26
Operating cost	36.11	54.77	36.98	56.08	36.98	56.09	40.15	60.89
Working capital cost	2.91	18.88	2.94	1.91	2.94	19.08	3.15	2.05
Capital cost	9.11	25.36	16.41	4.57	9.11	2.54	0.00	0.00
Import cost	40.63	0.00	34.84	0.00	40.03	0.00	91.75	0.00
Export revenue	−39.46	−0.00	−41.34	−0.00	−40.77	−0.00	−156.23	−0.00
Total cost	94.83	119.18	95.08	122.40	94.82	120.87	28.24	128.72

(*Table continues on the following page*)

Table 48 (*continued*)

Cost category	*Scenario IV*		*Scenario V*		*Scenario VI*		*Scenario VII*	
	Foreign exchange cost (U.S. dollars)	*Domestic cost (Egyptian pounds)*	*Foreign exchange cost (U.S. dollars)*	*Domestic cost (Egyptian pounds)*	*Foreign exchange cost (U.S. dollars)*	*Domestic cost (Egyptian pounds)*	*Foreign exchange cost (U.S. dollars)*	*Domestic cost (Egyptian pounds)*
Transport cost	16.99	16.57	16.28	15.87	17.21	16.78	15.96	15.57
Domestic raw materials cost	40.72	61.77	32.34	49.05	29.15	44.21	29.11	44.15
Operating cost	47.38	71.87	39.85	60.44	36.52	55.40	34.43	52.22
Working capital cost	3.88	2.52	3.18	2.07	2.96	1.92	2.85	1.85
Capital cost	51.88	14.45	9.11	2.54	15.39	4.29	9.11	2.54
Import cost	41.38	0.00	44.98	0.00	28.90	0.00	40.29	0.00
Export revenue	−289.14	−0.00	−120.66	−0.00	−439.46	−0.00	−40.77	−0.00
Total cost	−76.91[a]	167.17	25.08	129.96	90.66	122.59	90.97	116.31

Note: All costs are discounted to the beginning of the planning period.
a. Represents foreign exchange earnings.

Table 49. *Fertilizer Production and Consumption during the Planning Period, 1979–87*
(thousands of tons)

	No capacity expansion				*New capacity expansion* [a]			
Product	*Domestic production*	*Imports*	*Exports*	*Total consumption*	*Domestic production*	*Imports*	*Exports*	*Total consumption*
Calcium nitrate	192	0	0	192	81	0	0	81
Ammonium sulfate	72	0	0	72	72	0	0	72
CAN 33.5 percent	6,045	0	450	6,495	6,024	0	375	6,399
Urea	7,077	0	450	7,527	7,077	0	450	7,527
SSP	4,632	0	0	4,632	2,898	0	75	2,973
Powdered TSP	0	0	0	0	1,464	0	0	1,464
Granular TSP	0	1,134	0	1,134	0	258	0	258
Total	18,018	1,134	900	20,052	17,616	258	900	18,774

a. The reference solution.

Table 50. *The Domestic Resource Cost for the Various Scenarios*

Scenario	*Objective function value (millions of discounted U.S. dollars)*	*Domestic resource cost*			*Percentage of shadow exchange rate*			*Percentage of official exchange rate*		
		DRC_o	DRC_s	IDRC	DRC_o	DRC_s	IDRC	DRC_o	DRC_s	IDRC
Reference solution	177.28	0.1324	0.1255	0.1094	20.37	19.31	21.57	33.10	31.38	27.35
Scenario I	179.81	0.1362	0.1288	0.1544	20.96	19.81	23.75	34.06	32.20	38.60
Scenario II	179.14	0.1354	0.1273	0.1338	20.83	19.59	20.59	33.85	31.83	33.45
Scenario III	163.19	0.1262	0.1267	0.1260	19.41	19.49	19.38	31.55	31.67	31.50
Scenario IV	158.09	0.1559	0.1491	0.2308	23.99	22.94	35.50	38.99	37.28	57.69
Scenario V	161.96	0.1350	0.1275	0.1321	20.77	19.62	20.32	33.74	31.88	33.02
Scenario VI	178.66	0.1355	0.1286	0.1497	20.85	19.78	23.03	33.88	32.15	37.43
Scenario VII	172.31	0.1307	0.1220	0.0641	20.12	18.77	9.86	32.69	30.50	16.03

Note: Basis for comparison: foreign exchange cost: DRC_o = US$995.07 million for reference solution only, DRC_s = US$1,044.18 million, IDRC = US$163.70 million; domestic cost: IDRC = 111.65 million Egyptian pounds.

excess demand being satisfied by imports. As table 49 indicates, the major change in consumption that takes place if capacity expansion is permitted is the substitution of powdered triple superphosphate for some single superphosphate and imports. The higher-analysis TSP contributes significantly to meeting the demand for phosphorus nutrients, thus resulting in the reduction of domestic consumption of SSP and imports. Substitution in consumption also takes place on the nitrogen side, but to a much lesser extent; the change in the export pattern permits the substitution of CAN 33.5 percent for calcium nitrate.

These substitution effects are incorporated into the second measure. In this case, the foreign exchange cost of the entire program is also calculated on the assumption that all fertilizers consumed are imported, but the consumption pattern of these products is the one that is implicit with existing production capacity. This pattern is shown in the fourth column of table 49. The foreign exchange and domestic costs resulting from the various capacity-expansion scenarios are then obtained as before (shown in table 48). These cost components incorporate the substitution of final products resulting from the change in domestic production. The domestic resource cost is then obtained as before and is denoted by DRC_s in table 50.

The third measure of the domestic resource cost takes the existing capacity as given and computes a DRC for capacity expansion only. Thus, the foreign exchange and domestic costs are obtained for the no-capacity-expansion case (which includes the existing capacity) and obtains the same components for each of the capacity-expansion scenarios incorporating the substitution effect. The incremental domestic resource cost (IDRC) is then obtained as the ratio of the incremental domestic cost to the foreign exchange savings or earnings. This incremental cost thus represents the domestic cost associated with capacity expansion and substitution only. Since the model is structured to produce the minimum cost, the IDRC must always be less than the shadow exchange rate. If that is not the case, it implies that a less than optimal capacity expansion has occurred; that is, the product is being produced domestically when in fact it should have been imported. Further, the IDRC does not refer to a single project; it may also reflect multiple projects, as in Scenario IV. It is thus a measure that reflects sectoral capacity expansion.

Table 50 presents the three measures of domestic resource cost and of the resource cost coefficient as a percentage of the shadow and official exchange rate. In addition, the first column presents the objective function value. If domestic resource cost is considered first, the DRC measures in each case are less than both the shadow exchange rate and the official exchange rate, indicating that Egypt has a cost advantage in fertilizer production under any scenario. Further substitution in final consumption affects the DRC—that is, the values of DRC_o and DRC_s are not the same. In each case (except Scenario III), substitution causes a decline in the value of the DRC (that is, DRC_s is less than DRC_o). This is primarily because of the production of TSP (a high-analysis fertilizer) instead of SSP (a low-analysis fertilizer), which causes a reduction in the imports of phosphate fertilizers. There are also substitution effects in nitrogen consumption, which have a secondary influence on the DRC—that is, the substitution of CAN 33.5 percent and urea (both high-analysis fertilizers) for calcium nitrate (a low-analysis fertilizer).[14] Scenario III (which is a no-capacity-expansion case with unbounded exports) indicates a slight increase in the DRC—from a value of 0.1262 for DRC_o to a value of 0.1267 for DRC_s—because of substitution. This is because the high-analysis urea and CAN 33.5 are now exported rather than consumed and thus production and consumption of calcium nitrate become relatively larger. In addition, there is no substitution of TSP for SSP.

According to the incremental DRC, in each scenario the capacity expansion or strategy consistent with the scenario shows a sectoral comparative advantage for the expansion or strategy undertaken. Thus, the IDRC coefficients range from 19.38 percent to 35.50 percent of the shadow exchange rate. If, however, the domestic resource cost incorporating the substitution effects (DRC_s) is compared with the incremental value in resource cost (IDRC), the value of IDRC is less than that of the DRC_s only in the case of the reference solution (optimal capacity expansion) and Scenario III (unbounded exports). The DRC_s measure incorporates existing capacity plus capacity expansion, whereas the IDRC measure incorporates only capacity expansion. Thus, it is possible to say something about the relative efficiency of the new and the existing capacity.

In the two cases in which the IDRC is less than the DRC_s (reference solution and Scenario III), the difference indicates that the oppor-

14. This substitution leads to a higher foreign exchange cost of fertilizers, based on import prices, thus tending to lower the resource cost per unit of international value added.

tunity cost of earning or saving one dollar of foreign exchange associated with no capacity expansion would be greater than that associated with capacity expansion. In other words, capacity expansion (or Scenario III) has lowered the cost of earning foreign exchange.[15] In the case of the reference solution, the expansion of phosphoric acid capacity—and the resulting changes in production and consumption—has led to a lower cost to the system as a whole. The fact that Scenario III's IDRC is lower than its DRC_s (0.1262 as compared with 0.1267) is not surprising, since this scenario permits unlimited exports. Thus, the benefits of such a policy (that is, exports in excess of 100,000 tons a year) must be positive. Meanwhile, Scenario VII indicates that restrictions on the consumption of urea involve a cost to society (an IDRC of 0.0641 compared with a DRC_s of 0.1220).

For all the other scenarios, in which the IDRC is greater than the DRC_s, the implication is that the capacity expansion or the policy associated with the relevant scenario has raised the opportunity cost of earning or saving foreign exchange, relative to a no-capacity-expansion policy. Therefore, in the case of Scenario II, an expansion of phosphoric acid and nitrophosphates will raise the cost of earning foreign exchange relative to a do-nothing strategy. The same may be said of Scenario III, which incorporates a phosphoric acid plant with minimum production of calcium nitrate at Suez, and Scenario VI, which indicates that a complete import substitution policy involves an economic cost to the sector (an IDRC of 0.1497 as compared with a DRC_s of 0.1286).

The objective function value of the no-capacity-expansion case is 184.92 million Egyptian pounds, which is higher than the objective function values of the various scenarios shown in table 50. Thus, all the solutions presented are superior to the no-capacity-expansion case, and standard project appraisal methods could conceivably lead to the acceptance of each program, if presented without alternatives. The same point can be made regarding the DRC ratios, because in each case the ratio is less than the exchange rate. Thus,

15. If the foreign exchange cost of fertilizer valued at c.i.f. prices is greater than the foreign exchange cost of a no-capacity-expansion situation—which is the case in this study (US$1,044 million compared with US$164 million)—and if the IDRC is less than DRC_s, then the sectoral opportunity cost associated with capacity expansion will be less than that associated with no expansion, and vice versa.

Table 51. *The Ranking of the Scenarios According to Objective Function Value and Domestic Resource Cost*

Scenario	*Objective function value*	*Domestic resource cost* — *Without substitution* (DRC_o)	*With substitution* (DRC_s)	*Incremental* DRC (IDRC)
Reference solution	5	3	2	2
Scenario I	8	7	7	7
Scenario II	7	5	4	5
Scenario III	3	1	3	3
Scenario IV	1	8	8	8
Scenario V	2	4	5	4
Scenario VI	6	6	6	6
Scenario VII	4	2	1	1

an acceptable value of the DRC ratio is also consistent with a less than optimal pattern of investment.

Finally, as the ranking of the various scenarios in table 51 shows, there is no monotonic relationship between the objective function value and any of the three measures of DRC; that is, the ranking of scenarios is not invariant with the criterion (or DRC measure) chosen. Thus, a DRC ratio cannot be used as a guide to search for the best solution, because a lower DRC ratio may be associated with a higher cost investment program. For example, the lowest DRC_s and IDRC are associated with Scenario VII, which is ranked fourth from the point of view of the objective function, and the highest DRC value (for all three measures) is associated with Scenario IV, which has the lowest objective function value.[16]

This discrepancy in ranking is not surprising, however, since the four criteria are essentially different: namely, total (domestic plus foreign) cost minimization, minimization of the domestic opportunity cost of foreign exchange with and without substitution effects, and minimization of the incremental opportunity cost of foreign exchange. There is no reason to expect that the rankings based on

16. This point is also made in Ardy Stoutjesdijk and Larry Westphal, eds., *Industrial Investment Analysis Under Increasing Returns* (forthcoming).

total (domestic plus foreign) cost minimization will be identical to those based on the minimization of domestic costs per unit of international value added.

Two further points regarding the ranking of scenarios are of interest. First, rankings based on domestic resource cost with and without substitution are not the same; that is, if one chooses to use a DRC measure to rank projects, ignoring the substitution effects can be misleading. Second, rankings based on domestic resource cost with substitution effects are very similar to those based on the incremental DRC. In fact, there is only one difference; namely, Scenarios II and V reverse their rank order between these two measures. Thus, the rank correlation between these measures would be high.

A Sensitivity Analysis of the Results

A detailed sensitivity, or break-even, analysis of the results has been precluded by the high cost of computer runs. Several parameters have been examined, however, to provide an answer to the question: At what value of this parameter does the basic reference solution change? In effect, this is a single-parameter, break-even analysis that indicates the value of, say, the discount rate (the opportunity cost of capital) at which capacity expansion is not optimal, or the level of import prices at which imports become inefficient (as in the case of TSP) or efficient (as in the case of urea, CAN 33.5 percent, and SSP). That is, one can evaluate the break-even point alone rather than several solutions at varying discount rates or varying import prices. This provides a range within which the optimal solution remains feasible. Such an analysis is performed for the opportunity cost of capital; the investment cost; the exchange rate; the import prices for TSP, urea, CAN 33.5 percent, and SSP; and the transport cost for the reference solution. Finally, a brief description is given of the computer runs associated with alternative demand projections.

The opportunity cost of capital

The opportunity cost of capital assumed in this study is 10 percent. Given the usual problems associated with this parameter in most developing countries (LDCs), however, planners face an important question: If this value were an underestimate of the true cost of capital, does this affect the planned capacity expansion and the resultant change in the consumption and production patterns? In other words, how high must this cost of capital be for no capacity expansion to occur? Based on the assumption that the life of the plant will be fifteen years, this value is found to be 31.4 percent.[17] A longer plant life leads to a higher value of break-even cost of capital and vice versa, as is seen below:

Plant life years	*Break-even cost of capital (percent)*
5	18.6
10	29.6
15	31.4
20	31.8
25	31.9

Plant lives of more than fifteen years affect the break-even value of the opportunity cost only marginally; that is, a twenty-year plant life leads to a value of 31.8 percent and a twenty-five-year plant life to 31.9 percent. Compared with the value of 31.4 percent for a fifteen-year plant life, this is not a significant change. Plant lives of fewer than fifteen years lead to slightly larger changes; for example, a ten-year plant life leads to a break-even value of 29.6 percent for the cost of capital, and a five-year plant life to 18.6 percent. Thus, as plant life increases, the marginal changes in the break-even cost of capital decline. This analysis shows that, even if one chooses to make a pessimistic assumption on plant life, the phosphoric acid plant would be very robust over a large range of the cost of capital. Given this large range of flexibility in the choice of the cost of capital, one can state with some confidence that the erection of the phosphoric acid plant, and the accompanying changes in the production structure at Abu Zaabal from SSP to powdered TSP, should take place.

Investment costs

For any new capacity expansion that takes place, a relevant question is how sensitive is the erection of the new plant to the capital

17. This is determined by solving for the value of the cost of capital that equates the discounted net cost of the reference solution (capacity expansion) to the discounted net cost of the no-capacity-expansion case. An iterative procedure was used because of the nonlinearities introduced by the discount rate and the capital recovery factor, both of which are functions of the opportunity cost of capital.

cost used in the study? Since the only new capacity expansion in this study is the phosphoric acid plant, it is necessary to investigate only how high the capital cost of this plant could be before its construction became inefficient. This value is US$43.58 million—that is, two-and-a-half times as much as assumed in the study.[18]

The conversion of SSP to powdered TSP at Abu Zaabal has, however, been assumed to be a costless operation. This is not strictly true, although the cost involved is marginal (the estimate is between US$10,000 and US$20,000) and the conversion is simple enough to be performed locally, so that no foreign exchange need be involved. The range is large enough to accommodate errors in capital cost estimates or changes in the real value of the capital cost of the phosphoric acid plant and to make the necessary alterations to the SSP den to obtain powdered TSP.

The exchange rate

The major components of total cost affected by the exchange rate are the capital cost, the import price of raw materials and final product, and the foreign exchange component of the domestic cost. The basic issue of domestic production versus imports is thus affected by the relative incentive provided to either production or imports by the exchange rate. Since the foreign exchange cost is a fraction of the total cost, the incentive to import the final product will decline relative to producing the product domestically as the exchange rate increases; on the contrary, the relative incentive to produce domestically will decrease as the exchange rate declines.

The foreign exchange rate at which there will be no expansion of domestic capacity (that is, only imports) can be evaluated by calculating the various domestic resource costs, which measure comparative advantage. For the reference solution, the incremental domestic resource cost is 0.1094. This indicates that capacity expansion of the phosphoric acid plant (and the associated substitution in production and consumption) would be profitable as long as the exchange rate is greater than US$1 − 0.1094 Egyptian pounds, which is well below the official and shadow exchange rates. Thus,

18. This is determined by obtaining the incremental annual capital charge that is equivalent to the savings generated by the capacity-expansion solution over the no-capacity-expansion case. Since the site factor (1.3) and the capital recovery factor (0.1314) are known, the increment in the total capital can be obtained.

the break-even point that would reverse the optimal strategy is far too low to be of any concern.[19]

The import prices

The import prices for the final products used in this study are the long-term prices expected to prevail over the planning horizon. In the reference solution, there would be imports of TSP in the second and third time periods (18,000 tons a year and 68,000 tons a year, respectively), whereas there would be no imports of SSP, CAN 33.5 percent, or urea. In this section, two questions are raised. First, how high could the price of TSP rise before imports become infeasible?[20] Second, how low could the prices of SSP, CAN 33.5 percent, and urea fall before imports become feasible?[21]

In answer to the first question, the c.i.f. import price of TSP would have to rise to US$170 a ton before imports would be eliminated. Compared with the expected long-term price of US$150 a ton, there is about 14 percent flexibility before the break-even point is reached.

In response to the second question, imports of SSP would be efficient if the c.i.f. import price dropped to US$22.87 a ton. There could, however, be imports of SSP in the second time period if the price fell to US$37.90 a ton and in the third time period if the price fell to US$38.25 a ton. Compared with the c.i.f. import price of US$50 a ton, this indicates that a drop of 20 percent in the price would be necessary to make imports attractive. For CAN 33.5 percent, the break-even prices are US$65.73 a ton in the first period and US$47.58 a ton in the second and third periods.[22] For urea, the

19. This is particularly true in the case of Egypt, where the exchange rate is likely to be "sticking downwards" for some time to come. If labor were treated as a variable cost, however, this break-even exchange rate would be US$1 = 0.42 Egyptian pounds, which is above the official exchange rate.

20. This question is answered by selecting a representative governorate (Behera) that has all its P_2O_5 demand met by imports in the two time periods in the reference solution and the plant (Abu Zaabal) that would supply that governorate with the cheapest source of P_2O_5 if imports were not permitted.

21. In the case of SSP, CAN 33.5 percent, and urea, the governorate is chosen so that the difference in the transport cost associated with shipments from the plant and the port are minimized and so that the plant is the cheapest source of supply of the nutrient.

22. The decline in these prices can be explained by the decline in the capacity rental at Talkha.

Table 52. *Comparison of Break-even Import Prices and Import Price Used in the Planning Model for Selected Products*
(U.S. dollars per ton)

Product	*Break-even import price* 1980	1983	1986	*Import price (c.i.f.) used in the model*
SSP	22.87	37.90	38.25	50
CAN 33.5 percent	65.73	47.58	47.58	120
Urea	50.20	50.20	59.70	150

break-even prices are US$50.20 a ton in the first two time periods and US$59.70 a ton in the last period. As table 52 shows, the highest break-even import price for CAN 33.5 percent and urea is still considerably lower than the c.i.f. import price used in the study. Since import prices are unlikely to fall to such low levels, Egypt may be expected to retain its comparative advantage in these products.

Transport cost

No analysis is performed on the transport cost of final products, because the major changes expected to result from an increase in this cost would be an increase in total cost and an alteration in the shipment pattern. Such an analysis would require several high-cost computer runs, and these were not performed because the cost of obtaining the information did not seem to outweigh the associated benefits.

The transport cost of intermediate products is, however, a different case. The reference solution contains interplant shipments of ammonia from Suez to Helwan and no shipments of phosphoric acid from Abu Zaabal. Thus, two questions can again be raised. First, what increase in the transport cost of ammonia will lead to the production of ammonia at Helwan? Second, what decrease in the transport cost of phosphoric acid will lead to the shipment of the acid from Abu Zaabal to Kafr El Zayaat and to the subsequent production of TSP there?

Two possibilities exist at Helwan since ammonia can be produced either by using coke gas or by upgrading the system to use natural gas. Ammonia from coke-oven gas production would be feasible if the transport cost of ammonia increased by at least 61.59 Egyptian pounds a ton.[23] Since this amount is so large, one can be reasonably certain that shipment from Suez to Helwan would be preferable to ammonia production at Helwan from coke-oven gas. For ammonia production from natural gas, the necessary increase in the transport cost would be significantly smaller—3.52 Egyptian pounds a ton. This figure, however, ignores the variable cost component of the investment cost required for ammonia production from natural gas, and it is thus an underestimate. Consequently, the ammonia shipment activity appears to be stable. If, however, there are significant uncertainties in transport cost, then converting to production of ammonia from natural gas at Helwan should be investigated.

The actual transport cost of phosphoric acid from Abu Zaabal to Kafr El Zayaat is 6.05 Egyptian pounds a ton. To permit interplant shipment of this acid, the transport cost would have to decline to 3.20 Egyptian pounds a ton, almost a 50 percent decrease. Therefore, as long as the transport cost remains higher than 3.20 Egyptian pounds a ton, the shipment activity plus the conversion of SSP to TSP at Kafr El Zayaat remains a less than optimal policy.

Alternative demand projections

The demand projections provided by the Ministry of Agriculture appear to be subject to some uncertainty. The annual growth rate utilized in this study was 4.6 percent for nitrogen and 10.43 percent for phosphorus. An alternative annual growth rate suggested by the ministry was used for nitrogen consumption—6.9 percent. This was thought to be an expected maximum value, so higher growth rates were not considered. Given this growth rate, the model was rerun to determine the changes. It was found that no capacity expansion was necessary for the nitrogenous fertilizer industry over the entire planning period. This is not surprising in view of the excess capacity at Talkha and Suez. Thus, the higher growth rate causes the calcium nitrate plant at Suez and the calcium ammonium nitrate plant at Talkha I to operate nearly at full-capacity utilization.

No additional computer runs were carried out for the phosphate fertilizer growth rate, because the ministry and the Industrial Projects Department of the World Bank seemed to agree that the 10.43 percent annual growth was the expected maximum. Given the nature

23. This is obtained from the reduced cost of coke-oven gas ammonia production.

of the system, and since phosphorus consumption accounts for less than 15 percent of total nutrient consumption, it may be said that a higher growth rate would necessitate more imports, though no attempt has been made to determine the growth rate that would lead to capacity expansion over and above the phosphoric acid plant at Abu Zaabal.

Conclusions

Only the major results of the case study have been described in this chapter; nevertheless, it is clear that the planning methodology used in this study yields results that are specific enough to be meaningful at an operational level. Moreover, the information contained in the model's solution permits an analysis of the robustness of particular project proposals in the light of possible errors in crucial parameters. Finally, this approach can be used to determine the implications of specific scenarios regarding domestic production patterns, imports, and exports. Because of these properties, this planning methodology is a powerful tool of industrial investment analysis, giving results that provide an improved basis for the subsequent phase in the project cycle—that is, feasibility studies.

The major empirical conclusions of the case study are the following. First, Egypt is completely self-sufficient in nitrogen fertilizer with the existing capacity up to 1987. Triple superphosphate will need to be imported, however, in the 1982–84 period at the rate of 18,000 tons a year and in the 1985–87 period at the rate of 68,000 tons a year.

Second, the nitrogen fertilizer industry should produce calcium ammonium nitrate with 33.5 percent nutrient content at Aswan, Helwan, and Talkha I, thus moving away from the 31 percent variety.

Third, it is not economical to produce ammonia at Helwan using coke-oven gas; neither is it advisable to convert to a production process using natural gas. It is more economical to produce the required ammonia at Suez and ship it to Helwan over the entire planning period. Thus, Egypt needs to build the required ammonia movement facilities.

Fourth, calcium nitrate production at Suez is optimal at the level of 23,000 tons a year in the 1979–81 period and at only 1,000 tons a year and 2,000 tons a year in the two subsequent time periods. In practical terms, since the plant cannot operate at such low levels, these figures imply that it must shut down. The erection of a nitrophosphate complex producing a mixture of an equal-weight nitrophosphate (20–20–0) and calcium nitrate is not optimal and will involve an additional cost of 2.5 million Egyptian pounds to the fertilizer sector over the planning period 1979–87. A minimum level (150,000 tons a year) of calcium nitrate production at Suez also entails an additional cost to the sector of 1.9 million Egyptian pounds over the planning period. Thus, if some activity other than the optimal production pattern mentioned above must be undertaken at Suez, calcium nitrate production is superior to a combined nitrophosphate/calcium nitrate production activity.

Fifth, phosphorus demand can be adequately taken care of by the erection of a phosphoric acid (54 percent P_2O_5) plant with a capacity of 134,000 tons a year at Abu Zaabal in the first time period (1979–81) at a cost of US$23 million. The erection of this plant must be accompanied by a subsequent change in the production of the final product at Abu Zaabal from single superphosphate to powdered triple superphosphate.[24] This acid plant is robust (in the sense that it appears in all capacity-expansion scenarios) and has a high rate of return (31.4 percent) associated with it. This is one of the most important conclusions of the study.

Sixth, the production of phosphoric acid and powdered TSP at Abu Zaabal and the continued production of single superphosphate at Kafr El Zayaat and Assiout will satisfy domestic demand for phosphorus up to 1981. From 1982 to 1987, imports of TSP will be necessary. A policy of complete import substitution (or complete self-sufficiency) will cost the sector an additional 1.38 million Egyptian pounds over the planning period. (This is less than the cost to the sector of calcium nitrate production at Suez.) Such a policy entails the erection of a larger phosphoric acid plant (with a capacity of 214,000 tons a year) at Abu Zaabal in the first time period (1979–81) at a cost of about US$29 million, and the subsequent erection of a sulfuric acid plant in the second time period (1982–84) at the same location with a capacity of 146,000 tons a year at a cost of US$17 million. This must be accompanied by a conversion to production of powdered TSP at Abu Zaabal in the first time period and at Kafr El Zayaat in the second time period.

24. The cost of this conversion is marginal, about US$15,000.

Seventh, in all scenarios considered, an export-oriented strategy is beneficial to the sector, since Egypt possesses considerable comparative advantage. An export strategy without any capacity expansion will result in a savings of 14 million Egyptian pounds over the period under consideration, if Egypt can capture the required export market for urea.[25] As domestic demand increases, however, this will result in Egypt's relinquishing the captured export market to its competitors. In order to capture and to preserve an export market of 500,000 tons a year of final product, a phosphoric acid plant at Abu Zaabal and an ammonia urea complex (of 743,000 tons a year of urea) at Suez would have to be erected. Other locations not considered might be equally preferred; they would, however, need to have easy access to natural gas and good port facilities. The urea capacity expansion would have to be phased between the second and third time periods. The total investment cost for the acid plant and the new complex at Suez would amount to US$237 million. Such a strategy would result in a savings to the sector of 19 million Egyptian pounds. Capturing and maintaining a smaller export market of 250,000 tons a year would result in a smaller savings of 15 million Egyptian pounds and would entail the erection of only the phosphoric acid plant at Abu Zaabal.

Eighth, considerable concern has been voiced over the transport sector being the major bottleneck in the distribution of fertilizer. The study indicates that the total transport capacity used by the sector in 1975 is sufficient to transport fertilizers up to 1984. Only in the last time period (1985–87) is the 1975 transport capacity of 378 million ton-kilometers exceeded. The conversion to the higher-analysis fertilizers—urea and TSP—permits the desired distribution of the fertilizers to all the governorates since more nutrients are transported per ton of final product. Therefore, the necessary distribution of fertilizers can be accomplished with the 1975 transport capacity and, apart from replacement costs, major new investments will not be required to transport fertilizers until 1985.

Finally, a cost saving of 5 million Egyptian pounds can be achieved over the plan period if the farmers are prepared to use all the urea that is produced, instead of the traditional fertilizer. Therefore, educating the farmers could be beneficial, as long as the associated costs are less than 5 million Egyptian pounds.

25. The savings refer to the difference in the discounted total cost between the optimal-capacity-expansion case and the case incorporating the export strategy.

Appendix. Summary Tables of the Results of Scenarios I–VII

In this appendix, tables 53 to 59 present the summary results of Scenarios I–VII. These tables correspond to table 31, which gives the summary results of the reference solution to the dynamic planning model of the Egyptian fertilizer sector.

Table 53. *Summary of the Results of Scenario I*
(objective function value = 179.81 million Egyptian pounds)[a]

Category	*1980*	*1983*	*1986*
Cost (millions of Egyptian pounds)			
Transport cost	5.83	6.29	6.90
Domestic raw materials cost	13.16	14.86	16.06
Operating cost	17.33	19.11	20.05
Working capital cost	0.82	0.91	0.97
Capital cost	2.17	2.17	2.17
Import cost			
Raw materials	2.23	2.52	2.52
Final products	0.00	0.18	3.19
Export revenue	−3.90	−3.78	−3.78
Total cost	37.63	42.27	48.08
Total demand (thousands of tons)			
Nutrient demand	608	687	765
Nitrogen	496	552	607
Phosphorus	112	135	158
Fertilizer demand	1,695	1,922	2,033
Production (thousands of tons)			
Final products	1,795	2,022	2,133
Intermediate products	1,663	1,753	1,796
Capacity expansion (thousands of tons)			
Phosphoric acid (at Abu Zaabal)	134	0	0
Nitrophosphate/CN (at Suez)	88	0	0
Imports (thousands of tons)			
Final products (TSP)	0	3	53
Raw materials	137	158	158
Exports (thousands of tons)			
Final products	100	100	100

Table 53 (*continued*)

Category	*1980*	*1983*	*1986*
Shipments of final products to governorates from following plants (thousands of tons)			
Aswan (CAN 33.5 percent)	295	311	344
Helwan (CAN 33.5 percent + AS)	67	67	67
Kafr El Zayaat (SSP)	58	168	168
Assiout (SSP)	178	178	178
Suez (NP + CN)	54	79	79
Abu Kir (urea)	133	273	421
Talkha (CAN 33.5 percent + urea)	740	681	613
Abu Zaabal (TSP)	163	163	163
Total shipments	1,695	1,922	2,033
Interplant shipments of intermediate products from following plants (thousands of tons)			
Aswan	—	—	—
Helwan	—	—	—
Kafr El Zayaat (sulfuric acid to Abu Zaabal)	1	1	1
Assiout	—	—	—
Suez (ammonia to Helwan)	36	36	36
Abu Kir	—	—	—
Talkha	—	—	—
Abu Zaabal	—	—	—
Total shipments	37	37	37

Note: Detail may not sum to totals because of rounding.
a. Discounted total cost in 1975 Egyptian pounds for the period 1979–87.

Table 54. *Summary of the Results of Scenario II*
(objective function value = 179.14 million Egyptian pounds)[a]

Category	*1980*	*1983*	*1986*
Cost (millions of Egyptian pounds)			
Transport cost	6.21	6.46	7.04
Domestic raw materials cost	13.25	14.79	15.99
Operating cost	17.45	19.03	19.96
Working capital cost	0.82	0.91	0.96
Capital cost	1.21	1.21	1.21
Import cost			
Raw materials	2.24	2.52	2.52
Final products	0.00	1.07	4.07
Export revenue	−3.78	−3.78	−3.78
Total cost	37.39	42.19	47.97
Total demand (thousands of tons)			
Nutrient demand	608	687	765
Nitrogen	496	552	607
Phosphorus	112	135	158
Fertilizer demand	1,695	1,922	2,033
Production (thousands of tons)			
Final products	1,860	2,065	2,176
Intermediate products	1,723	1,791	1,833
Capacity expansion (thousands of tons)			
Phosphoric acid (at Abu Zaabal)	134	0	0
Imports (thousands of tons)			
Final products (TSP)	0	18	68
Raw materials	138	158	158
Exports (thousands of tons)			
Final products	100	100	100
Shipments of final products to governorates from following plants (thousands of tons)			
Aswan (CAN 33.5 percent)	295	311	344
Helwan (CAN 33.5 percent + AS)	57	39	39
Kafr El Zayaat (SSP)	69	168	168
Assiout (SSP)	178	178	178
Suez (CN)	150	150	150
Abu Kir (urea)	133	272	421
Talkha (CAN 33.5 percent + urea)	715	683	613
Abu Zaabal (TSP)	163	163	163
Total shipments	1,760	1,965	2,076

Table 54 (*continued*)

Category	*1980*	*1983*	*1986*
Interplant shipments of intermediate products from following plants (thousands of tons)			
Aswan	—	—	—
Helwan	—	—	—
Kafr El Zayaat (sulfuric acid to Abu Zaabal)	1	1	1
Assiout	—	—	—
Suez (ammonia to Helwan)	24	24	24
Abu Kir	—	—	—
Talkha (ammonia to Helwan)	7	—	—
Abu Zaabal	—	—	—
Total shipments	32	25	25

Note: Detail may not sum to totals because of rounding.
a. Discounted total cost in 1975 Egyptian pounds for the period 1979–87.

Table 55. *Summary of the Results of Scenario III*
(objective function value = 163.19 million Egyptian pounds)[a]

Category	*1980*	*1983*	*1986*
Cost (millions of Egyptian pounds)			
Transport cost	6.13	6.41	6.79
Domestic raw materials cost	16.28	16.32	16.37
Operating cost	20.09	20.17	20.26
Working capital cost	0.95	0.95	0.95
Capital cost	0.00	0.00	0.00
Import cost			
Raw materials	1.53	1.53	1.53
Final products	4.54	7.54	10.55
Export revenue	−18.49	−13.55	−8.64
Total cost	31.03	39.37	47.81
Total demand (thousands of tons)			
Nutrient demand	608	687	765
Nitrogen	496	552	607
Phosphorus	112	135	158
Fertilizer demand	1,896	2,024	2,153
Production (thousands of tons)			
Final products	2,336	2,346	2,358
Intermediate products	1,748	1,757	1,767
Capacity expansion (thousands of tons)			
None	0	0	0
Imports (thousands of tons)			
Final products (TSP)	76	126	176
Raw materials	77	77	77
Exports (thousands of tons)			
Final products	440	323	206
Shipments of final products to governorates from following plants (thousands of tons)			
Aswan (CAN 33.5 percent)	344	344	344
Helwan (CAN 33.5 percent + AS)	92	92	92
Kafr El Zayaat (SSP)	168	168	168
Assiout (SSP)	178	178	178
Suez (CN)	153	163	175
Abu Kir (urea)	5	123	240
Talkha (CAN 33.5 percent + urea)	787	787	787
Abu Zaabal (SSP)	168	168	168
Total shipments	1,896	2,024	2,153

Table 55 (*continued*)

Category	*1980*	*1983*	*1986*
Interplant shipments of intermediate products from following plants (thousands of tons)			
Aswan	—	—	—
Helwan	—	—	—
Kafr El Zayaat	—	—	—
Assiout	—	—	—
Suez (ammonia to Helwan)	24	21	19
Abu Kir	—	—	—
Talkha (ammonia to Helwan)	12	15	17
Abu Zaabal	—	—	—
Total shipments	36	36	36

Note: Detail may not sum to totals because of rounding.

a. Discounted total cost in 1975 Egyptian pounds for the period 1979–87.

Table 56. *Summary of the Results of Scenario IV*
(objective function value = 158.09 million Egyptian pounds)[a]

Category	1980	1983	1986
Cost (millions of Egyptian pounds)			
Transport cost	6.21	6.23	6.96
Domestic raw materials cost	16.91	21.55	25.28
Operating cost	20.89	24.51	28.02
Working capital cost	1.01	1.21	1.40
Capital cost	1.21	10.21	12.48
Import cost			
Raw materials	2.47	2.52	2.52
Final products	0.00	1.07	4.07
Export revenue	−19.39	−27.30	−35.49
Total cost	29.29	30.81	45.24
Total demand (thousands of tons)			
Nutrient demand	608	687	765
Nitrogen	496	552	607
Phosphorus	112	135	158
Fertilizer demand	1,748	1,911	2,089
Production (thousands of tons)			
Final products	2,248	2,561	2,934
Intermediate products	1,953	2,108	2,348
Capacity expansion (thousands of tons)			
Phosphoric acid (at Abu Zaabal)	134	0	0
Ammonia (at Suez)	0	431	0
Urea (at Suez)	0	424	319
Imports (thousands of tons)			
Final products (TSP)	0	18	68
Raw materials	152	158	158
Exports (thousands of tons)			
Final products	500	650	845
Shipments of final products to governorates from following plants (thousands of tons)			
Aswan (CAN 33.5 percent)	344	344	344
Helwan (CAN 33.5 percent + AS)	92	92	92
Kafr El Zayaat (SSP)	69	168	168
Assiout (SSP)	178	178	178
Suez (CN + urea)	87	9	125
Abu Kir (urea)	27	169	231
Talkha (CAN 33.5 percent + urea)	787	787	787
Abu Zaabal (TSP)	163	163	163
Total shipments	1,748	1,911	2,089

Table 56 (*continued*)

Category	*1980*	*1983*	*1986*
Interplant shipments of intermediate products from following plants (thousands of tons)			
Aswan	—	—	—
Helwan	—	—	—
Kafr El Zayaat (sulfuric acid to Abu Zaabal)	1	1	1
Assiout	—	—	—
Suez (ammonia to Helwan)	36	36	36
Abu Kir	—	—	—
Talkha	—	—	—
Abu Zaabal	—	—	—
Total shipments	37	37	37

Note: Detail may not sum to totals because of rounding.
a. Discounted total cost in 1975 Egyptian pounds for the period 1979–87.

Table 57. *Summary of the Results of Scenario V*
(objective function value = 161.96 million Egyptian pounds)[a]

Category	*1980*	*1983*	*1986*
Cost (millions of Egyptian pounds)			
Transport cost	5.69	6.10	6.97
Domestic raw materials cost	15.09	16.96	17.31
Operating cost	18.34	21.01	21.66
Working capital cost	0.89	1.01	1.04
Capital cost	1.21	1.21	1.21
Import cost			
Raw materials	2.24	2.52	2.52
Final products	0.00	1.06	5.86
Export revenue	−10.50	−12.48	−10.69
Total cost	32.96	37.39	45.87
Total demand (thousands of tons)			
Nutrient demand	608	687	765
Nitrogen	496	552	607
Phosphorus	112	135	158
Fertilizer demand	1,685	1,968	2,056
Production (thousands of tons)			
Final products	1,935	2,265	2,353
Intermediate products	1,737	1,960	2,035
Capacity expansion (thousands of tons)			
Phosphoric acid (at Abu Zaabal)	134	0	0
Imports (thousands of tons)			
Final products (TSP)	0	18	98
Raw materials	138	158	158
Exports (thousands of tons)			
Final products	250	297	297
Shipments of final products to governorates from following plants (thousands of tons)			
Aswan (CAN 33.5 percent)	297	344	344
Helwan (CAN 33.5 percent + AS)	92	92	92
Kafr El Zayaat (SSP)	69	168	77
Assiout (SSP)	178	178	178
Suez (CN)	12	87	175
Abu Kir (urea)	133	148	240
Talkha (CAN 33.5 percent + urea)	740	787	787
Abu Zaabal (TSP)	163	163	163
Total shipments	1,685	1,968	2,056

Table 57 (*continued*)

Category	*1980*	*1983*	*1986*
Interplant shipments of intermediate products from following plants (thousands of tons)			
Aswan	—	—	—
Helwan	—	—	—
Kafr El Zayaat (sulfuric acid to Abu Zaabal)	1	1	1
Assiout	—	—	—
Suez (ammonia to Helwan)	36	36	19
Abu Kir	—	—	—
Talkha	—	—	—
Abu Zaabal	—	—	—
Total shipments	37	37	37

Note: Detail may not add to totals because of rounding.
a. Discounted total cost in 1975 Egyptian pounds for the period 1979–87.

Table 58. *Summary of the Results of Scenario VI*
(objective function value = 178.66 million Egyptian pounds)[a]

Category	*1980*	*1983*	*1986*
Cost (millions of Egyptian pounds)			
Transport cost	6.12	6.45	7.16
Domestic raw materials cost	13.15	15.08	16.69
Operating cost	17.01	18.48	20.52
Working capital cost	0.81	0.91	1.01
Capital cost	1.52	2.43	2.43
Import cost			
Raw materials	2.32	2.76	3.22
Final products	0.00	0.00	0.00
Export revenue	−3.50	−3.78	−3.78
Total cost	37.43	42.34	47.25
Total demand (thousands of tons)			
Nutrient demand	608	667	765
Nitrogen	496	552	607
Phosphorus	112	135	158
Fertilizer demand	1,680	1,737	2,002
Production (thousands of tons)			
Final products	1,780	1,831	2,102
Intermediate products	1,669	1,838	1,954
Capacity expansion (thousands of tons)			
Phosphoric acid (at Abu Zaabal)	214	0	0
Sulfuric acid (at Abu Zaabal)	0	146	0
Imports (thousands of tons)			
Final products	0	0	0
Raw materials	141	160	182
Exports (thousands of tons)			
Final products	100	100	100
Shipments of final products to governorates from following plants (thousands of tons)			
Aswan (CAN 33.5 percent)	317	311	344
Helwan (CAN 33.5 percent + AS)	67	67	67
Kafr El Zayaat (SSP)	52	0	76
Kafr El Zayaat (TSP)	0	91	93
Assiout (SSP)	178	105	178
Suez (CN)	23	1	3
Abu Kir (urea)	133	281	421
Talkha (CAN 33.5 percent)	297	247	188
Talkha (urea)	443	465	465
Abu Zaabal (TSP)	168	168	168
Total shipments	1,680	1,737	2,002

Table 58 (*continued*)

Category	*1980*	*1983*	*1986*
Interplant shipments of intermediate products from following plants (thousands of tons)			
Aswan	—	—	—
Helwan	—	—	—
Kafr El Zayaat (sulfuric acid to Abu Zaabal)	8	0	0
Assiout	—	—	—
Suez (ammonia to Helwan)	36	36	36
Abu Kir	—	—	—
Talkha	—	—	—
Abu Zaabal (phosphoric acid to Kafr El Zayaat)	—	67	68
Total shipments	44	103	104

Note: Detail may not add to totals because of rounding.
a. Discounted total cost in 1975 Egyptian pounds for the period 1979–87.

Table 59. *Summary of the Results of Scenario VII*
(objective function value = 172.31 million Egyptian pounds)[a]

Category	*1980*	*1983*	*1986*
Cost (millions of Egyptian pounds)			
Transport cost	5.45	6.24	6.70
Domestic raw materials cost	13.65	14.79	16.12
Operating cost	15.56	17.90	19.56
Working capital cost	0.79	0.88	0.96
Capital cost	1.21	1.21	1.21
Import cost			
Raw materials	2.24	2.52	2.52
Final products	0.00	1.07	4.07
Export revenue	−3.78	−3.78	−3.78
Total cost	35.12	40.83	47.36
Total demand (thousands of tons)			
Nutrient demand	608	667	765
Nitrogen	496	552	607
Phosphorus	112	135	158
Fertilizer demand	1,563	1,830	1,997
Production (thousands of tons)			
Final products	1,663	1,930	2,096
Intermediate products	1,350	1,591	4,730
Capacity expansion (thousands of tons)			
Phosphoric acid (at Abu Zaabal)	134	0	0
Imports (thousands of tons)			
Final products (TSP)	0	18	68
Raw materials	138	158	158
Shipments of final products to governorates from following plants (thousands of tons)			
Aswan (CAN 33.5 percent)	253	344	344
Helwan (CAN 33.5 percent + AS)	14	67	67
Kafr El Zayaat (SSP)	69	168	168
Assiout (SSP)	178	178	178
Suez (CN)	0	3	3
Abu Kir (urea)	421	421	421
Talkha (CAN 33.5 percent + urea)	465	487	653
Abu Zaabal (TSP)	163	163	163
Total shipments	1,563	1,830	1,997

Table 59 (*continued*)

Category	*1980*	*1983*	*1986*
Interplant shipments of intermediate products from following plants (thousands of tons)			
Aswan	—	—	—
Helwan	—	—	—
Kafr El Zayaat (sulfuric acid to Abu Zaabal)	1	1	1
Assiout	—	—	—
Suez (ammonia to Helwan)	14	36	36
Abu Kir	—	—	—
Talkha	—	—	—
Abu Zaabal	—	—	—
Total shipments	15	37	37

Note: Detail may not add to totals because of rounding.
a. Discounted total cost in 1975 Egyptian pounds for the period 1979–87.

Appendix

Computer-Readable Representation of the Model

```
GAMS 0    E G Y P T I A N   FERTILIZER MODEL                                  01/30/80  16.44.20  PAGE     1
          SET DEFINITIONS

   SET I  PLANT LOCATIONS  /

          ASWAN
          HELWAN
          ASSIOUT
          KAFR-EL-ZT

          SUEZ
          TALKHA
          ABU-KIR
          ABU-ZAABAL
                           /

       J  DEMAND REGIONS    /

          ALEXANDRIA      ALEXANDRIA
          BEHERA          DAMANHUR
          GHARBIA         TANTA
          KAFR-EL-SH      KARE EL-SHEIKH
          DAKAHLIA        EL MANSURA

          DAMIETTA        DAMIETTA
          SHARKIA         ZAGAZIG
          ISMAILIA        ISMAILIA
          SUEZ            SUEZ
          MENOUFIA        SHIBIN EL KOM

          KALUBIA         BENHA
          GIZA            GIZA
          BENI-SUEF       BENI-SUEF
          FAYOUM          EL-FAYOUM
          MINIA           EL-MINIA

          ASSIOUT         ASSOIUT
          NEW-VALLEY      EL KHARGA
          SOHAG           SOHAG
          QUENA           QUENA
          ASWAN           ASWAN
                                    /
       L  EXPORT PORTS OF EXIT     /

          ALEXANDRIA
          SUEZ
                                    /
       M  PRODUCTIVE UNITS          /

          SULF-A-S    SULFURIC ACID: SULFUR
          SULF-A-P    SULFURIC ACID: PYRITES
          NITR-ACID   NITRIC ACID
          AMM-ELEC    AMMONIA: WATER ELECTROLYSIS
          AMM-C-GAS   AMMONIA: COKE GAS

          AMM-N-GAS   AMMONIA: NATURAL GAS
          AMM-R-GAS   AMMONIA: REFINERY GAS
```

```
         PHOS-ACID    PHOSPHORIC ACID
         C-AMM-NITR   CALCIUM AMMONIUM NITRATE
         AMM-SULF     AMMONIUM SULFATE

         UREA
         AMM-PHOS     AMMONIUM PHOSPHATE
         SSP          SINGLE SUPERPHOSPHATE
         TSP          TRIPLE SUPERPHOSPHATE
         NITRO-PHOS   NITROPHOSPHATES
                          /
      P  PROCESSES        /

         SULF-A-S     SULFURIC ACID: SULFUR
         SULF-A-P     SULFURIC ACID: PYRITES
         NITR-ACID    NITRIC ACID
         AMM-ELEC     AMMONIA: WATER ELECTROLYSIS
         AMM-C-GAS    AMMONIA: COKE GAS

         AMM-N-GAS    AMMONIA: NATURAL GAS
         AMM-R-GAS    AMMONIA: REFINERY GAS
         PHOS-ACID    PHOSPHORIC ACID
         CAN-260      CALCIUM AMMONIUM NITRATE: 26.0 PCT
         CAN-310      CALCIUM AMMONIUM NITRATE: 31.0 PCT

         CAN-335      CALCIUM AMMONIUM NITRATE: 33.5 PCT
         AMM-SULF     AMMONIUM SULFATE
         UREA
         MAP          MONAMMONIUM PHOSPHATE
         DAP          DIAMMONIUM PHOSPHATE

         SSP-155      SINGLE SUPERPHOSPHATE: 15.5 PCT
         TSP-POW      TRIPLE SUPERPHOSPHATE: POWDERED
         TSP          TRIPLE SUPERPHOSPHATE: GRANULAR
         NITROPHOS    NITROPHOSPHATE: C-NTR AND NP-20-20
                                            /
      G  UPGRADING (CONVERSION) ACTIVITIES  /

         AMM-C-N      AMMONIA:  COKE-OVEN TO NATURAL GAS
                           /
      CQ NUTRIENTS         /

         N            NITROGEN
         P205         PHOSPHORUS
                                         /
      CF FINAL PRODUCTS (FERTILIZERS)    /

         UREA
         C-NITR       CALCIUM NITRATE
         CAN-260      CALCIUM AMMONIUM NITRATE: 26.0 PCT
         CAN-310      CALCIUM AMMONIUM NITRATE: 31.0 PCT
         CAN-335      CALCIUM AMMONIUM NITRATE: 33.5 PCT
         AMM-SULF     AMMONIUM SULFATE

         MAP          MONAMMONIUM PHOSPHATE
```

```
          DAP          DIAMMONIUM PHOSPHATE
          SSP-155      SINGLE SUPERPHOSPHATE: 15.5 PCT
          TSP-POW      TRIPLE SUPERPHOSPHATE: POWDERED
          TSP          TRIPLE SUPERPHOSPHATE: GRANULAR
          NP-20-20     NITROPHOSPHATE 20-20-0
                                     /
       CI INTERMEDIATE PRODUCTS      /

          AMMONIA
          CO2
          NITR-ACID    NITRIC ACID
          SULF-ACID    SULFURIC ACID
          PHOS-ACID    PHOSPHORIC ACID
                                                    /
       CS INTERMEDIATES FOR SHIPMENT / AMMONIA, SULF-ACID, PHOS-ACID /

       CR DOMESTIC RAW MATERIALS AND MISCELLANEOUS INPUTS  /

          EL-ASWAN     ELECTRICITY FROM ASWAN DAM
          COKE-GAS     COKE-OVEN GAS
          NAT-GAS      NATURAL GAS
          REF-GAS      REFINERY GAS
          PHOS-ROCK    PHOSPHATE ROCK

          LIMESTONE
          EL-SULFUR    ELEMENTAL SULFUR
          PYRITES
          ELECTRIC     ELECTRICITY
          BF-GAS       BLAST-FURNACE GAS

          WATER        COOLING WATER
          STEAM
          BAGS
          LABOR
                                 /
       T  TIME PERIODS           /

          1979-81
          1982-84
          1985-87
                                                   /

 SET IP  COPY OF PLANT LOCATIONS

     JP  COPY OF MARKETING CENTERS

     TP COPY OF TIME PERIODS

     C  UNION OF ALL PRODUCTS AND RAW MATERIALS;

 IP(I)=YES; JP(J)=YES; TP(T)=YES; C(CF)=YES; C(CI)=YES; C(CR)=YES;
```

```
GAMS 0   E G Y P T I A N   FERTILIZER MODEL                                01/30/80  16.44.20  PAGE    4
         CONSUMPT-ON AND DEMAND DATA

                 TABLE CF75  CONSUMPTION OF FERTILIZER 1974-75 (1000 TPY)

                         CAN-260    CAN-310    CAN-335  AMM-SULF        UREA

          ALEXANDRIA                             5.0        3.0          1.0
          BEHERA             1.0                25.0       90.0         35.0
          GHARBIA                               17.0       60.0         28.0
          KAFR-EL-SH         1.0                10.0       45.0         22.0
          DAKAHLIA           1.0                26.0       60.0         20.0

          DAMIETTA                               2.0       15.0          8.0
          SHARKIA            1.0                31.0       50.0         28.0
          ISMAILIA                               4.0        6.0          2.0
          SUEZ                                   1.0
          MENOUFIA           1.0                24.0       21.0         30.0

          KALUBIA                               25.0       16.0          7.0
          GIZA                                  40.0        6.0          2.0
          BENI-SUEF          1.0                15.0        1.0         20.0
          FAYOUM             1.0                20.0        6.0         20.0
          MINIA              2.0        15.0    35.0        1.0         41.0

          ASSIOUT            1.0        20.0    26.0        1.0         27.0
          NEW-VALLEY                                                     1.0
          SOHAG                         65.0     3.0                     7.0
          QUENA                         95.0     2.0                     3.0
          ASWAN                         40.0

             +           SSP-155   C-250-55  C-300-100        DAP

          ALEXANDRIA         8.0
          BEHERA            64.0         1.0        .1         .1
          GHARBIA           57.0         1.0        .2         .1
          KAFR-EL-SH        25.0         2.0        .1
          DAKAHLIA          52.0         1.0

          DAMIETTA           5.0
          SHARKIA           43.0         1.0        .1
          ISMAILIA           4.0
          SUEZ               1.0
          MENOUFIA          33.0         2.0        .1         .1

          KALUBIA           22.0         1.0                   .1
          GIZA              14.0         1.0        .1
          BENI-SUEF         13.0         3.0
          FAYOUM            17.0         1.0
          MINIA             50.0         3.0        .2         .1

          ASSIOUT           35.0         5.0        .1
          NEW-VALLEY         1.0
          SOHAG             20.0         1.0
          QUENA              8.0
          ASWAN              8.0
```

```
           TABLE DEM80  DEMAND PROJECTIONS FOR 1980 (1000TPY)

              N   P205

 MEDIUM   496   112
 HIGH     542   112


  PARAMETER ETA UREA CONSUMPTION RESTRICTION / 1979-81 = .60
                                               1982-84 = .75
                                               1985-87 = .85 /

  SET C75 FERTLIZERS USED IN 1975 / C-250-55, C-300-100 /; C75(CF)=YES;


           TABLE  ALPHA  NUTRIENT CONTENT

                   N        P205

 UREA          .46
 C-NITR        .155
 CAN-260       .26
 CAN-310       .31
 CAN-335       .335

 AMM-SULF      .206
 MAP           .11        .54
 DAP           .18        .46
 SSP-155                  .155
 TSP-POW                  .46

 TSP                      .46
 NP-20-20      .20        .20
 C-250-55      .25        .055
 C-300-100     .30        .10

  PARAMETERS CN75     CONSUMPTION OF NUTRIENTS 1974-75 (1000 TPY)
             RDC      REGIONAL DISTRIBUTION OF CONSUMPTION
             CINC     CONSUMPTION INCREMENT
             DB       DEMAND IN NUTRIENTS (1000 TPY)
             MIDYEAR / 1979-81=1980, 1982-84=1983, 1985-87=1986 / ;

  CN75(J,CQ)        = SUM(C75, ALPHA(C75,CQ)*CF75(J,C75));
  CN75("TOTAL",CQ)  = SUM(J, CN75(J,CQ));
  RDC(J,CQ)         = CN75(J,CQ)/CN75("TOTAL",CQ);
  CINC(CQ)          = (DEM80("MEDIUM",CQ) - CN75("TOTAL",CQ))/5;
  DB(CQ,J,T)        = RDC(J,CQ)*(CN75("TOTAL",CQ) + CINC(CQ)*(MIDYEAR(T)-1975));

  PARAMETERS EH  TOTAL EXPORT RESTRICTION        (1000 TPY)
             EB  MAXIMUM EXPORT BY PRODUCT       (1000 TPY);

  EH(T) = 100;  EB(T) = 25;
```

```
         TABLE ROAD  ROAD DISTANCES (KMS)

                   ABU-KIR KAFR-EL-ZT     TALKHA ABU-ZAABAL     HELWAN

  ALEXANDRIA            16        119        187        210        244
  BEHERA                76         42        120         50        184
  GHARBIA              150         20         55         65        122
  KAFR-EL-SH           145         20         35        105        162
  DAKAHLIA             208         58          3        138        152

  DAMIETTA             267        131         66        216        233
  SHARKIA              240         78         58         60        110
  ISMAILIA             365        241        146        142        173
  SUEZ                 370        246        298        224        178
  MENOUFIA             157         33         90        154        109

  KALUBIA              190         66         81         97         76
  GIZA                 287        133        146         48          9
  BENI-SUEF            359        248        261        163        105
  FAYOUM               341        230        243        145         88
  MINIA                384        372        386        288        230

  ASSIOUT              616        504        518        420        362
  NEW-VALLEY           815        703        717        619        561
  SOHAG                715        603        617        519        461
  QUENA                858        746        760        662        604
  ASWAN               1134       1022       1036        938        880

      +               SUEZ    ASSIOUT      ASWAN

  ALEXANDRIA           362        607       1135
  BEHERA               288        547       1065
  GHARBIA              226        485       1003
  KAFR-EL-SH           266        525       1043
  DAKAHLIA             219        515       1033

  DAMIETTA             286        596       1114
  SHARKIA              214        473        991
  ISMAILIA              89        536       1054
  SUEZ                            541       1059
  MENOUFIA             213        472        990

  KALUBIA              180        439        957
  GIZA                 169        372        890
  BENI-SUEF            270        257        775
  FAYOUM               252        308        826
  MINIA                394        132        650

  ASSIOUT              527                   518
  NEW-VALLEY           726        199        519
  SOHAG                626         99        419
  QUENA                769        242        276
  ASWAN               1045        518
```

```
         TABLE RAIL   INTERPLANT RAIL DISTANCES (KMS)

               ABU-KIR KAFR-EL-ZT     TALKHA ABU-ZAABAL     HELWAN

 KAFR-EL-ZT        128
 TALKHA            196         58
 ABU-ZAABAL        219         85        138
 HELWAN            253        142        155         57
 SUEZ              371        246        298        224        178
 ASSIOUT           616        504        518        420        362
 ASWAN            1134       1022       1036        938        880
 EXPORT-PTS         16        104        199        210        166

     +            SUEZ    ASSIOUT      ASWAN

 ASSIOUT           527
 ASWAN            1045        518
 EXPORT-PTS         10        583       1087


         TABLE IMPD IMPORT DISTANCES (KMS)

               BARGE      ROAD

 ABU-KIR          16
 KAFR-EL-ZT      104         6
 TALKHA          199
 ABU-ZAABAL      210        .1
 HELWAN          183
 SUEZ            346        50
 ASSIOUT         583
 ASWAN          1087        10


 PARAMETERS MUF   TRANSPORT COST (LE PER TON): FINAL PRODUCTS
            MUFV  TRANSPORT COST (LE PER TON): IMPORTED FINAL PRODUCTS
            MUE   TRANSPORT COST (LE PER TON): EXPORTS
            MUI   TRANSPORT COST (LE PER TON): INTERPLANT SHIPMENT
            MUR   TRANSPORT COST (LE PER TON): IMPORTED RAW MATERIALS ;

   RAIL(I,IP) = RAIL(I,IP) + RAIL(IP,I);
   ROAD(J,"IMPORT-PTS") = MIN(ROAD(J,"ABU-KIR"),ROAD(J,"SUEZ"));

   MUF(I,J)     = ( .5 + .0144*ROAD(J,I)             )$ROAD(J,I);
   MUFV(J)      = ( .5 + .0144*ROAD(J,"IMPORT-PTS")  )$ROAD(J,"IMPORT-PTS");
   MUE(I)       = ( .5 + .0300*RAIL("EXPORT-PTS",I)  )$RAIL("EXPORT-PTS",I);
   MUI(I,IP)    = (3.5 + .0300*RAIL(I,IP)            )$RAIL(I,IP);
   MUR(I)       = (1.0 + .0030*IMPD(I,"BARGE")       )$IMPD(I,"BARGE")
                + ( .5 + .0144*IMPD(I,"ROAD" )       )$IMPD(I,"ROAD ");
```

```
          TABLE A  INPUT-OUTPUT COEFFICIENT

               C-NITR  CAN-260  CAN-310  CAN-335  AMM-SULF    UREA    MAP    DAP

 NITR-ACID      -.66     -.60     -.71     -.76
 LIMESTONE      -.35     -.26     -.12     -.04
 PHOS-ACID                                                          -.99   -.87
 AMMONIA                 -.16      -.20    -.21       -.26    -.58  -.15   -.23
 CO2                                                          -.58

 SULF-ACID                                            -.76
 C-NITR          1.0
 CAN-260                  1.0
 CAN-310                           1.0
 CAN-335                                    1.0

 AMM-SULF                                              1.0
 UREA                                                          1.0
 MAP                                                                  1.0
 DAP                                                                         1.0

 ELECTRIC                                              -19     -75    -22    -22
 WATER                    -49      -49      -49        -17
 STEAM                    -.4      -.4      -.4               -1.5    -.1    -.15
 BAGS            -22      -23      -23      -23        -22     -22     -2    -22

     +         SSF-155    TSP   TSP-POW  NITROPHOS

 SULF-ACID      -.41
 PHOS-ROCK      -.62   -.35      -.35      -.27
 PHOS-ACID             -.74      -.74
 NITR-ACID                                 -.51
 AMMONIA                                   -.064

 SSP-155         1.0
 TSP                    1.0
 TSP-POW                          1.0
 NP-20-20                                   .427
 C-NITR                                     .573

 ELECTRIC        -14    -28       -23       -52
 WATER            -6               -2       -19
 STEAM                  -.1       -.2       -.3
 BAGS            -22    -22       -23       -23


     +          PHOS-ACID   SULF-A-S   SULF-A-P  NITR-ACID

 PHOS-POCK        -2.35
 EL-SULFUR                   -.334
 PYRITES                                -.826
 AMMONIA                                           -.292
 PHOS-ACID        1.0
 SULF-ACID        -1.80        1.0        1.0
```

```
NITR-ACID                                                   1.0

ELECTRIC            -144         -50          -75          -231
WATER                 -4         -20          -60           -.6

    +          AMM-ELEC   AMM-N-GAS   AMM-R-GAS   AMM-C-GAS

EL-ASWAN          -12.0
NAT-GAS                       -33.0
REF-GAS                                    -.98
COKE-GAS                                                 -2.0
AMMONIA             1.0         1.0         1.0           1.0
CO2                             1.0         1.0           1.0

ELECTRIC                        -33         -50         -1960
BF-GAS                                                   -609
WATER                           -10         -14          -700
STEAM                                                      -4



        TABLE B  CAPACITY UTILIZATION COEFFICIENT

           C-NITR  CAN-260  CAN-310  CAN-335  AMM-SULF    UREA    MAP    DAP

C-NITR        1.0
C-AMM-NITR              1.0      1.0      1.0
AMM-SULF                                             1.0
UREA                                                         1.0
AMM-PHOS                                                            1.0    1.0

    +      SSP-155    TSP    TSP-POW   NITROPHOS

C-NITR                                    .573
SSP            1.0              1.0
TSP                    1.0
NITRO-PHOS                               1.0

    +      PHOS-ACID    SULF-A-S    SULF-A-P   NITR-ACID

PHOS-ACID       1.0
SULF-A-S                     1.0
SULF-A-P                                1.0
NITR-ACID                                           1.0

    +      AMM-ELEC   AMM-N-GAS   AMM-R-GAS   AMM-C-GAS

AMM-ELEC        1.0
AMM-N-GAS                   1.0
AMM-R-GAS                               1.0
AMM-C-GAS                                           1.0
```

```
 PARAMETER PJ  IMPORT PRICE (CIF US$ PER TON 1975)   /

PYRITES        17.5
EL-SULFUR      55

UREA          150
CAN-260       100
CAN-310       110
CAN-335       120
AMM-SULF       75
MAP           220
DAP           210
SSP-155        80
TSP-POW       115
TSP           150
NP-20-20      150
                                                    /

       TABLE PD  DOMESTIC RAW MATERIAL PRICES

           LIMESTONE  NAT-GAS  COKE-GAS  REF-GAS  EL-ASWAN  PHOS-ROCK
*             LE/TON  LE/MSCF   LE/MNCM  LE/MNCM    LE/MWH     LE/TON

 ABU-KIR                  .56
 KAFR-EL-ZT                                                       5.0
 TALKHA          1.2      .56
 ABU-ZAABAL                                                       4.0
 HELWAN          1.2      .60       16
 SUEZ            1.2      .65                 8                   6.0
 ASSIOUT                                                          3.5
 ASWAN           1.2                                   1


  PARAMETER PMISC  MISC. MATERIAL COST   /

 ELECTRIC  .007   LE/KWH
 BF-GAS    .007   LE/CM
 WATER     .031   LE/CM
 STEAM    1.25    LE/TON
 BAGS      .28    LE/UNIT
 LABOR  360.      LE/MANYEAR
                                        /

  PARAMETER PE   EXPORT PRICE;   PE(CF) = PV(CF)*.70;

  PD(I,CR)$PMISC(CR) = PMISC(CR);
```

```
         TABLE DCAP  DESIGN CAPACITY OF PLANTS (T/DAY)

            C-NITR  C-AMM-NITR  AMM-SULF   UREA   SSP   SULF-A-S    SULF-A-P

 ABU-KIR                                   1500
 KAFR-EL-ZT                                       600       200          50
 TALKHA                 1000               1650
 ABU-ZAABAL                                       600       542         227
 HELWAN                  364
 SUEZ           758                  200
 ASSIOUT                                          600       250
 ASWAN                  1100

     +      NITR-ACID  AMM-ELEC  AMM-N-GAS  AMM-R-GAS  AMM-C-GAS

 ABU-KIR                              1000
 TALKHA          1050                 1600
 HELWAN           282                                        172
 SUEZ             572                            230
 ASWAN            800       450

*  TALKHA.AMMONIA =  400 TALKHA I + 1200 TALKHA II


 PARAMETER CAPUT  CAPACITY UTILIZATION FACTOR     /

 ABU-KIR    .9  ,  KAFR-EL-ZT    .85 ,  TALKHA    .9  ,  ABU-ZAABAL  .85
 HELWAN     .7  ,  SUEZ          .7  ,  ASSIOUT   .9  ,  ASWAN       1.0
                                                                        /


 PARAMETER K INITIAL CAPACITY (1000 TPY); K(M,I) = .33*CAPUT(I)*DCAP(I,M);



         TABLE TS  TIME SUMMATION MATRIX

            1979-81  1982-84  1985-87
   1979-81     1
   1982-84     1        1
   1985-87     1        1        1


   SET TT TIME LAG MATRIX / 1979-81.1982-84, 1982-84.1985-87 /
```

```
        TABLE  INV  INVESTMENT COST

*   FIX        FIXED COST IN MILL. US$
*   PROP       VARIABLE COST IN 1000 US$/TON/YEAR

               FIX      PROP

 AMM-SULF      3.2      32.1
 UREA         16.7      52.2
 AMM-PHOS      4.5      32.4
 SSP           7.5      25.5

 TSP           7.0      34.2
 NITRO-PHOS    8.0      70.0
 SULF-ACID     8.5      33.0
 AMM-N-GAS    47.9     103.8
 PHOS-ACID    10.0      57.0


  PARAMETER OMEGA  FIXED-CHARGE PORTION OF INVESTMENT OR LABOR
            NU     VARIABLE PORTION OF INVESTMENT OR LABOR
            HB     MAXIMUM CAPCITY EXPANSION
            F      CAPACITY  CONVERSION
            SF     SITE FACTOR  ;

  SF = 1.3*.001;
  OMEGA(M)          = SF*INV(M,"FIX");   NU(M)       = SF*INV(M,"PROP");
  OMEGA("AMM-C-N")  = SF*20.0;
  OMEGA("LABOR")    = .5;

  HB(M)  = 500 ;

  F("AMM-C-GAS","AMM-C-N","HELWAN") =  K("AMM-C-GAS","HELWAN");
  F("AMM-C-GAS","AMM-C-N","HELWAN") = -K("AMM-C-GAS","HELWAN");



  PARAMETERS SIGMA    CAPITAL RECOVERY FACTOR
             DELTA    DISCOUNT FACTOR
             LIFE     LIFE OF PRODUCTIVE UNIT
             SER      SHADOW EXCHANGE RATE
             RHO      OPPORTUNITY COST OF CAPITAL;

  LIFE = 15;  RHO = .1; SER = .65;

  SIGMA    = RHO*(1+RHO)**LIFE/((1+RHO)**LIFE-1);
  DELTA(T) = (1+RHO)**(1976-MIDYEAR(T))
           + (1+RHO)**(1975-MIDYEAR(T))
           + (1+RHO)**(1974-MIDYEAR(T));
```

```
    VARIABLES  Z      PROCESS LEVEL                                  (1000 TPY)
               XF     DOMESTIC SHIPMENT ACTIVITY: FINAL PRODUCTS     (1000 TPY)
               XI     DOMESTIC SHIPMENT ACTIVITY: INTERMEDIATES      (1000 TPY)
               VF     IMPORTS: FINAL PRODUCTS                        (1000 TPY)
               VR     IMPORTS: RAW MATERIALS                         (1000 TPY)

               E      EXPORTS                                        (1000 TPY)
               U      DOMESTIC RAW MATERIAL PURCHASES                (UNITS)
               H      CAPACITY EXPANSION                             (1000 TPY)
               UP     BINARY VARIABLE: UPGRADING
               Y      BINARY VARIABLE: EXPANSION

               PSI    TOTAL COST (DISCOUNTED)     (1000 LE)
               PSIK   CAPITAL COST                (1000 LE PER YEAR)
               PSIP   DOMESTIC RECURRENT COST     (1000 LE PER YEAR)
               PSIL   TRANSPORT COST              (1000 LE PER YEAR)
               PSIM   WORKING CAPITAL COST        (1000 LE PER YEAR)
               PSII   IMPORT COST                 (1000 LE PER YEAR)
               PSIE   EXPORT REVENUE              (1000 LE PER YEAR)

    EQUATIONS  OBJ    OBJECTIVE FUNCTION  (1000 LE DISCOUNTED)
               MBD    MATERIAL BALANCE ON DEMAND              (1000 TPY)
               MBU    MATERIAL BALANCE ON UREA CONSUMPTION    (1000 TPY)
               MBF    MATERIAL BALANCE ON FINAL PRODUCTS      (1000 TPY)
               MBI    MATERIAL BALANCE ON INTERMEDIATES       (1000 TPY)

               MBR    MATERIAL BALANCE ON RAW MATERIALS       (1000 TPY)
               MBL    MATERIAL BALANCE ON LABOR
               CC     CAPACIY CONSTRAINT                      (1000 TPY)
               ME     MAXIMUM CAPACITY EXPANSION              (1000 TPY)
               EX     MUTUAL EXCLUSIVITY CONSTRAINT           (UNITY)

               ECC    EXPORT CONSTRAINT BY COMMODITY AND PLANT  (1000 TPY)
               ECA    AGGREGATE EXPORT CONSTRAINT               (1000 TPY)
               ECMAX  EXPORT CONSTRAINT BY MARKET SHARE: MAXIMUM(1000 TPY)
               ECMIN  EXPORT CONSTRAINT BY MARKET SHARE: MINIMUM(1000 TPY)
               AK     ACCOUNTING: CAPITAL COST CHARGES     (1000 LE PER YEAR)

               AP     ACCOUNTING: DOMESTIC RECURRENT COST(1000 LE PER YEAR)
               AL     ACCOUNTING: TRANSPORT COST         (1000 LE PER YEAR)
               AM     ACCOUNTING: WORKING CAPITAL        (1000 LE PER YEAR)
               AI     ACCOUNTING: IMPORT COST            (1000 LE PER YEAR)
               AE     ACCOUNTING: EXPORT REVENUE         (1000 LE PER YEAR);

   MBD(CQ,J,T)..   SUM((CF,I), ALPHA(CF,CQ)*XF(CF,I,J,T))

               + SUM(CF, ALPHA(CF,CQ)*VF(CF,J,T)) =G= DB(CQ,J,T);


   MBU(J,T)..      SUM(I, ALPHA("UREA","N")*XF("UREA",I,J,T))

               + ALPHA("UREA","N")*VF("UREA",J,T) =L= ETA(T)*DB("N",J,T);
```

```
MBF(CF,I,T)..   SUM(P, A(CF,P)*Z(P,I,T)) =G= SUM(J, XF(CF,I,J,T)) + E(CF,I,T);

MBI(CI,I,T)..   SUM(P, A(CI,P)*Z(P,I,T)) + SUM(IP, XI(CI,IP,I,T))$CS(CI)
               =G= SUM(IP, XI(CI,I,IP,T))$CS(CI);

MBR(CR,I,T)..   SUM(P, A(CR,P)*Z(P,I,T)) + U(CR,I,T)$PD(I,CR)
                                         + VR(CR,I,T)$PV(CR) =G= 0 ;

MBL(I,T)..      U("LABOR",I,T) =G= SUM(TP$TS(T,TP), SUM(M,
                OMEGA("LABOR")*Y(M,I,TP) + NU("LABOR")*H(M,I,TP)));

CC(I,M,T)..     SUM(P, B(M,P)*Z(P,I,T)) =L= K(M,I)
              + SUM(TP$TS(T,TP), .9*H(M,I,TP) + SUM(G, F(M,G,I)*UP(G,I,TP)));

ME(I,M,T)..     H(M,I,T) =L= HB(M)*Y(M,I,T);

EX(G,I)..       SUM(T, UP(G,I,T)) =L= 1 ;

ECC(CF,I,T)..   E(CF,I,T)  =L=  EB(T);

ECA(T)..        SUM((CF,I), E(CF,I,T)) =L= EH(T);

ECMAX(T)..      SUM((CF,I,TP)$TT(T,TP), E(CF,I,TP)) =L=
                1.3*SUM((CF,I), E(CF,I,T));

ECMIN(T)..      SUM((CF,I,TP)$TT(T,TP), E(CF,I,TP)) =G=
```

```
                 SUM((CF,I), E(CF,I,T));

 OBJ..   PSI =E= SUM(T, DELTA(T)*(PSIK(T) + PSIP(T) + PSIL(T) + PSIM(T)
                 + PSII(T) - PSIE(T)));

 AK(T)..     PSIK(T) =E= SER*SUM(TP$TS(T,TP), SIGMA*(
                                SUM((I,M), OMEGA(M)*Y(M,I,TP) + NU(M)*H(M,I,T))
                              + SUM((I,G), OMEGA(G)*UP(G,I,TP))));

 AP(T)..     PSIP(T) =E= SUM((CR,I), PD(I,CR)*U(CR,I,T));


 AL(T)..     PSIL(T) =E= SUM(CF, SUM((I,J), MUF(I,J)*XF(CF,I,J,T))
                                  + SUM(J, MUFV(J)*VF(CF,J,T))
                                  + SUM(I, MUE(I)*E(CF,I,T)))
                          + SUM(CS, SUM((I,IP), MUI(I,IP)*XI(CS,I,IP,T)))
                          + SUM(CR, SUM(I, MUR(I)*VR(CR,I,T)));

 AM(T)..     PSIM(T) =E= .025*(PSIP(T) + SUM((CR,I), PV(CR)*VR(CR,I,T)));

 AI(T)..     PSII(T) =E= SER*SUM((CF,J), PV(CF)*VF(CF,J,T))
                          + SER*SUM((CR,I), PV(CR)*VR(CR,I,T));

 AE(T)..     PSIE(T) =E= SER*SUM((CF,I), PE(CF)*E(CF,I,T));
```

```
VARIABLES    TYPE     REFERENCES

A            PARAM         REF       693       695       698   DEFINED       382       DCL       382
AE           EQU       DEFINED       742       DCL       684
AI           EQU       DEFINED       739       DCL       683
AK           EQU       DEFINED       724       DCL       678
AL           EQU       DEFINED       731       DCL       681
ALPHA        PARAM         REF       261       687       688       690       691   DEFINED       234       DCL       234
AM           EQU       DEFINED       737       DCL       682
AP           EQU       DEFINED       728       DCL       680
B            PARAM         REF       704   DEFINED       457       DCL       457
C            SET       DEFINED     3*162       DCL       160
CAPUT        PARAM         REF       574   DEFINED       567       DCL       567
CC           EQU       DEFINED       704       DCL       670
CF           SET           REF       536     2*687     2*688     3*693       711       713       715       716       718
                           719       731       732       733     2*739     2*742   DEFINED       102   CONTROL       162
                           231       536       687       688       693       711       713       715       716       718
                           719       731       739       742       DCL       102
CF75         PARAM         REF       261   DEFINED       165       DCL       165
CI           SET           REF     3*695     2*696   DEFINED       118   CONTROL       162       695       DCL       118
CINC         PARAM         REF       265       272   DEFINED       264       DCL       257
CN75         PARAM         REF       262     2*263       264       265       272   DEFINED       261       262       DCL
                           255
CQ           SET           REF       261       262     2*263     2*264     3*265       687     2*688   DEFINED        97
                       CONTROL       261       262       263       264       265       687       DCL        97
CR           SET           REF     2*538     3*698     2*699     2*728       735     2*737     2*740   DEFINED       128
                       CONTROL       162       538       698       728       735       737       740       DCL       128
CS           SET           REF       695       696       734   DEFINED       126   CONTROL       734       DCL       126
C75          SET           REF     2*261   DEFINED     2*231   CONTROL       261       DCL       231
DB           PARAM         REF       272       688       691   DEFINED       265       DCL       258
DCAP         PARAM         REF       574   DEFINED       543       DCL       543
DELTA        PARAM         REF       639       721   DEFINED       635       DCL       627
DEM80        PARAM         REF       264   DEFINED       219       DCL       219
E            VAR           REF       693       711       713       715       716       718       719       733       742
                           DCL       648
EB           PARAM         REF       272       711   DEFINED       270       DCL       268
ECA          EQU       DEFINED       713       DCL       675
ECC          EQU       DEFINED       711       DCL       674
ECMAX        EQU       DEFINED       715       DCL       676
ECMIN        EQU       DEFINED       718       DCL       677
EH           PARAM         REF       272       713   DEFINED       270       DCL       267
ETA          PARAM         REF       691   DEFINED       227       DCL       227
EX           EQU       DEFINED       709       DCL       672
F            PARAM         REF       639       705   DEFINED       621       622       DCL       611
G            SET           REF     2*705       709     2*726   DEFINED        93   CONTROL       705       709       726
                           DCL        93
H            VAR           REF       702       705       707       725       DCL       650
HB           PARAM         REF       707   DEFINED       619       DCL       610
I            SET           REF     2*369     2*372     2*374     2*375     2*376     2*377     2*574       687       690
                         3*693     2*695       696     3*698       699       701     2*702     2*704     3*705     2*707
                           709       711       713       715       716       718       719     2*725       726     2*728
                         2*731     2*733     2*734     2*735       737       740       742   DEFINED         4   CONTROL
```

REFERENCE MAPS

```
VARIABLES    TYPE     REFERENCES

                             162       369       372       374       375       376       538       574       687       690
                             693       695       698       701       704       707       709       711       713       715
                             716       718       719       725       726       728       731       733       734       735
                             737       740       742       DCL         4
IMPD         PARAM           REF     2*376     2*377   DEFINED       349       DCL       349
INV          PARAM           REF     2*615   DEFINED       589       DCL       589
IP           SET             REF     2*369     2*375       695       696     2*734   DEFINED       162   CONTROL       369
                             375       695       696       734       DCL       154
J            SET             REF       261       262       263       265     2*370     2*372     2*373       687     2*688
                             690     2*691       693     2*731     2*732       739   DEFINED        17   CONTROL       162
                             261       262       263       265       370       372       373       687       690       693
                             731       732       739       DCL        17
JP           SET         DEFINED       162       DCL       156
K            PARAM           REF       621       622       704   DEFINED       574       DCL       574
L            SET         DEFINED        43       DCL        43
LIFE         PARAM           REF     2*634   DEFINED       632       DCL       628
M            SET             REF       574     2*615     2*702     2*704     2*705     3*707     4*725   DEFINED        48
                         CONTROL       574     2*615       619       701       704       707       725       DCL        48
MBD          EQU         DEFINED       687       DCL       663
MBF          EQU         DEFINED       693       DCL       665
MBI          EQU         DEFINED       695       DCL       666
MBL          EQU         DEFINED       701       DCL       669
MBR          EQU         DEFINED       698       DCL       668
MBU          EQU         DEFINED       690       DCL       664
ME           EQU         DEFINED       707       DCL       671
MIDYEAR      PARAM           REF       265       272       635       636       637   DEFINED       259       DCL       259
MIN          FUNCT           REF       370
MUE          PARAM           REF       379       733   DEFINED       374       DCL       365
MUF          PARAM           REF       379       731   DEFINED       372       DCL       363
MUFV         PARAM           REF       379       732   DEFINED       373       DCL       364
MUI          PARAM           REF       379       734   DEFINED       375       DCL       366
MUR          PARAM           REF       379       735   DEFINED       376       DCL       367
NU           PARAM           REF       639       702       725   DEFINED       615       DCL       609
OBJ          EQU         DEFINED       721       DCL       662
OMEGA        PARAM           REF       639       702       725       726   DEFINED       615       616       617       DCL
                             608
P            SET             REF     2*693     2*695     2*698     2*704   DEFINED        68   CONTROL       693       695
                             698       704       DCL        68
PD           PARAM           REF       540       698       728   DEFINED       509       538       DCL       509
PE           PARAM           REF       540       742   DEFINED       536       DCL       536
PMISC        PARAM           REF     2*538   DEFINED       524       DCL       524
PSI          VAR             REF       721       DCL       654
PSIE         VAR             REF       722       742       DCL       660
PSII         VAR             REF       722       739       DCL       659
PSIK         VAR             REF       721       724       DCL       655
PSIL         VAR             REF       721       731       DCL       657
PSIM         VAR             REF       721       737       DCL       658
PSIP         VAR             REF       721       728       737       DCL       656
PV           PARAM           REF       536       540       699       737       739       740   DEFINED       491       DCL
                             491
RAIL         PARAM           REF     2*369     2*374     2*375   DEFINED       329       369       DCL       329
RDC          PARAM           REF       265       272   DEFINED       263       DCL       256
RHO          PARAM           REF     3*634       635       636       637   DEFINED       632       DCL       630
ROAD         PARAM           REF     2*370     2*372     2*373       379   DEFINED       275       370       DCL       275
```

```
         REFERENCE MAPS

VARIABLES  TYPE     REFERENCES

SER        PARAM        REF      724      739      740      742  DEFINED      632      DCL      629
SF         PARAM        REF    2*615      616  DEFINED      614      DCL      612
SIGMA      PARAM        REF      639      724  DEFINED      634      DCL      626
T          SET          REF      265      635      636      637      687    2*688      690    3*691    3*693
                      2*695      696    2*698      699    2*701      704      705    2*707      709    2*711
                      2*713      715      716      718      719    5*721    2*722    2*724      725    2*728
                      2*731      732      733      734      735    3*737    2*739      740    2*742  DEFINED
                        147  CONTROL      162      265    2*270      635      687      690      693      695
                        698      701      704      707      709      711      713      715      718      721
                        724      728      731      737      739      742      DCL      147
TP         SET          REF      701    2*702    3*705    2*715    2*718      724      725      726  DEFINED
                        162  CONTROL      701      705      715      718      724      DCL      158
TS         PARAM        REF      701      705      724  DEFINED      578      DCL      578
TT         SET          REF      715      718  DEFINED      586      DCL      586
U          VAR          REF      698      701      728      DCL      649
UP         VAR          REF      705      709      726      DCL      651
VF         VAR          REF      688      691      732      739      DCL      645
VR         VAR          REF      699      735      737      740      DCL      646
XF         VAR          REF      687      690      693      731      DCL      643
XI         VAR          REF      695      696      734      DCL      644
Y          VAR          REF      702      707      725      DCL      652
Z          VAR          REF      693      695      698      704      DCL      642

SETS

  C          UNION OF ALL PRODUCTS AND RAW MATERIALS
  CF         FINAL PRODUCTS (FERTILIZERS)
  CI         INTERMEDIATE PRODUCTS
  CQ         NUTRIENTS
  CR         DOMESTIC RAW MATERIALS AND MISCELLANEOUS INPUTS
  CS         INTERMEDIATES FOR SHIPMENT
  C75        FERTILIZERS USED IN 1975
  G          UPGRADING (CONVERSION) ACTIVITIES
  I          PLANT LOCATIONS
  IP         COPY OF PLANT LOCATIONS
  J          DEMAND REGIONS
  JP         COPY OF MARKETING CENTERS
  L          EXPORT PORTS OF EXIT
  M          PRODUCTIVE UNITS
  P          PROCESSES
  T          TIME PERIODS
  TP         COPY OF TIME PERIODS
  TT         TIME LAG MATRIX

PARAMETERS

  A          INPUT-OUTPUT COEFFICIENT
  ALPHA      NUTRIENT CONTENT
  B          CAPACITY UTILIZATION COEFFICIENT
  CAPUT      CAPACITY UTILIZATION FACTOR
  CF75       CONSUMPTION OF FERTILIZER 1974-75 (1000 TPY)
  CINC       CONSUMPTION INCREMENT
```

```
PARAMETERS

  CN75       CONSUMPTION OF NUTRIENTS 1974-75 (1000 TPY)
  DB         DEMAND IN NUTRIENTS (1000 TPY)
  DCAP       DESIGN CAPACITY OF PLANTS (T/DAY)
  DELTA      DISCOUNT FACTOR
  DEM80      DEMAND PROJECTIONS FOR 1980 (1000TPY)
  EB         MAXIMUM EXPORT BY PRODUCT       (1000 TPY)
  EH         TOTAL EXPORT RESTRICTION        (1000 TPY)
  ETA        UREA CONSUMPTION RESTRICTION
  F          CAPACITY  CONVERSION
  HB         MAXIMUM CAPCITY EXPANSION
  IMPD       IMPORT DISTANCES (KMS)
  INV        INVESTMENT COST
  K          INITIAL CAPACITY (1000 TPY)
  LIFE       LIFE OF PRODUCTIVE UNIT
  MIDYEAR
  MUE        TRANSPORT COST (LE PER TON): EXPORTS
  MUF        TRANSPORT COST (LE PER TON): FINAL PRODUCTS
  MUFV       TRANSPORT COST (LE PER TON): IMPORTED FINAL PRODUCTS
  MUI        TRANSPORT COST (LE PER TON): INTERPLANT SHIPMENT
  MUR        TRANSPORT COST (LE PER TON): IMPORTED RAW MATERIALS
  NU         VARIABLE PORTION OF INVESTMENT OR LABOR
  OMEGA      FIXED-CHARGE PORTION OF INVESTMENT OR LABOR
  PD         DOMESTIC RAW MATERIAL PRICES
  PE         EXPORT PRICE
  PMISC      MISC. MATERIAL COST
  PV         IMPORT PRICE (CIF US$ PER TON 1975)
  RAIL       INTERPLANT RAIL DISTANCES (KMS)
  RDC        REGIONAL DISTRIBUTION OF CONSUMPTION
  RHO        OPPORTUNITY COST OF CAPITAL
  ROAD       ROAD DISTANCES (KMS)
  SER        SHADOW EXCHANGE RATE
  SF         SITE FACTOR
  SIGMA      CAPITAL RECOVERY FACTOR
  TS         TIME SUMMATION MATRIX

VARIABLES

  E          EXPORTS                                        (1000 TPY)
  H          CAPACITY EXPANSION                             (1000 TPY)
  PSI        TOTAL COST (DISCOUNTED)    (1000 LE)
  PSIE       EXPORT REVENUE             (1000 LE PER YEAR)
  PSII       IMPORT COST                (1000 LE PER YEAR)
  PSIK       CAPITAL COST               (1000 LE PER YEAR)
  PSIL       TRANSPORT COST             (1000 LE PER YEAR)
  PSIM       WORKING CAPITAL COST       (1000 LE PER YEAR)
  PSIP       DOMESTIC RECURRENT COST    (1000 LE PER YEAR)
  U          DOMESTIC RAW MATERIAL PURCHASES                (UNITS)
  UP         BINARY VARIABLE: UPGRADING
  VF         IMPORTS: FINAL PRODUCTS                        (1000 TPY)
  VR         IMPORTS: RAW MATERIALS                         (1000 TPY)
  XF         DOMESTIC SHIPMENT ACTIVITY: FINAL PRODUCTS     (1000 TPY)
  XI         DOMESTIC SHIPMENT ACTIVITY: INTERMEDIATES      (1000 TPY)
  Y          BINARY VARIABLE: EXPANSION
  Z          PROCESS LEVEL
```

```
EQUATIONS

  AE        ACCOUNTING: EXPORT REVENUE         (1000 LE PER YEAR)
  AI        ACCOUNTING: IMPORT COST            (1000 LE PER YEAR)
  AK        ACCOUNTING: CAPITAL COST CHARGES   (1000 LE PER YEAR)
  AL        ACCOUNTING: TRANSPORT COST         (1000 LE PER YEAR)
  AM        ACCOUNTING: WORKING CAPITAL        (1000 LE PER YEAR)
  AP        ACCOUNTING: DOMESTIC RECURRENT COST(1000 LE PER YEAR)
  CC        CAPACIY CONSTRAINT                   (1000 TPY)
  ECA       AGGREGATE EXPORT CONSTRAINT                (1000 TPY)
  ECC       EXPORT CONSTRAINT BY COMMODITY AND PLANT  (1000 TPY)
  ECMAX     EXPORT CONSTRAINT BY MARKET SHARE: MAXIMUM(1000 TPY)
  ECMIN     EXPORT CONSTRAINT BY MARKET SHARE: MINIMUM(1000 TPY)
  EX        MUTUAL EXCLUSIVITY CONSTRAINT        (UNITY)
  MBD       MATERIAL BALANCE ON DEMAND           (1000 TPY)
  MBF       MATERIAL BALANCE ON FINAL PRODUCTS   (1000 TPY)
  MBI       MATERIAL BALANCE ON INTERMEDIATES    (1000 TPY)
  MBL       MATERIAL BALANCE ON LABOR
  MBR       MATERIAL BALANCE ON RAW MATERIALS    (1000 TPY)
  MBU       MATERIAL BALANCE ON UREA CONSUMPTION (1000 TPY)
  ME        MAXIMUM CAPACITY EXPANSION           (1000 TPY)
  OBJ       OBJECTIVE FUNCTION  (1000 LE DISCOUNTED)
```

Index